The Tet Offensive

C000127714

With Americans turning against the war in ever greater numbers, struggles for power between the government and the military, and no end in sight to the fighting, the Tet Offensive of 1968 proved to be the turning point of the Vietnam War. In *The Tet Offensive*, historian William Thomas Allison provides a clear, concise overview of the major events and issues surrounding the Tet Offensive, and compiles carefully selected primary sources to illustrate the complex military, political, and public decisions that made up Tet.

The Tet Offensive is composed of two parts: an accessible, well-illustrated narrative overview, and a collection of core primary source documents. Throughout the narrative, historiographic questions are addressed within the text to highlight discussion among historians over pivotal points of debate. The objectively selected documents provide students with raw material from which to gain insight into these events through their own analysis, and to improve their ability to discuss and understand the importance of historical scholarship. Approachable and insightful, *The Tet Offensive* is not only a great introduction to reading history through primary sources, it is an essential tool for understanding what made the Tet Offensive such an important turning point of the Vietnam War.

William Thomas Allison is Professor of History at Weber State University in Ogden, Utah. He is author of *Military Justice in Vietnam: The Rule of Law in an American War*, and *American Diplomats in Russia: Case Studies in Orphan Diplomacy*, among other books.

The Tet Offensive

A Brief History with Documents

William Thomas Allison

Routledge
Taylor & Francis Group

NEW YORK AND LONDON

First published 2008
by Routledge
270 Madison Ave, New York, NY 10016

Simultaneously published in the UK
by Routledge
2 Park Square, Milton Park, Abingdon, Oxon OX14 4RN

*Routledge is an imprint of the Taylor & Francis Group,
an informa business*

© 2008 Taylor and Francis Group, LLC

Typeset in Times by RefineCatch Limited, Bungay, Suffolk
Printed and bound in the United States of America
on acid-free paper by Edwards Brothers, Inc

All rights reserved. No part of this book may be reprinted or
reproduced or utilized in any form or by any electronic,
mechanical, or other means, now known or hereafter
invented, including photocopying and recording, or in any
information storage or retrieval system, without permission in
writing from the publishers.

Trademark Notice: Product or corporate names may be
trademarks or registered trademarks, and are used only for
identification and explanation without intent to infringe.

Library of Congress Cataloging-in-Publication Data
Allison, William Thomas.
The Tet Offensive : a brief history with documents / William Thomas
Allison.
    p. cm.
ISBN13: 978–0–415–95680–2 (hbk)
ISBN10: 0–415–95680–3 (hbk: alk. paper)
ISBN13: 978–0–415–95681–9 (pbk)
ISBN10: 0–415–95681–1 (pbk: alk. paper)
[etc.]
1. Tet Offensive, 1968. 2. Tet Offensive, 1968–Sources. I. Title.
DS557.8.T4A52 2008
959.704'342–dc22

                                        2007033629

ISBN10: 0–415–95680–3 (hbk)
ISBN10: 0–415–95681–1 (pbk)
ISBN10: 0–203–93177–7 (ebk)

ISBN13: 978–0–415–95680–2 (hbk)
ISBN13: 978–0–415–95681–9 (pbk)
ISBN13: 978–0–203–93177–6 (ebk)

Contents

Acknowledgements

The genesis of this book came from several years of teaching courses on the Vietnam War, the United States since 1865, American Military History, and American Diplomatic History, wherein primary documents always play a key role in the course. The Tet Offensive, an event that took place when I was just over one year old, stands out in American history as a pivotal moment in the Vietnam War as well as an ideal case study for teaching historical method. The purpose of this book is to study both.

I am grateful to Routledge for supporting such a book. Kimberly Guinta and her staff at Routledge, especially Matthew Kopel, have been patient, professional, and generous in their guidance and help in producing this volume. Staff, archivists, and historians at the National Archives at College Park, Maryland; the Lyndon B. Johnson Presidential Library at Austin, Texas; the U.S. Army Center for Military History at Fort Lesley J. McNair in Washington, D.C.; the Marine Corps History Division at Quantico, Virginia; and the Vietnam Archive at Texas Tech University in Lubbock, Texas, were wonderfully helpful. Erik Villard and Janet Valentine of the U.S. Army Center of Military History were especially generous with their assistance and time. Angela Swaner and Jennifer Allison helped transcribe documents.

I am indebted to several colleagues who offered suggestions and support, including Sara Dant Ewert and Stephen Francis at Weber State University, and Dale Clifford of the University of North Florida. My father, Tommy Allison, who served in the Marine Corps in Vietnam in 1968–69, always had good comments and observations, and, as always, supported my efforts. To my wife Jennifer, thanks for walking the dog without me for so many evenings while I sat strapped to the computer.

Bill Allison
Ogden, Utah

Illustrations

FIGURES

TABLES

Abbreviations

ARVN	Army of the Republic of (South) Vietnam
BEQ	Bachelor Enlisted Quarters
Bn	Battalion
BOQ	Bachelor Officer Quarters
CIA	Central Intelligence Agency
CIDG	Civilian Irregular Defense Groups
CIO	Central Intelligence Organization
CMIC	Combined Military Interrogation Center
COFRAM	Control Fragmentation Munitions
CONUS	Continental United States
CORDS	Civil Operations and Revolutionary Development Support
COSVN	Central Office of South Vietnam
CTZ	Corps Tactical Zone
DMZ	Demilitarized Zone
DoD	Department of Defense
DRV	Democratic Republic of Vietnam (North Vietnam)
FW	Free World Forces
FY	Fiscal Year
GVN	Government of (South) Vietnam
H&I	Harassment and Interdiction
JCS	Joint Chiefs of Staff
JUSPAO	Joint U.S. Public Affairs Office
KIA	Killed in Action
LOC	Lines of Communication
LST	Landing Ship, Tank
MAC	Military Assistance Command
MACV	Military Assistance Command, Vietnam
Medcap	Medical Civil Action Program
MP	Military Police
MRF	Mobile Riverine Force
NLF	National Liberation Front

NLFSV	National Liberation Front, South Vietnam
NVA	North Vietnamese Army, also known as the People's Army of Vietnam
OSD	Office of the Secretary of Defense
OSD (ISA)	Office of the Assistant Secretary of Defense for International Security Affairs
PAVN	People's Army of Vietnam
PLAF	People's Liberation Armed Forces, also known as the Viet Cong, the military wing of the National Liberation Front
POL	Petrol, Oil, Lubricants
RD	Revolutionary Development
RF/PF	Regional Forces/Popular Forces
RLT	Regimental Landing Team
ROK	Republic of Korea
RVNAF	Republic of (South) Vietnam Armed Forces
TAC	Tactical Air Command
VC	Viet Cong, also known as the People's Liberation Armed Forces, the military wing of the National Liberation Front
WIA	Wounded in Action

Chronology

January 8–26, 1967	American forces conduct Operation Cedar Falls to root out PLAF forces in the Iron Triangle region of South Vietnam.
February 22–April 1, 1967	American and ARVN forces conduct Operation Junction City to destroy PLAF and PAVN sanctuaries near the Cambodian border.
April 1967	Thirteenth Plenum of the Lao Dong Party in Hanoi approves Resolution 13, which calls for a general uprising in South Vietnam to achieve victory as soon as possible.
July 7, 1967	The Central Committee of the Lao Dong Party in Hanoi makes the decision to proceed with the General Offensive–General Uprising phase.
August 3, 1967	President Johnson announces call for 10 percent surtax on all individual and business income.
September 3, 1967	South Vietnamese elect Nguyen Van Thieu president and Nguyen Cao Ky vice president.
September 11–October 31, 1967	PAVN forces attack Marines at Con Thien.
September 29, 1967	In a speech at San Antonio, Texas, President Johnson offers a bombing halt in exchange for beginning substantive peace negotiations.
October 21, 1967	100,000 march in protest of the war from the Lincoln Memorial to the Pentagon.

October 25, 1967	The Central Committee of the Lao Dong Party in Hanoi approves Resolution 14, which authorizes the General Offensive–General Uprising.
November 1, 1967	In a memo to President Johnson, Secretary of Defense Robert McNamara recommends change of strategy in Vietnam, including a bombing halt over North Vietnam and scaling back the American ground combat role in South Vietnam.
November 2, 1967	The Wise Men meet at the White House, approving Johnson's war policies.
November 3–December 1, 1967	Battle of Dak To.
November 11, 1967	President Johnson begins the "Success Campaign" on Veterans' Day with speeches at eleven military installations across the United States.
November 13, 1967	On a trip to Washington, American Ambassador to South Vietnam Ellsworth Bunker states progress is being made in South Vietnam.
November 16, 1967	While in Washington for consultations with President Johnson, General William Westmoreland declares that progress is being made and American withdrawal could commence in less than two years.
November 29, 1967	White House announces Secretary of Defense Robert McNamara will become President of the World Bank.
November 30, 1967	Minnesota Democratic Senator Eugene McCarthy announces he will run for president in 1968.
December 10, 1967	General Westmoreland anticipates the Communists will mount a broad offensive at an undetermined date.
December 15, 1967	MACV turns over defense of Saigon to ARVN forces and South Vietnamese national police.
January 20, 1968	North Vietnamese siege against Marines at Khe Sanh begins.
January 29, 1968	Tet holiday ceasefire begins for ARVN forces.

January 30, 1968	Communist forces in some parts of South Vietnam prematurely begin Tet attacks.
January 31, 1968	Tet Offensive begins.
February 24, 1968	Battle of Hue effectively ends with ARVN capture of the Imperial Palace from PAVN forces in the Citadel.
February 27, 1968	*CBS News* anchorman Walter Cronkite tells national television audience that the conflict in Vietnam will end in stalemate.
February 28, 1968	Chairman of the Joint Chiefs of Staff General Earle Wheeler submits request for 206,000 additional forces to President Johnson.
March 1, 1968	Clarke Clifford sworn in as Secretary of Defense, replacing Robert McNamara.
March 12, 1968	President Johnson defeats Senator Eugene McCarthy in New Hampshire primary by slim margin.
March 16, 1968	Senator Robert Kennedy announces candidacy for President. At the South Vietnamese village of My Lai, hundreds of civilians are massacred by two companies of the American Division while on a mission to root out PLAF snipers.
March 22, 1968	General Westmoreland is recalled to become Army Chief of Staff, to be replaced by General Creighton Abrams as commander of MACV.
March 25–26, 1968	President Johnson gathers another meeting of the so-called Wise Men at the White House. The group concludes that no more forces should be deployed to Vietnam and that negotiations should be pursued.
March 31, 1968	President Johnson addresses the nation about Vietnam and announces a bombing halt and that he is seeking to begin negotiations with North Vietnam. He also announces that he will not seek reelection.
April 8, 1968	Siege at Khe Sanh officially ends.
April 22, 1968	Secretary of Defense Clark Clifford

	announces the beginning of "Vietnamization," in which the South Vietnamese will gradually take over responsibility for fighting the war.
May 12, 1968	President Johnson announces formal peace negotiations will begin in Paris.
May 1968	PAVN and PLAF forces stage next phase of Tet Offensive. Known as Mini-Tet, the attacks are beaten back by American and ARVN forces at great cost to the North Vietnamese.
June 17, 1968	American forces abandon Khe Sanh.
August–September 1968	PAVN and PLAF forces stage last Tet Offensive attacks, which are again defeated by American and ARVN forces.
October 31, 1968	President Johnson announces a halt to all bombing over North Vietnam.
November 5, 1968	Republican Richard Nixon is elected President of the United States.
June 8, 1969	First American troops withdraw from South Vietnam.
January 23, 1973	President Nixon announces Paris Peace Accords.
March 29, 1973	Last American troops withdraw from South Vietnam.
April 30, 1975	PAVN forces capture Saigon, ending the Vietnam War.
July 11, 1995	President William J. Clinton announces normalization of relations with the Democratic Republic of Vietnam.

Introduction

For many participants and historians, the Tet Offensive was the pivotal event of the American war in Vietnam. During the Tet Lunar New Year holiday at the end of January 1968, the North Vietnamese People's Army of Vietnam (PAVN) and the military forces of the National Liberation Front (NLF) in South Vietnam, known as the People's Liberation Armed Forces (PLAF) or Viet Cong (VC), staged daring attacks across South Vietnam on over sixty district towns, thirty-six of forty-four provincial capitals, and the major cities, among dozens of other targets. So began the *Tet Mau Than*, the New Year of the Monkey. In the end, the attacks were beaten back by the Americans and South Vietnamese, along with Free World Military Forces from Australia, New Zealand, Thailand, South Korea, and the Philippines, but not without dramatic consequences for the United States, South Vietnam, and North Vietnam. Despite the apparent military success in stopping the broad offensive, the Tet attacks left an indelible mark on South Vietnam, the American public, and American politics. By the end of March 1968, American strategy in the war had changed and President Lyndon Johnson decided not to run for reelection and to seek peace, finally admitting that the war could not be won on American terms alone.

In accordance with Communist doctrine and Vietnamese mythology and tradition, Tet was to be the historic General Offensive, which would in turn inspire the General Uprising among the South Vietnamese people, and bring a decisive and final victory. For the NLF revolutionaries in South Vietnam, Tet was the great effort to mortally weaken, if not completely destroy, the corrupt and fragile South Vietnamese government (GVN). For the GVN, the Tet Offensive, as it unfolded, was the best opportunity to show the people in the countryside as well as the Americans that it had strength and could defeat the NLF insurgency. For the United States, Tet became the moment in this long war where the decision to win, pull out, or continue as before, would have to be made.

The photographs and television news footage of the Tet Offensive are permanent reminders of the significance of this event. Television news footage of the fighting in and around the American Embassy in Saigon, the summary execution of a VC agent by the head of the South Vietnamese National Police, the intense house-to-house fighting in Hue, the long siege on Khe Sanh, Walter Cronkite telling his national television audience that it was time for change, and an embattled President Lyndon Johnson telling the American people that he would not seek reelection—these and many other images from the Tet Offensive have become iconic images of the American war in Vietnam.

Historians continue to debate many questions concerning the Tet Offensive. What did North Vietnam hope to achieve in this apparent all-or-nothing effort? Were American and South Vietnamese forces caught completely by surprise? What was the purpose of the North Vietnamese siege of Khe Sanh? What role did same-day television reporting have upon public opinion during and after the Tet Offensive? Was Tet really a military defeat for the North Vietnamese and the Viet Cong but yet also a psychological victory? Did the North Vietnamese purposefully sacrifice the Viet Cong for political reasons? Why did President Johnson finally decide to change direction? These and many other questions continue to draw the attention of historians. The questions themselves help shed light on this most controversial of American wars; the range of answers also holds relevance upon questions about American conflicts today.

The purpose of this brief volume is to provide students with an overview of the primary events leading to and during the Tet Offensive as well as the impact of Tet during the months that followed. It is not meant to be definitive, exhaustive, or the "final word," but rather to stir questions among students to inspire further examination of this event in particular and expose students to primary document analysis. Throughout the overview, historiographic questions will be addressed to expose students to historical discussion over what most observers consider the pivotal event of the Vietnam War. The documents provide students with raw material from which to glean insight into this event through their own analysis. Selection of the documents was objective, with the goal of giving students a basic primary source base for the events related to the Tet Offensive. No doubt others might have chosen some different documents while not including others. As a teaching tool, the primary goals of this text are to allow students to discuss the major issues, analyze primary documents, and decide upon their own interpretation of the Tet Offensive, while learning about the historian's craft.

The text begins with an overview of the political and military situation leading up to the outbreak of the Tet attacks, including North Vietnamese planning and objectives of the offensive, the status of the GVN and its military forces, and the Johnson administration's campaign to convince the American public of progress in Vietnam. Then follow sections on the offensive itself, including indications to American military leaders that an offensive was looming, the outbreak of attacks in Saigon, particularly assaults on the American Embassy and South Vietnamese government buildings, the battle for the old imperial city of Hue, and the siege of the Marine outpost at Khe Sanh. The reaction to Tet will then be briefly examined, including the impact Tet had upon the GVN, the NLF and PLAF, and the North Vietnamese government and its regular forces. General William Westmoreland's request for more troops, changes in American public opinion, and the Johnson administration's internal debate on war policy will also be discussed. Throughout the text, "historiographic points" examine what historians and other authors have said about major questions concerning the Tet Offensive. A chronology of events is provided at the beginning of the book, and a selected bibliography concludes the text.

Most wars have their turning points or pivotal moments: Saratoga or the Cowpens in the American War for Independence; Gettysburg, Vicksburg, or Antietam in the American Civil War; Stalingrad or the invasion of Normandy during World War II; and Dien Bien Phu in the French Indochina War, just to name a few. For many who participated in the American war in Vietnam and for many who study the conflict, Tet stands out as the key event.

Part I

The Tet Offensive

Background

The situation before Tet

The United States, North Vietnam, and South Vietnam each had unique difficulties as the war entered 1968. At the end of 1967, the war had cost the United States over sixteen thousand deaths and over fifty-three thousand wounded since 1960, with the vast majority of those casualties occurring after the American buildup began in 1964–65. South Vietnam had lost over fifty thousand killed and over eighty thousand wounded since the North Vietnamese military effort began in earnest in 1960. PAVN and PLAF forces had lost perhaps as many as 200,000 killed and untold thousands wounded. As pressure mounted in the United States to show progress in the war and in stabilizing the South Vietnamese government, so too did pressure increase in North Vietnam to bring a successful close to the conflict.

The American political and military context

The American war in Vietnam had evolved from a comparatively small advisory effort in the late 1950s to build up South Vietnamese forces and establish stable government in South Vietnam, which had been divided from its northern neighbor since the end of the French Indochina War in 1954, to a major Americanized war effort involving over 480,000 American forces by 1967. As North Vietnam and the NLF became more aggressive in their war for unification in 1963–4, it became more apparent that South Vietnam could not fight on its own. Questions about South Vietnamese military effectiveness, combined with a weak government and enemy attacks directed against American forces and installations, served to convince the Johnson administration in 1965 to begin "Americanizing" the war.

This was not a total war effort like that the United States had mounted against Germany and Japan in World War II. Because of the world geo-political situation, this war was a limited war, a conflict that was part of the broader Cold War between the United States and its allies and the Communist sphere dominated by the Soviet Union and China. American Cold War strategy dictated that the United States assist South Vietnamese resistance against North Vietnamese aggression. With American prestige at stake, the United States felt compelled to defend smaller, lesser-developed nations against Communist aggression.

President Lyndon Johnson attempted to conduct the war in Vietnam in a manner that did not directly threaten the Soviet Union or China, to avoid a broader general war, and that did not overburden the American economy. Johnson's ambitious domestic agenda, his Great Society programs, would be jeopardized by a large war in far-away Southeast Asia. Thus, escalation was gradual from 1964 through 1967 and the United States did not invade North Vietnam and resisted calls from the military to conduct sizeable incursions into Laos and Cambodia. The military relied upon the draft to augment the professional force that was fighting in Vietnam, manning the Demilitarized Zone (DMZ) in Korea, and deterring a Soviet invasion of Western Europe. To avoid the perception of a larger war, the Johnson administration did not mobilize the reserves, did not institute price controls and rationing in the United States, and generally did not attempt to unify broad support for the war.

Under the command of General William Westmoreland, Military Assistance Command, Vietnam (MACV) adopted a three-pronged strategy as the American role in the conflict increased in 1965 (Figure 1). One part of this approach was a strategy of attrition using tactics that came to be known as "search and destroy." American and South Vietnamese Army (ARVN) units would patrol the jungles and countryside to make contact with Viet Cong forces, and then call in massive American firepower from either artillery or air assets, or both, to lay a swath of destruction upon enemy positions. Commanders measured success through body counts, literally by counting corpses found on the battlefield. The objective of such a strategy was to kill or injure as many enemy soldiers as possible to make the cost of continuing the war too high, thus breaking the enemy's will to fight. The other part of the strategy was interdiction to stop the flow of men and material into South Vietnam from North Vietnam and along the Ho Chi Minh Trail through Laos and Cambodia. Massive bombing along the trail and a series of firebases just south of the DMZ along the 17th Parallel that divided North and South Vietnam attempted to stop what became a very sophisticated and efficient logistical system from North Vietnam. The third part of the American approach to the war in Vietnam involved bombing of selected targets in North Vietnam, with the dual hope of hurting the ability of the North Vietnamese to supply its troops and Viet Cong units in the south and coercing North Vietnam to the peace table to guarantee an independent and free South Vietnam.

This military strategy was initiated to support American efforts to establish stable democratic government in South Vietnam, which had made little progress. Creating a stable government that respected the rule of law and

Figure 1   General William C. Westmoreland, Commanding General, MACV, watches the ceremonies on the arrival of the Royal Thai Volunteer Regiment in Vietnam, September 1967.

Source: National Archives.

avoided the abyss of corruption, and that could thus establish trust and legitimacy with the Vietnamese people, proved extremely difficult. Pacification programs tried to improve life and sway the rural peasantry from the NLF camp. This campaign of "winning hearts and minds," as the vernacular at the time called it, was separate from the military campaign, but nonetheless encountered problems of poor administration and corruption. By 1967, reports concluded that the VC still largely controlled the countryside.

Corruption had always existed in South Vietnam, but the problem had been considerably exacerbated by the massive influx of American military and luxury goods into South Vietnam. Stabilizing the South Vietnamese economy, with extensive government corruption and an insurgency war underway in the countryside and American dollars unintentionally competing for preeminence with Vietnamese piasters, was an equally daunting undertaking. Despite a Herculean effort on the part of American military advisors and billions of dollars in equipment and training, the South Vietnamese military also remained questionable as an independent and effective fighting force. In 1965, the Johnson administration concluded that the GVN and its military could not successfully fight the NLF insurgency. Facing limited strategic options, Johnson decided to escalate the American presence and Americanize the war rather than withdraw from South Vietnam completely.

American military operations since beginning the escalation in 1965 had been dramatic but marginally effective. Using ARVN forces to protect the cities allowed Westmoreland to use American Army and Marine units to conduct operations in the countryside, the control of which would in turn allow pacification programs to have their fullest effect. The bombing campaign designed to force North Vietnam to the peace table and stop support of the VC insurgents in the South had been extensive and expensive, but in over two years Operation Rolling Thunder had failed to achieve either objective. Search and destroy operations involving air insertion of American forces, such as Operation Starlite in 1965 and Operation Junction City in February 1967, often succeeded in the short term in stopping PLAF and PAVN movements, but enemy forces frequently returned to the areas weeks later. Ground operations designed to corral PLAF forces in a particular area and destroy them with massive firepower, such as Operation Cedar Falls in January 1967, also had some short-term impact but little lasting effect. Viet Cong units in the Iron Triangle region northwest of Saigon reoccupied many positions evacuated because of Cedar Falls soon after the operation ended. The significant impact such operations did have was to force the PLAF to relocate sanctuaries across the border into Cambodia, which for the United States only threatened to broaden a limited war that American political leaders had hoped to contain in South Vietnam.

Despite inflicting heavy casualties, none of these approaches seemed to be making real progress toward ending the conflict on American terms. PLAF units quickly learned how to minimize casualties from American search and destroy missions, mainly through an uncanny ability to melt back into the forest and jungle through a series of tunnels and well-hidden trails. The interdiction campaign along the DMZ and the Ho Chi Minh Trail had little effect, as the trail's design allowed for repairs to be made while men and material continued uninterrupted along nearby detour routes. The amount of material transported down the trail from North Vietnam actually had increased year to year through 1968. Bombing was frequently disrupted because of the weather, especially during the rainy season, and much of the trail ran just outside Vietnam along the border with Laos and Cambodia, which further complicated ground and air operations to destroy the trail.

By 1967, the over 100,000 sorties of the air campaign against North Vietnam were no closer to bringing Ho Chi Minh to the peace table than approximately twenty-five thousand sorties flown in 1965. Sophisticated Soviet and Chinese air defense systems made bombing missions even more dangerous, inefficient, and costly, as pilots now had to spend more time against air defense targets rather than on important military, industrial, and logistical targets. More and more American aircraft were shot down over North Vietnam, with dozens of pilots and crew taken prisoner, some being held in North Vietnamese prisoner-of-war camps for more than seven years by the time the American war ended in early 1973.

American casualties and financial costs of the war mounted quickly. The war effort was beginning to have an adverse effect on the American economy, particularly on the value of the dollar. The war was now costing American taxpayers over $2 billion per month, which annually amounted to about 3 percent of the Gross National Product (compared to 12 percent during the Korean War and over 40 percent for World War II). In August 1967, Johnson proposed a 10 percent surcharge on all income tax returns to help offset increasing military expenditures so he could continue his Great Society domestic agenda.

Daily casualty reports appeared in newspapers and nightly on network television news. Draft resistance increased by 1967 and anti-war protests were also on the rise in number and intensity. On October 21, 1967, over 100,000 gathered on the Washington Mall to protest the draft with a march on the Pentagon (Figure 2). Abbie Hoffman and Norman Mailer gave speeches, while Peter, Paul, and Mary sang protest songs from the steps of the Lincoln Memorial. Nearly half of the crowd crossed the Potomac River to the Pentagon, where thousands of hippies tried to levitate the building as an exorcism of the evil inside it. Hundreds were arrested, but it was clear to many that whether or not one agreed with the war, an increasingly larger segment of the country was turning against it.

Convinced that the anti-war movement was responsible for his downturn in the polls, Johnson ordered the Central Intelligence Agency (CIA) to begin surveillance and harassment of anti-war protest leaders and others who questioned his policies. The CIA's Operation Chaos ultimately created files on over seven thousand Americans involved one way or another with the anti-war movement. Public opinion polls by mid-1967 clearly showed the American people were tiring of the war and concerned about the lack of progress as measured against the increasing cost in casualties and money. In late summer, two-thirds of the American public no longer supported President Johnson's leadership of the nation, and by early fall, for the first time more Americans than not thought Vietnam was a mistake.

Figure 2 Protesters on the Washington Mall before marching to the Pentagon, October 21, 1967.

Source: National Archives.

The war seemed to be making little headway and was perhaps even stuck—thus the frequent characterizations of the war as a quagmire or stalemate. Once hawkish senators and congressmen began questioning Johnson's war policies. General William Westmoreland and the Joint Chiefs of Staff (JCS) proposed plans that would expand the war into Laos and Cambodia, even north of the DMZ into North Vietnam, with an increased total force of 542,000 American troops in country by mid-1968. Westmoreland had become convinced that what analysts called the "cross-over point," the point at which PAVN and PLAF units could no longer replace losses in the field, was near. The troop increase would provide an overwhelming offensive force that could then wipe out the PLAF in the South and deter PAVN operations south of the DMZ. But Johnson could not afford the domestic economic and political price of calling up the reserves while also increasing monthly draft allotments, and therefore allowed only a fraction of what Westmoreland had requested.

In May 1967, Johnson acceded to Westmoreland's request to militarize the pacification program. Since the beginning of American involvement in Vietnam, pacification programs had been decentralized and under the operation of numerous agencies, often at cross-purposes. Westmoreland longed to centralize the disorganized programs under the control of MACV. Under the new Civil Operations and Revolutionary Development Support agency (CORDS), pacification became not only centralized, but militarized. Despite the effort to get pacification and military operations on the same page, military operations tended to undo the work pacification had achieved. The village secured and improved through pacification might get in the way of a military operation and be destroyed, thus alienating hundreds of villagers from American and South Vietnamese influence.

Secretary of Defense William McNamara, who had been a principal architect of the American involvement in Vietnam since the Kennedy years, became disillusioned with Westmoreland's strategy and the war in general. In the spring of 1967, he began offering a string of proposals to Johnson that would restrict bombing of the North and pull American forces back into secure enclaves in order to turn the fighting back over to the South Vietnamese. Concerned at the lack of real progress toward establishing a secure independent South Vietnamese state, convinced that Ho Chi Minh and the North Vietnamese would carry the fight for years, and worried that American prestige abroad was suffering because of what critics charged was excessive bombing of what amounted to a Third World country, McNamara concluded the war was unwinnable. Caught in a difficult political position at home, Johnson rejected McNamara's ideas and in the end replaced McNamara with Clark Clifford in March 1968.

For the increasingly beleaguered President, Vietnam had become a military and financial problem and a political dilemma. Facing difficult choices and an upcoming presidential election year, Johnson and his administration went on the offensive in 1967 to shore up support for the war while at the same time opening doors for a settlement with North Vietnam. In a September 1967 speech delivered in San Antonio, Texas, Johnson offered a new platform for peace negotiations to Ho Chi Minh. The so-called San Antonio plan offered Hanoi a bombing halt in exchange for opening real negotiations and a promise that North Vietnam would not take advantage of the bombing halt to move more men and supplies down the Ho Chi Minh Trail into South Vietnam. Instead of bombing to coerce the North Vietnamese to the peace table, Johnson now took the opposite tack of offering a bombing halt to achieve the same purpose. North Vietnam, however, adhered to its original set of conditions for a settlement: a complete bombing halt, the full withdraw of American troops, and the establishment of a new coalition government including the NLF in South Vietnam.

On November 1 and 2, Johnson convened a group of foreign policy and military advisors from current and past presidential administrations to discuss Vietnam. He had called together such gatherings before, but this time Johnson needed to know if he was on the right path to success in Vietnam. Polls and the economy, in addition to differing government and press reports from Vietnam, had created increasing doubt among the American people, if not Johnson himself. Known as the "Wise Men," this gathering included former Secretary of State Dean Acheson, longtime presidential advisor and soon to be Secretary of Defense Clark Clifford, Supreme Court Justice Abe Fortas, Generals Maxwell Taylor and Omar Bradley, former Ambassador to the Soviet Union and Great Britain and Johnson's Ambassador-at-Large Averill Harriman, former Ambassador to South Vietnam Henry Cabot Lodge, Jr., CIA Director Richard Helms, and members of the Johnson administration, such as Secretary of Defense Robert McNamara, National Security Advisor Walt Rostow, and White House Press Secretary George Christian, among others (Figure 3). They met for several hours over the

Figure 3 The Wise Men meet in the Cabinet Room of the White House, November 2, 1967. Depicted: (clockwise) Robert Murphy, Ambassador Averell Harriman, Dean Acheson, General Omar Bradley, General Maxwell Taylor, Justice Abe Fortas, Clark Clifford, Secretary of State Dean Rusk, President Lyndon B. Johnson, Secretary of Defense Robert McNamara, Douglas Dillon, McGeorge Bundy.

Source: Lyndon Baines Johnson Presidential Library.

course of two days, which included briefings by Army General Earle Wheeler, the Chairman of the Joint Chiefs of Staff, and George Carver from the CIA. Johnson attended briefly during the second day. In the end, the Wise Men recommended turning more of the day-to-day combat operations over to the South Vietnamese, limiting bombing of the north, and perhaps most importantly urging the White House to do a better job communicating to the American public its strategy in Vietnam. Satisfied that the Wise Men thought he was on the right track in Vietnam, Johnson took the recommendations under advisement.

Also on November 1, Secretary of Defense McNamara sent Johnson a memorandum outlining his thoughts on the war. McNamara urged a change of course, noting that the current strategy would not bring the United States any closer to success in Vietnam by the end of 1968. Such a lack of progress would further risk American public support of the war, which would in turn jeopardize public support of Johnson's ambitious domestic agenda. Internationally, support of the war had never been strong, but to continue the present path would erode what little international support remained. McNamara advised against sending more troops to Vietnam and expanding military operations into North Vietnam, but otherwise supported Johnson's policies in Vietnam. The Wise Men did not see the McNamara memorandum.

The Johnson administration initiated an intensive public relations campaign in late 1967. The so-called Success or Progress Campaign was designed to persuade the increasing number of doubters that American policies in Vietnam were indeed working and progress was being made. On Veterans' Day weekend, Johnson gave stirring speeches at several military bases, including Fort Benning and Camp Pendleton. Johnson brought Ambassador to South Vietnam Ellsworth Bunker and General Westmoreland home in November to make the rounds on television news programs and give public speeches espousing success in Vietnam (Figure 4). Westmoreland told the nation that the strategy of attrition against the North Vietnamese and Viet Cong insurgents, combined with the growing strength of the South Vietnamese government, would inevitably allow the United States to decrease its troop commitment in Vietnam. Offering optimism and encouragement, Westmoreland even predicted that in two years' time American troops should be able to begin coming home. The beginning of the end, Westmoreland claimed, had begun. The campaign had worked. While questions from naysayers did not abate completely, the intensity from critics calmed somewhat by the end of the year.

Johnson topped off the Success Campaign with a trip to the large American base at Cam Rahn Bay in South Vietnam just before Christmas, where he passed out medals and spoke to the troops, vowing to stay the course (Figure 5). In January, Johnson told the nation in his State of the

Figure 4 At the White House in November 1967, President Lyndon B. Johnson reads a document as General William Westmoreland waits.

Source: Lyndon Baines Johnson Presidential Library.

Union address that loss of public support at this critical point in the war would signal to the North Vietnamese that America had lost its will to carry the fight. According to the Johnson administration, the United States was winning the unusual war in far-off Southeast Asia and, if the American people would be a bit more patient, a satisfactory end-state could be achieved. The paradox became, however, that if the American public lost its patience, then Johnson would not have the time needed to win the war.

The South Vietnamese political and military context

South Vietnam had struggled politically, economically, and militarily since the end of the French Indochina War in 1954. American money and advisors gradually took over supporting the South Vietnamese government from France in the mid-1950s, with the goal of establishing a stable long-term government and a military effective enough to defend the nation against outside aggression as well as from internal threats. The coup overthrowing the American-backed leader of South Vietnam, Ngo Dinh Diem, in 1963 had resulted in a series of military and civilian governments that had finally

Figure 5 President Lyndon B. Johnson visits troops Cam Ranh Bay in South Vietnam, December 23, 1967.

Source: Lyndon Baines Johnson Presidential Library.

settled with the rise of Nguyen Van Thieu as head of state in February 1965, strongly supported by the young and westernized South Vietnamese Air Force General Nguyen Cao Ky. In what amounted to a fraudulent election, Thieu and Ky were elected president and vice president, respectively, in 1967. Since the coup against Diem in November 1963, at least seven different governments had come and gone in South Vietnam. Corruption reigned in Saigon, with the government, including Thieu and Ky, the worst offender.

By the end of 1967, South Vietnamese political and military leaders knew they could not survive without the continued assistance and presence of the United States, and were thus caught in the dilemma of having to improve governance and military effectiveness to show the United States results, yet knowing that if the results were too good, the United States would begin to withdraw its support. The United States had been doing the bulk of the fighting since 1965, thus the South Vietnamese military, while certainly not sitting idle, did not have the experience it would might otherwise have had. Lack of experience, government corruption, and a failure to gain legitimacy in the countryside hampered South Vietnam's progress toward stabilization and independence from American assistance (Figure 6).

The military forces of South Vietnam boasted over 350,000 men among its army, navy, air force, and Marines. Each branch of the South Vietnamese military was equipped with American weapons, technology, and other equipment, but often with World War II-era rifles and outdated American artillery and armor. At the end of 1967, for example, only a few elite units between the ARVN and South Vietnamese Marines had modern M-16 rifles. Over twelve thousand American military and civilian personnel worked with these forces as advisors, logistical experts, intelligence operatives, and the like. Results, however, did not live up to expectations. Of ten ARVN divisions, only four were considered by American advisors to be combat effective. Poor training, ineffective leadership, and endemic corruption had made the South Vietnamese military virtually impotent. There were exceptions, such as the airborne and marine units, which performed remarkably well.

In addition to the regular South Vietnamese military forces, there were over 150,000 men in the so-called Regional Forces and just under 150,000 in the Popular Forces. Both operated and were organized much like a local militia. American Special Forces, the now famous Green Berets, trained and commanded over forty-two thousand Vietnamese in Civilian Irregular Defense Groups (CIDG), which were posted along the Cambodian and

Figure 6 Honolulu Conference, February 8, 1966, at Camp Smith, Hawaii. From left to right, Secretary of Defense Robert McNamara, South Vietnamese Prime Minister Nguyen Cao Ky, President Lyndon B. Johnson and South Vietnamese Lieutenant General Nguyen Van Thieu.

Source: Lyndon Baines Johnson Presidential Library.

Laotian borders. The CIDG conducted scouting and interdiction operations with only marginal effectiveness. In the cities, such as Saigon and Da
Nang, a seventy-thousand man National Police Force maintained security,
though they were not trained for regular combat. Over the years, tradition
dictated leaves for large segments of the South Vietnamese military and
truces were often arranged with PLAF forces during special holidays so that
soldiers could return to their homes to visit family. Tet, the lunar New Year,
was one such holiday.

The South Vietnamese government and military did not inspire a great
deal of confidence in the Vietnamese people or American advisors. American
pressure on South Vietnamese government and military officials was
immense, to say the least. Both the government and the military needed to
show progress toward stability, strength, and effectiveness, but neither
seemed to be moving forward at an appropriate pace to show real progress.

The North Vietnamese political and
military context

North Vietnam fought with confidence and a committed national effort for
over two decades. Ho Chi Minh's Communist forces had defeated the
French, in part by building a conventional fighting force from an effective
guerilla force. Since its decision to unify Vietnam through a war of unification in 1960, PAVN and PLAF forces had become increasingly better
equipped and organized, and experienced. Greater American involvement
in the war forced North Vietnamese leaders to turn to a strategy of exhaus-
tion. North Vietnamese war planners reasoned that American political leaders and the American public could not endure a long, costly war. Knowing
that defeating the United States militarily was doubtful, North Vietnam
accepted the notion that outlasting the United States would bring a settlement favorable to North Vietnamese objectives.

Guerilla units would continue the fight in the South while PAVN forces
gained strength for the final campaign. Gaining trust and legitimacy from
the people in the countryside of South Vietnam by making the South
Vietnamese government look bad was the primary political strategy, while
inflicting heavy casualties on American forces to cause the United States to
withdraw from South Vietnam was the primary military objective. Both
would hopefully assure a negotiated settlement where a new government
with a Communist majority would be installed to govern South Vietnam.
For North Vietnam, a war of unification against the United States would
have to be a long war, but one that in the end would result in victory for
the North.

By early 1968, American intelligence estimated that roughly half of the
Communist regular combat units, also called main-force battalions, in

South Vietnam consisted of PAVN regulars, numbering perhaps as many as fifty thousand men. PLAF units were divided into two different groups. Main-force units engaged in regular combat, while paramilitary or guerilla units served as guides, performed logistics functions, and conducted small ambush operations. PLAF main-force units numbered some sixty thousand men, while paramilitary forces may have had as many as 400,000 men and women serving. Unlike the American troops, who served twelve-month tours of duty (thirteen for Marines) and returned to the United States, PAVN and PLAF troops served for the duration of the conflict. The only ticket home was a disabling wound, and daily life in the PAVN and PLAF, much more so than that of their American enemy, was grueling and uncomfortable.

The North Vietnamese understood that they could not overcome the superiority of American firepower, so they adopted tactics to minimize its impact. Other than inaccurate rockets and mortars, PLAF units mostly did without heavy weapons such as artillery. While PAVN forces did have some Soviet-built tanks and artillery, these did not often come into play in the South until later in the war. To counter American firepower, PAVN and PLAF units instead used hit-and-run tactics, striking with lethal rapidity then withdrawing before American firepower could be brought to bear upon them. Meticulous planning, especially in reconnaissance and withdrawal routes, also helped minimize casualties and losses of valuable equipment. Because the objective of North Vietnamese military strategy was to inflict as many casualties as possible, holding positions was not a priority. PAVN and PLAF units rarely held static or captured positions for more than a brief period before withdrawing into the dense bush and jungle to safe areas.

Over the years, the North Vietnamese government had become dependent upon Soviet and Chinese support, and by the mid-1960s had done a remarkable job of playing one off against the other to set up a situation where both competed to be the primary supporter of the North Vietnamese war effort. It was in the interest of both the Soviet Union and China to hurt American prestige among lesser-developed nations and to support insurgents and others against American forces and national interests in such regions, which could produce great gains for Communist influence internationally at less risk and cost than a direct encounter with the United States. Both the Soviet Union and China supplied North Vietnam with all sorts of military material, including sophisticated air defense systems around Hanoi and countless tons of weapons that were transported along the Ho Chi Minh Trail to PAVN and PLAF units in South Vietnam.

By 1967, the North Vietnamese government faced a crucial decision in how it would continue the war. Basically, the choice was either to continue as before, relying upon a strategy of outlasting the United States and undermining the South Vietnamese government, or to stage a massive offensive to deal American and South Vietnamese morale such a blow that a negotiated settlement resulting in an American withdrawal would come sooner rather than later. The choice hinged upon the North Vietnamese capability to continue a protracted war for an indefinite period.

North Vietnamese planning and objectives

By mid-1967, North Vietnamese and Viet Cong units were feeling the effects of American-led attacks. While they never suffered a decisive defeat, the costs of engaging American forces and their superior firepower were beginning to tell. Since a decision among the top North Vietnamese leadership in 1966 to seek a decisive victory at an opportune point in the war, North Vietnamese leaders had discussed the idea of a general offensive to force the United States to withdraw from Vietnam and irreversibly weaken the South Vietnamese government. The problem, however, came in establishing favorable battlefield conditions to initiate such an offensive. The United States had continued its steady escalation of forces in South Vietnam, and although PAVN and PLAF tactics were designed to minimize casualties, American firepower was having an adverse effect. Moreover, as the war settled into a stalemate in 1967, the lack of progress toward victory had an adverse effect on morale, especially among the NLF insurgents in the South.

Under such conditions, then, a decisive victory was needed sooner rather than later. The concept of the General Offensive that would in turn cause and gain momentum from a General Uprising among the general population against the South Vietnamese government guided planning for what would become known as the Tet Offensive. Discussions of such an offensive may have begun as early as 1966 and the general idea of an offensive and uprising was authorized for planning at the Thirteenth Plenum in April 1967. The idea seems to have found its earliest support with Le Duan, the Secretary-General of the ruling Lao Dong Party, and General Nguyen Chi Thanh. Le Duan had become highly critical of the lack of progress in the effort to unify North and South Vietnam and urged a more aggressive strategy to take advantage of the weakness of South Vietnamese military forces and the decline in American public support of the war. General Thanh proposed a broad attack on the major urban centers of South Vietnam, cities such as Hue, Da Nang, and of course Saigon, by PAVN and PLAF main-force and guerilla units. Both Thanh and Le Duan rationalized that such an offensive, while not without high risks, would solidify Communist influence in the countryside; take the fight to the cities to undermine the South Vietnamese government; and cause American public opinion to swing firmly against the war. Influence in the countryside had become a particular concern, not so much because of the success of American pacification programs, but because more people were moving to the cities. Controlling the countryside did not preclude the need to now gain influence in the cities. Thanh reasoned that broad attacks would inflict such large casualties on American forces that the United States would withdraw. Under these conditions, then, a negotiated settlement could be reached that would bring complete victory sooner rather than later. Thanh presented his ideas to the Political Bureau in June 1967.

General Vo Nguyen Giap, perhaps North Vietnam's best-known general, who had led Ho Chi Minh's forces at Dien Bien Phu in 1954 and was now Minister of Defense, was skeptical that the United States would simply withdraw and was extremely reluctant to risk PAVN main-force units (Figure 7). Attacking the cities would expose PAVN and PLAF forces to American firepower, unlike the strategy of hit-and-run tactics, which allowed forces to melt back into the cover of jungle or to safe havens. Giap's caution found many adherents within North Vietnam's political and military leadership,

Figure 7 North Vietnamese General Vo Nguyen Giap.
Source: Corbis.

and Thanh's death in July 1967 may have allowed Giap to succeed in getting a less ambitious plan ultimately approved in July 1967.

The plan called for the offensive to begin during the Tet holiday at the end of January 1968. Giap overcame initial misgivings about the timing of the offensive by citing the historical precedent of the successful 1789 Tet attack by Vietnamese patriots against Chinese occupiers in Hanoi. In fact, the idea of General Offensive and General Uprising is borrowed heavily from Maoist Communist theory. According to this concept, a war of liberation or revolution began with Resistance, wherein insurgent forces fought their enemy in the countryside, maintaining the initiative while building strength. Once strength was achieved, the General Offensive would begin the final phase of the war, in which the General Uprising would overthrow the government and install a new government dominated by the insurgent party. In Vietnam's unique historical context, the General Uprising held much more resonance than in China. Vietnam had been dominated by China for centuries, then again by France. In both instances, the uprising by the people against foreign occupiers played significant roles in achieving independence. A General Uprising in 1945, according to Vietnamese tradition, began the movement toward declaring independence from France. Thus, North Vietnam was able to play upon tradition and history to move into this phase of its war to unify Vietnam. The plan itself was called General Offensive–General Uprising—*Tong Cong Kich–Ton Khoi Nghia.*

Giap's plan involved multiple phases, beginning with a preparatory phase beginning in September 1967. The initial phase included attacks on outlying regions, even along the border with Cambodia and Laos, to draw American and South Vietnamese forces away from urban centers. This phase would give PAVN and PLAF units time to plan specific missions for the General Offensive and build up forces and weapons caches in staging areas for the assault on the cities and other targets. Gaining experience with new tactics and communications was imperative during this phase. Part of the preparatory phase also included diplomatic initiatives designed to mask preparations for the offensive and divide South Vietnamese and American leadership on the direction of the war. One such initiative was the December 1967 offer from Hanoi to open negotiations in exchange for an unconditional bombing halt.

The next phase would be the mass attacks across South Vietnam on American and South Vietnamese military targets, government centers, including provincial capitals, and the cities, beginning January 31, 1968. Massive propaganda would be included in this phase in the hope of encouraging defections from the South Vietnamese military to PAVN and Viet Cong forces. The final phase was contingent upon the success of the Tet holiday attacks. If the General Uprising failed or the South Vietnamese military was not destroyed, for example, weeks, even months, of continuous attacks would wear down American and South Vietnamese forces in pursuit of the original objectives. For North Vietnam and the NLF forces in the South, the Tet Offensive, as it unfolded in 1968, actually lasted through the summer of that year.

Historiographic point

What was the purpose of the Tet Offensive?

The PAVN official history states that the objectives of the Tet Offensive were to:

- annihilate and cause the total disintegration of the bulk of the puppet army, overthrow the puppet regime at all administrative levels, and place all governmental power in the hands of the people;
- annihilate a significant portion of the American military's troop strength and destroy a significant portion of his war equipment in order to prevent the American forces from being able to carry out their political and military missions;
- on this basis, crush the American will to commit aggression and force the United States to accept defeat in South Vietnam and end all hostile actions against North Vietnam. In addition, using this as our basis, we would achieve the immediate goals of the revolution, which were independence, democracy, peace, and neutrality in South Vietnam, and then move toward achieving peace and national unification.[1]

General Tran Van Tra, commander of PAVN forces in South Vietnam from 1965 through 1973 and who commanded the Tet attack on Saigon in 1968, cited similar objectives and purpose.[2] General Tran Do, the operational planner of the offensive in South Vietnam, suggested that the main objective had been to undermine the South Vietnamese military and government, but having an impact in the United States had been an unintended but fortunate consequence.[3] American General William Westmoreland characterized the purpose of Tet as a "go for broke" effort to score a decisive victory. Westmoreland placed less emphasis on the General Uprising, focusing instead on the North Vietnamese willingness to show the Americans that the United States could win only with an enormously increased military effort and cost in casualties and money. He was convinced the supreme objective was to inflict a "catastrophic Dien Bien Phu" during a critical presidential election year to break the will of the American people. Both objectives would give the North

Vietnamese the advantage at the negotiating table, since American and South Vietnamese resolve would assuredly be weakened.[4]

Historians and other writers generally agree on the above description of North Vietnamese purpose and objectives in the Tet Offensive. James H. Willbanks maintains that the Tet campaign was meant to end the stalemate that characterized the war in 1967 by provoking an uprising across South Vietnam, shattering South Vietnamese military forces, and forcing the United States to accept that the war was hopeless.[5] William Duiker suggests the purpose was to force the withdrawal of American forces and the creation of a coalition government dominated by the NLF.[6] James Arnold focuses on the political objectives that could be achieved by a stunning military attack, namely convincing the American public that the war was unwinnable, which would in turn force the Johnson administration to change its Vietnam policy.[7] Journalist Don Oberdorfer, who reported from Vietnam for the *Washington Post*, states that at the very least the North Vietnamese wanted to bring the conflict to a head and force the United States to make a decision to stay in or pull out. At most, according to Oberdorfer, the North Vietnamese hoped for the complete destruction of the South Vietnamese military and the overthrow of the South Vietnamese government.[8]

Writer and historian Gabriel Kolko insists that the primary purpose of the military offensive was political—to instill dissent in the South Vietnamese and American governments to force a change in policy, hopefully toward a negotiated settlement where North Vietnam would have the upper hand.[9] For Marilyn Young, the main objective of the Tet Offensive was to force the United States to begin de-escalation, while hoping rather than depending upon some sort of decisive battle or the collapse of the South Vietnamese government.[10] Political scientist William Turley suggests that North Vietnamese objectives ranged from optimistic to more realistic in the hope of grand achievements but content to settle for less confident results. For Turley, the most optimistic objective was to destabilize the South Vietnamese government to the point of collapse then establish a coalition government. Without the South Vietnamese government, Turley reasons, the United States would have no "puppet" to support and would thus hasten its withdrawal. Otherwise, North Vietnamese leaders were content to at least convince the United States that its limited war strategy had failed and to pursue a negotiated settlement.[11]

Gary R. Hess, an historian of American foreign relations, contends that the North Vietnamese wanted to exploit an overextended American military and economy that was losing public support at home. The Tet Offensive, Hess suggests, was to inflict such massive casualties on American forces that the Johnson administration would have to reconsider the military, financial, and political costs of continuing the war. Such a military strike would also cause South Vietnamese leaders to lose faith in their American allies, thus dividing the alliance. North Vietnamese leaders ultimately hoped that the Tet Offensive would move the conflict into a brief fighting-while-negotiating phase.[12] Historian George Donelson Moss maintains that the General Uprising was the key objective if any success in the Tet attacks was to be achieved. Without the uprising and subsequent overthrow of the South Vietnamese government, a coalition government was impossible, thus making a negotiated settlement improbable.[13]

Ronnie E. Ford claims that the Tet Offensive was never meant to be a "go for broke" effort to quickly win the war, but rather the offensive was a "continual process" of attacks and uprisings to gain strength as the war entered a fighting-while-negotiating phase.[14] Another historian of the Vietnam War, George C. Herring, notes that while the North Vietnamese at the least hoped the offensive would begin a fighting-while-negotiating phase, the maximum result was to be the collapse of the South Vietnamese government, the withdrawal of American forces, and a new coalition government under NLF control.[15]

The Tet campaign

The first phase of the Tet Offensive began in the fall of 1967. Because the final plan and authorization was not issued until December 1967 and planning had been so secretive, PLAF units in particular had little time to prepare for highly visible and dangerous missions. Many chains of command had to be reorganized as units were reconfigured to meet whatever operation they were assigned. Operational security was paramount to the success of the initial Tet attacks. Such stress on secrecy, however, had the unintended consequence of leaving many officers and units in the dark as to how their particular mission fit into a broader operation. Moving large amounts of material and thousands of troops along infiltration routes across the DMZ and down the Ho Chi Minh Trail was also a major security hazard. New recruits were needed to fill out under-strength units, which trained hard to make the paradigm shift from guerilla-style tactics to urban warfare methods required for fighting in the cities. Preparing for the offensive was a tremendous and risky undertaking.

The Border Battles

In order to draw American forces away from the cities and train PAVN and PLAF forces in tactics for holding positions, the North Vietnamese conducted several attacks in border areas, especially near the Cambodian and Laotian borders and the DMZ. General Westmoreland believed these attacks were in part designed to give North Vietnam control of provinces just south of the DMZ, in particular Quang Tri, and in preparation for decisive engagement at the Marine outpost at Khe Sanh, located just a few miles from the border with Laos and fifteen miles south of the DMZ. I Corps Tactical Zone (CTZ) encompassed the northern provinces of South Vietnam and American forces there conducted mostly interdiction operations to prevent North Vietnamese infiltration across the DMZ and the border with Laos (Figure 8). To conduct such operations, I CTZ commanders had built a string of outposts and fire bases at places like Con

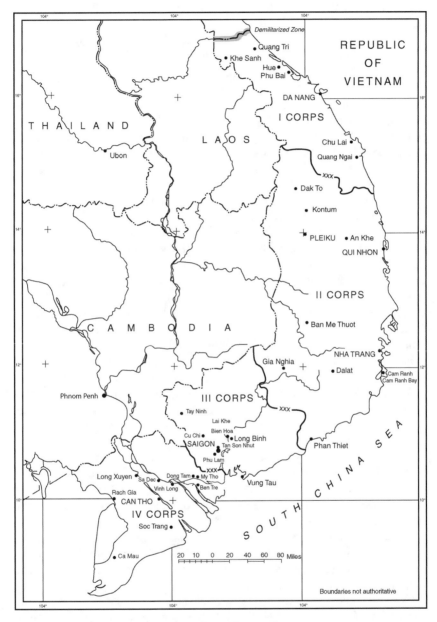

Figure 8 The Republic of Vietnam with Corps Tactical Zones.

Source: U.S. Army Center of Military History.

Thien, Camp Carroll, the Rockpile, and Khe Sanh, which would play a major role in the upcoming events.

PAVN forces staged major attacks on Con Thien in July and September while conducting a continuous artillery barrage on the base through the end of October. The Marines at Con Thien withstood the barrages and repelled the attacks. PAVN forces stopped their assault at the end of October. By attacking a static fortified position, PAVN forces had to expose themselves to American firepower. Mortars, artillery, naval gunfire, and B-52 air strikes pounded PAVN forces, which suffered very heavy losses. In October, ARVN units repelled a PAVN attack on a border outpost at Song Be in the III CTZ, while Viet Cong and PAVN forces staged a joint assault on an ARVN outpost at Loc Ninh, near the Cambodian border. Units from the American 1st Infantry Division were called in to help repel the well-coordinated but very costly assaults. Over the course of five days, PAVN and PLAF launched numerous human-wave assaults on fortified positions.

The twenty-two day battle at and around the border post at Dak To, a U.S. Special Forces camp in the Central Highlands border region, severely bloodied both sides for no strategic advantage. American intelligence picked up the movement of PAVN units into the region, causing Westmoreland to redeploy, though not permanently, several American and ARVN battalions to repel the attack. Beginning November 17, PAVN forces engaged American and ARVN units in a chain of battles that killed an estimated fourteen hundred PAVN troops and wounded hundreds more, while costing the Americans and South Vietnamese near 360 killed and more than a thousand wounded.

These PAVN and PLAF attacks, known collectively as the "Border Battles," were part of Giap's plan to lure American and ARVN forces away from the cities. Because of the mobility of these forces, however, few were permanently relocated, leaving most to return to their original posts. The cost to PAVN and PLAF units involved in these assaults was indeed high, as American firepower was able to pound massive exposed concentrations of enemy troops. American intelligence noted that it had been unusual for PAVN and PLAF units to stage such massive attacks, attempt to hold static positions, and take such high casualties.

By December 1967, North Vietnamese assaults in remote areas and the increase in movement along the Ho Chi Minh Trail had signaled to American intelligence analysts that a big enemy push was near. The problem was pinpointing when and where the attack or attacks would come. Captured documents indicated major attacks would soon take place at key bases and towns like Pleiku and Ban Me Thuot. Other captured documents were filled with political encouragement for the upcoming decisive battle that would win the war, another key piece of intelligence indicating something major. PLAF and PAVN desertions decreased markedly, and captured enemy soldiers taunted interrogators by boasting that the war would soon be over.

In December, Westmoreland even warned General Earle Wheeler, the Chairman of the Joint Chiefs of Staff, that President Johnson and the American public should be prepared for a large-scale North Vietnamese offensive in the not too distant future.

By January, MACV became convinced that a major assault would take place. Conventional wisdom pointed to an assault by PAVN forces across the DMZ and Laotian borders in northern South Vietnam. Few suspected an all-out assault across all of South Vietnam even though there were several indications that just such an assault would take place. Some, including Westmoreland, believed that movement of enemy forces in other parts of the country was probably a feint to draw American forces away from the north, especially from the besieged base at Khe Sanh. Westmoreland thought Khe Sanh was where Giap had decided to stage the decisive Dien Bien Phu-like battle. Part of the American reluctance to accept intelligence indicating an all-out offensive was that the Americans believed North Vietnam did not have the capability to carry out such an offensive.

Nonetheless, Westmoreland eventually became concerned enough to recommend to the government of South Vietnam that the traditional Tet holiday truce be completely cancelled. South Vietnamese President Thieu waffled, first decreasing the cease-fire order from forty-eight to thirty-six hours beginning January 29, then canceling the cease-fire altogether on the evening of January 30, just hours before the Tet attacks began. Thousands of South Vietnamese troops were on leave, traveling to their hometowns to spend the holiday with family, as tradition dictated. In a cautious move, Westmoreland redeployed several American units in the last days of January, fearing that the all-out offensive might indeed take place. Westmoreland put American forces across South Vietnam on highest alert early in the day on January 30. The South Vietnamese government inexplicably lifted the ban on fireworks for the Tet holiday. That night, fireworks went off across Saigon and other cities in festive celebrations of the lunar new year initiating the Year of the Monkey.

Historiographic point

Did American intelligence fail in predicting the Tet Offensive?

One of the key questions about the Tet Offensive involves the apparent surprise experienced by American and South Vietnamese forces when the attacks broke out in the early hours of January 31, 1968. Should American forces have been better prepared for the attacks? Did intelligence analysis fail to provide adequate warning?

John Prados, an historian of the Vietnam War, suggests that the indicators of a broad, countrywide offensive were clear. Even in the few days before January 31, intelligence signaled an imminent attack. As to why Westmoreland and others did not interpret these signals as such, Prados claims Westmoreland had already made up his mind that the main thrust of the offensive would occur in the northern provinces, notably at Khe Sanh. He had reckoned that the attacks would begin perhaps right after the Tet holiday. North Vietnamese deception convinced Westmoreland that the main attacks would occur elsewhere, not in the cities, certainly not in Saigon. In that sense, according to Prados, the Americans were caught by surprise: they failed to interpret the events, movements, captured documents, and other indicators because they viewed these incidents through the wrong lens.[16]

James J. Wirtz agrees with Prados but offers even broader failures in the intelligence analysis. Wirtz argues that in part because of the Success Campaign during the fall of 1967, intelligence analysts in Vietnam produced reports that fit with the prevailing notion that the United States was winning the war. Indicators that a massive offensive was imminent would not have supported the rhetoric of progress. Moreover, American interpretations of the Border Battles and other fights in 1967 more often than not attributed Communist movements as reaction to American military initiatives rather than North Vietnamese preparation for a broad offensive. For Wirtz, the two general mistakes the Americans made that caused the scope of Tet to be a surprise were the failure to recognize the fact that existing beliefs no longer accounted for events leading up to the Tet Offensive and the failure to recognize enemy mistakes and act upon them. In the end, according to Wirtz, Westmoreland had to make a choice between a decisive engagement against Khe Sanh or a broad general offensive. Based upon his beliefs, upon what he wanted to happen, and upon the way he and others chose to interpret intelligence, he decided Khe Sanh was the target while the attacks that took place in the cities were diversions.[17]

The bureaucratic disconnect among the CIA, MACV intelligence, GVN intelligence resources, and other intelligence organizations operating in Vietnam and Washington, D.C., according to Ronnie Ford, created an atmosphere conducive to non-cooperation. Disagreements over enemy strength, the so-called Order of Battle crisis of 1967, and intentions led to a breakdown in intelligence sharing during the months and weeks leading up to the Tet Offensive. As a consequence, bringing together information at the top levels of command did not occur as it should have.[18]

Historian Larry Cable states that there was no failure in gathering intelligence leading up to the Tet attacks. Rather, the failure came in the way intelligence analysts and top-level commanders chose to interpret the intelligence. Doctrine, bureaucracy, overlapping intelligence parameters, and a lack of a process for synthesizing intelligence contributed to a skewed view of enemy intentions that fit with the institutional view of the war. In other words, Westmoreland and others saw what they wanted to see, rather than what was there.[19] James Willbanks agrees with this view of the intelligence leading up to Tet, noting, "when intelligence indicators coincide with preferences, predisposition, and preexisting beliefs, the real message behind the gathering intelligence may be lost."[20]

The Battle of Khe Sanh

Beginning as a small outpost to monitor infiltration across the DMZ in 1962, Khe Sanh by 1967 had become a large installation complete with 1,500-ft steel-planked runway. Aside from the runway, only the treacherous and mostly unpaved Route 9 served as a supply link to the base. A Marine regiment took over the outpost from Army Special Forces in January 1967. Located on what amounted to a large but low plateau with heavily wooded hills overlooking about half of the area, Khe Sanh was an excellent location from which to launch interdiction patrols near the Laotian border and the DMZ. The outpost had seen plenty of action since its inception. During late April and early May 1967, PAVN units attempted to take a triangular series of hills that surrounded the base from which they could shell Khe Sanh with ease. These hills, 861, 881 North, and 881 South (named so because of their height in meters), had to be retaken by Marine units in vicious fighting. Once secure, the Marines built strong fortified positions atop each of these and other surrounding hills to better defend the main base at Khe Sanh (Figure 9).

Beginning in September, PAVN forces began massing near Khe Sanh; by December perhaps as many as twenty thousand PAVN troops were deployed to the area. American intelligence indicated that elite units from Hanoi were present and that Giap himself was in command. This and other indicators led Westmoreland to believe that the North Vietnamese were planning a major assault on the post to inflict a Dien Bien Phu-like defeat upon American forces. Rather than evacuate the outpost, Westmoreland reinforced it to lure PAVN forces into the open where they could be annihilated by American firepower.

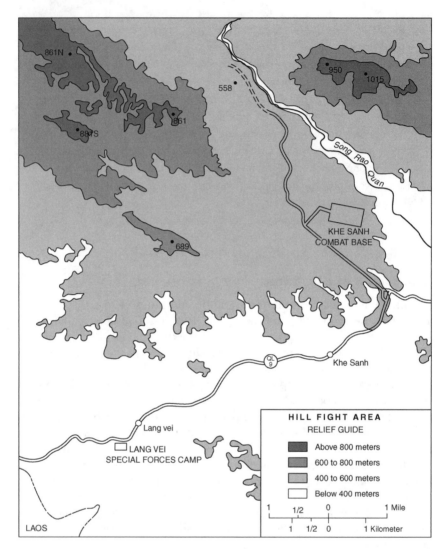

Figure 9 Khe Sanh area, including hills and Lang Vei Special Forces Camp.

Source: Willard Pearson, *The War in the Northern Provinces, 1966–1968* (Washington, D.C.: Department of the Army, 1975, 16).

In January, intelligence from Marine patrols and reconnaissance missions from the nearby Army Special Forces Camp at Lang Vei indicated a large PAVN presence in the area. Some PAVN deserters alerted the Marines at Khe Sanh that an attack was imminent. Westmoreland ordered contingency plans to relieve the base if it was in danger of being overrun. One plan involved the deployment of over fifty American combat battalions to the north. The other, Operation Niagara, was a massive aerial bombardment of the hills surrounding Khe Sanh once the PAVN assault began.

In the pre-dawn darkness of January 21, PAVN mortars and rockets began shelling hills 881 South and 861. Fierce fighting ensued, as PAVN human-wave attacks assaulted Marine posts atop these hills. Khe Sanh itself came under intense fire, including a lucky shell that struck the ammunition dump near the runway. The Marines lost much of their ammunition in the explosion, forcing perilous re-supply from airdrops and touch-and-go landings by C-130 cargo planes and other aircraft. PAVN units cut Route 9 the same day. Operation Niagara commenced as Marine patrols and aerial reconnaissance pinpointed PAVN positions for one of the most intensive aerial bombardments in history, which continued, aside from interruptions because of poor weather, through March 31. Marine and Air Force fighter-jets conducted over twenty-four thousand sorties around Khe Sanh against North Vietnamese positions, while Air Force B-52s flew at least 2,700 missions in support of the besieged base.

The American public followed the Battle of Khe Sanh in daily news-papers and nightly on television network news. It appeared that the biggest battle of the war was underway. President Johnson had a sand-table map of the base constructed in the situation room of the White House, where he closely followed the battle each day, sometimes picking bombing targets himself (Figure 10). Television news likened the battle to Dien Bien Phu, which is the type of decisive victory Westmoreland believed Giap hoped to achieve. The analogy was questionable, however, as where the French garrison at Dien Bien Phu had been isolated and difficult to reinforce, the Marines at Khe Sanh enjoyed daily re-supply (although access to fresh water was a logistical problem) and near-constant air cover, and maintained most hilltop positions throughout the battle. Nonetheless, in the American public's mind, Khe Sanh and Dien Bien Phu were near synonymous.

As the Tet Offensive got underway on January 30–31, the six thousand Marines at Khe Sanh endured bombardment and assault from over twenty thousand PAVN forces in the hills surrounding the base. Senior commanders in Vietnam debated the merit of holding the base, some believing the out-post was untenable and of no strategic value considering the present crisis. Westmoreland, however, maintained that the assault on Khe Sanh was the main thrust of the North Vietnamese offensive. President Johnson agreed, hoping Westmoreland would seize the opportunity to deal the North Vietnamese a mortal blow, thereby buying the president valuable political time for increasing support for the war. At one point, Chairman of the Joint Chiefs of Staff General Wheeler asked Westmoreland if tactical nuclear weapons would be necessary to relieve the garrison. Westmoreland replied

Figure 10 The map table of Khe Sanh in the White House Situation Room, February 15, 1968. Depicted left to right: Press Secretary George Christian, President Lyndon B. Johnson, General Robert Ginsburgh, Walt Rostow.

Source: Lyndon Baines Johnson Presidential Library.

that such extreme measures were not likely to be needed, but he did not dismiss the idea entirely.

PAVN forces overran the Special Forces camp at Lang Vei on February 7. Much to the shock of the Americans, PAVN forces had used least a dozen Soviet-made PT-76 tanks in the assault, which was over in a matter of minutes. The presence of tanks in the area led the Marines at Khe Sanh to believe the North Vietnamese intended to overrun the garrison. On February 10, however, five PAVN infantry battalions were redeployed to Hue, which the North Vietnamese attacked and actually captured as part of the Tet Offensive. The last major PAVN assault on Khe Sanh came on the night of February 29–March 1 and was repelled with great cost to the North Vietnamese (Figure 11). By March 10, it appeared that the North Vietnamese had withdrawn more forces and the intensity of the assaults noticeably decreased. It appears that the failure of the Tet attacks elsewhere had convinced Giap that Khe Sanh was either no longer needed as a diversionary operation or no longer worth the price of overrunning.

Beginning April 1, the Army's 1st Cavalry Division and ARVN airborne troops began clearing Route 9 to relieve the Marines at Khe Sanh. Operation Pegasus opened the road completely by April 8, and by April 18 the Marines

Figure 11 PAVN forces advance at Khe Sanh, February 1968.
Source: U.S. Army Center of Military History.

had been fully relieved. The Army occupied Khe Sanh with little harassment from the few remaining PAVN units in the area until June, when it was decided that the base held no strategic use and was thus destroyed and abandoned. PAVN losses were undoubtedly great, but no firm figure can be placed on North Vietnamese killed and wounded. Some estimates range as high as ten to fifteen thousand, while the official body count of enemy dead yielded only 1,602. Between the seventy-seven day battle, Operation Pegasus, and air operations connected to the Khe Sanh battle, the United States lost over four hundred killed and almost a thousand wounded.

Historiographic point

What was the purpose of the North Vietnamese attack against the outpost at Khe Sanh?

Was that attack on Khe Sanh a diversion for the other Tet Offensive attacks across South Vietnam, or did Giap intend to overrun and destroy the base in the hope of a Dien Bien Phu-like victory? The purpose of the assault on the outpost is still debated. To be sure, Khe Sanh must be considered in the overall context of the Tet Offensive. General Giap himself stated this about Khe Sanh:

> Khe Sanh was not that important to us. Or it was only to the extent that it was to the Americans. It was the focus of attention in the United States because their prestige was at stake, but to us it was part of the greater battle that would begin after Tet. It was only a diversion, but one to be exploited if we could cause many casualties and win a big victory. As long as they stayed in Khe Sanh to defend their prestige they said it was important; when they abandoned it they said it had never been important.[21]

In his memoir, General Westmoreland had this to say about the significance of Khe Sanh:

> After deliberate consideration, I ruled out abandoning Khe Sanh. To have done so would have been to cooperate with the enemy's grand design for seizing the two northern provinces and his constant efforts to carry the fight into the populated areas. . . . None of us was blind to the possibility that the North Vietnamese might try to make of Khe Sanh another Dien Bien Phu, yet we were aware of marked differences in the two situations and were convinced we could hold Khe Sanh with a relatively small ground force if augmented by tremendous firepower.[22]

Journalist Neil Sheehan contends that Khe Sanh was a major diversion, calling it the "biggest lure of the war," and that Giap did not intend for the battle to be another Dien Bien Phu.[23] Historian John Prados maintains that Hanoi probably "did not have a fixed plan at all but a set of strategic goals toward which it aimed." To Prados, the original intention of the North Vietnamese cannot be known, but at the beginning of the assault it seems to have been to "pursue a real siege." Then, as the battle continued into March, the North Vietnamese vacillated between overwhelming the base and continuing the siege depending upon the progress of the overall offensive.[24]

George R. Vickers, a sociologist who has studied the Vietnam War extensively, contends that Giap had no design for a Dien Bien Phu redux and only used Khe Sanh to prevent American forces from being able to reinforce urban centers attacked during the Tet Offensive.[25] This interpretation matches General Tran Van Tra's assertion that the attack on Khe Sanh was launched to "draw a large number of U.S. and Saigon puppet troops from the inner cities to this remote but important area, to divert the enemy's attention and thus help our urban forces in the secret deployment of their units."[26]

Historian Peter Brush doubts that at the beginning of the siege the primary objective of the North Vietnamese was to overrun Khe Sanh. Instead, Brush maintains that the operation was a very successful diversion. Having achieved the diversion, however, Brush thinks Giap was tempted to then achieve some sort of victory over American forces there.[27] James Willbanks suggests that the large number of forces Giap committed to and sacrificed at Khe Sanh indicates that the North Vietnamese indeed wanted to take the base. Such large force, Willbanks contends, was more than enough to hold six thousand Marines in their positions for diversionary purposes. Perhaps, says Willbanks, Giap had plans for the large force depending upon success early in the Tet Offensive.[28]

William Turley believes that the "level of effort was sufficient to sustain a credible diversion," but not to attempt to overrun the base if the United States was determined to defend it. For Turley, a diversion was the primary purpose of the North Vietnamese attack on Khe Sanh.[29] James J. Wirtz holds to the diversion interpretation as well, adding that Khe Sanh, while costly to the North Vietnamese, achieved its objective to mask the real Tet attacks.[30] General Phillip Davidson dismisses diversion as the purpose of Khe Sanh as "obvious nonsense." Instead, Davidson believes that Giap intended to use momentum gained from Tet victories around South Vietnam to stage a climatic set-piece battle to decisively defeat the Americans. Ironically, this is precisely what Westmoreland wanted Khe Sanh to be against the North Vietnamese.[31]

Author Ang Cheng Guan contends that Giap never meant for Khe Sanh to be another Dien Bien Phu, nor was it solely intended as a diversion. Instead, according to Guan, Khe Sanh was "part and parcel of an overall strategy" in the General Offensive–General Uprising plan in the north, particularly in the coastal area around Quang Tri province. For Guan, Khe Sanh should not be examined by itself, but rather as part of the overall Tet Offensive.[32]

Tet begins

In the early morning hours of January 31, over sixty-seven thousand PAVN and Viet Cong troops, plus several thousand guerilla forces, attacked targets across South Vietnam. This first wave of assaults hoped to inflict as much damage as possible and capture key targets, holding them until reinforcements could arrive. Surprise was crucial, but much of the surprise was lost when some units began their attacks prematurely on January 29 at places such as Pleiku, Qui Nhon, Ban Me Thuot, and Nha Trang. In order to allow its soldiers to enjoy the Tet holiday, the North Vietnamese government announced in late January that Tet would begin on the evening of January 29 rather than January 30, thus perhaps contributing to the confusion for some PLAF and PAVN commanders. Many, but not all, American and ARVN units went on high alert on the eve of Tet. In so many towns and cities across South Vietnam, Tet celebrations went on as normal—that is, until it became apparent that what many thought were fireworks were actually mortars, rockets, and gunfire.

The scope of the attacks surprised Westmoreland and the American high command. Nonetheless, the American and South Vietnamese rapidly responded after the initial confusion faded. Except for extended fighting in the Cholon district of Saigon and at the old imperial city of Hue, American and ARVN forces repelled most of the attacks in a matter of hours and in some cases a few days. Considering that over half of ARVN troops were on holiday leave and some American units were not on alert, the failure of the first wave of assaults is extraordinary. Air and ground mobility allowed American and ARVN forces to deploy with speed and lethal efficiency. PAVN and PLAF reinforcements failed to get to where they were most needed. The populace did not heed the call for the historic General Uprising and instead largely remained indoors. The South Vietnamese government did not waver and the attacks failed to shatter ARVN forces. Rather, it was the PLAF that was arguably shattered, as PLAF units led many of the assaults in the cities and, lacking reinforcement, were pounded by American and ARVN forces (Figure 12).

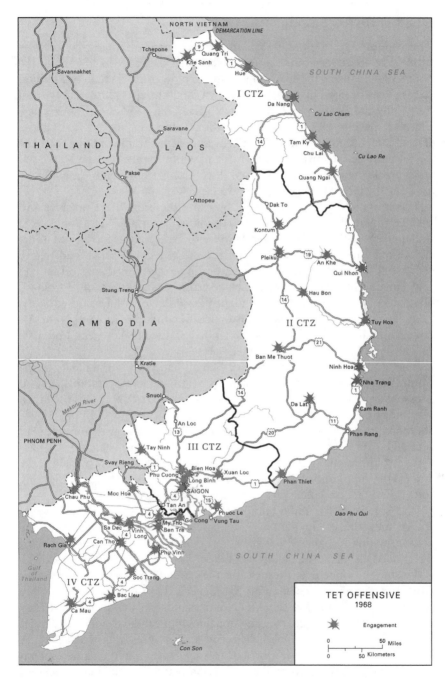

Figure 12 The Tet Offensive.

Source: U.S. Army Center of Military History.

The battle for Saigon

The capital city of South Vietnam had changed dramatically because of the war. Refugees poured into the city daily to escape the fighting in the countryside, causing the city's population to grow from less than two million to over three million in a matter of a few years. The city offered safety from Viet Cong cadres and a chance, though often not a good one, to start a new life after having left family and tradition behind in one's home village. Because of the multitudes of refugees and dense traffic coming into the city, it had been relatively easy over the previous months for the Viet Cong to smuggle weapons and infiltrate Viet Cong troops into safe houses strategically located near Tet Offensive targets.

Just after midnight on January 31, over four thousand Viet Cong men and women organized in eleven assault battalions began their attacks to seize and hold objectives in the city center for perhaps as long as forty-eight hours before reinforcements organized outside the city could arrive and relieve them. In all, at least three divisions were organized for attacks on Saigon and surrounding areas, which included the headquarters of the South Vietnamese Joint General Staff, Independence Palace (which housed President Thieu's office), the National Broadcasting Station, Tan Son Nhut Air Base, and, most symbolically for the United States, the American Embassy, in addition to numerous other targets.

Since December 1967, security for Saigon had been in the hands of the South Vietnamese to allow American forces to conduct operations in rural areas. Many South Vietnamese national police and ARVN troops in Saigon were not on duty as the attacks began, and only the 716th Military Police Battalion, a single battalion of about a thousand men, was thinly spread guarding over 130 American military and government installations. These forces would be the initial reaction force to the attacks. Few of them were trained in urban combat and most were woefully unprepared for the fighting they would face on January 31 and during the following days.

The attack on the radio station began about 3:00 a.m., when twenty PLAF men dressed in South Vietnamese riot-police gear arrived at the station, telling the guard that they were reinforcements. When the guard questioned them, he was shot and killed. The men quickly swarmed the radio station, where over the airwaves they were to play recorded messages from Ho Chi Minh encouraging the General Uprising to overthrow the government. Fortunately, the ARVN commander in the area had already cut the station's power and transmission lines to the radio tower several miles away on a prearranged signal when it was clear something was wrong. A lone PLAF machine gunner atop a nearby apartment building killed several ARVN troops arriving to retake the station before he was finally silenced. The enemy inside the station nonetheless found themselves surrounded and trapped. They destroyed as much of the broadcasting equipment as they could while defending themselves against ARVN troops assaulting the building. In what would become the common characteristics of most Tet attacks, reinforcements failed to arrive. After a six-hour fight, the PLAF men in the station were all killed.

Posing as ARVN troops, another unit of PLAF forces attacked the Independence Palace at about 1:30 a.m. Not surprisingly, the Palace was one of the most heavily guarded buildings in Saigon. After blasting the staff entrance gate with rockets, the thirty-four PLAF sappers charged into the compound only to be met with ferocious gunfire from the guards inside. The survivors withdrew to a nearby apartment building and held out for two days. Only two of the thirty-four survived. The attack on the Navy Headquarters, where the objective was to seize nearby docked ships to transport reinforcements from coastal areas to Saigon as part of the General Uprising, met a similar fate, except that all of the PLAF sappers were killed in a matter of minutes. At the Armored Command and Artillery Command compound in Saigon, sappers hoping to capture tanks and artillery found no tanks and no working artillery pieces. As at the radio station, reinforcements were nowhere to be seen in each of these attacks.

At the Joint General Staff headquarters, PLAF sappers were supposed to coordinate their assault on Gate 5 with a local force battalion's attack on Gate 4. The arrival of an American military police patrol jeep disrupted the attack on Gate 5, allowing the ARVN guards inside the gates to fully secure the entrance. The attack on Gate 5 did not begin until five hours later, at 7:00 a.m. This time, the local force unit breached the defenses and gained entry into the compound. Incredibly, the attackers could have taken control of the headquarters at this point but instead chose to wait for reinforcements, which, of course, did not arrive. ARVN airborne troops and South Vietnamese Marines destroyed the PLAF local force unit in just a few hours. President Thieu arrived by helicopter to the Joint General Staff headquarters by noon, making it his emergency base of operations.

Other attacks materialized in the pre-dawn darkness. Several American bachelor officer quarters (BOQs), were struck, including BOQ Number 3, where sixteen American military police were killed. PLAF units occupied the Phu Tho Racetrack, a horseracing venue located at the junction of several key roads in the Cholon district of Saigon. The racetrack was occupied early in the morning as a location from which to dispatch incoming reinforcements. As the primary attacks failed, remaining PLAF units congregated in the area surrounding the racetrack, while reinforcements failed to materialize. PLAF resistance in the area, however, was strong. It took American and ARVN units, including the use of helicopter gunships, all day to secure the area and the facility.

Despite securing the racetrack, PLAF units mounted several counter-attacks to retake the facility while the fighting continued for several more days in Cholon. Densely populated, poor, and packed with tenement housing, Cholon had been a haven for NLF agents in Saigon for years as well as the center for the Saigon black market. On February 4, people living in Cholon were told to leave the area, which was then declared a free-fire zone, meaning that anyone found in Cholon would be considered enemy. Massive firepower was used to root out the PLAF in Cholon. By the end of the campaign, which took until March 7, Cholon was in ruins and hundreds of civilians had been killed, thousands wounded, and thousands more made homeless (Figure 13).

Just outside the city, PLAF assault teams hit Tan Son Nhut Air Base and the nearby air base at Bien Hoa and the huge Army installation at Long Binh. American reinforcements arrived by helicopter and road to Long Binh, where they assisted base security forces in repelling human-wave assaults. Many participants noted that the PLAF stood their ground and

Figure 13 Three Vietnamese women move back into the Cholon area after a Viet Cong attack that left a two-block area leveled, in hopes of salvaging meager belongings.

Source: National Archives.

fought rather than withdrawing, which had been the norm. At Tan Son Nhut, PLAF battalions attacked the base from three sides. The Americans had been truly caught by surprise at Tan Son Nhut, and had it not been for the coincidental presence of an ARVN airborne battalion awaiting transport to another sector, the PLAF assault may have done much more damage than it did. Almost every American and ARVN soldier and officer who could carry a weapon was involved in repulsing the assault.

On February 1, one of the most graphic and remembered images of the war was captured on film by Associate Press photographer Eddie Adams and NBC cameraman Vo Suu. General Nguyen Ngoc Loan, the chief of the South Vietnamese National Police, summarily executed an NLF officer with a single shot to the young man's head from his revolver. The context for the incident was straightforward. Martial law had been declared in Saigon and any unauthorized person found carrying a weapon could be shot on the spot. Such was the case in this instance. The film footage of the execution, showing the body collapsing and blood spurting from the wound, had a resounding impact. Because of satellite technology and the time difference between Saigon and New York, the film was on NBC's *Hunter–Brinkley Report* that very night and Eddie Adams' photograph of the bullet's impact was on the front page of most major newspapers the next morning. Over fifteen million saw the film footage on the evening news, yet NBC received only ninety letters protesting showing the horrifying uncensored footage on television. Suddenly, the brutality of the war was in living rooms across the United States (Figure 14).

Of all the attacks on Saigon that day, none held such drama and symbolism for the American public as the PLAF sapper attack on the American Embassy. For American commanders, the attack was more of a nuisance than a major assault, and as they gradually recognized the scope of the Tet attacks the comparatively minor assault on the Embassy compound held little relevance. For the American public and media, and President Johnson, the assault on the Embassy, which by treaty and tradition is American soil, after all the talk of making progress in South Vietnam was a true and deep shock. With the Saigon Press Corps billeted just blocks away, the Embassy attack received a great deal of attention.

The multi-story building inside a compound surrounded by an eight-foot tall reinforced concrete wall had opened in September 1967 and symbolized American power and influence in Vietnam. It should be no surprise that the Embassy was a target. Nineteen PLAF sappers, some of whom had just been recruited from the countryside, were basically conducting a symbolic suicide mission. From a nearby garage the group made their way unchallenged by South Vietnamese police who saw the two vehicles driving erratically and without lights. American military police managed to seal the enormous steel front gate as the sappers approached. At 2:47 a.m., a guard inside the

Figure 14 General Nguyen Ngoc Loan, head of the South Vietnamese National Police, executes Viet Cong Captain Nguyen Van Lem during the Tet Offensive in Saigon, February 1, 1968.

Source: Associated Press Images.

Embassy radioed that the compound was under attack. Outside, along the high wall, one sapper ignited a satchel charge, blowing a 3 ft-wide hole in the concrete. Most of the team rushed in, their lieutenant the first to fall dead, into a hail of gunfire from the handful of guards inside. Despite outnumbering the guards, the PLAF sappers faltered and took cover on the grounds. Because the gate had been sealed shut, military police outside could not get in. The few sappers that remained outside the wall killed two military police before being killed or captured.

As dawn arrived, an intense battle to retake the Embassy grounds ensued. American commanders had decided to wait for daylight to destroy the remaining sappers, knowing that other Americans were inside the Embassy building and in other buildings in the compound. The crowd of reporters and news cameramen recorded the battle. Under pressure from Washington, where President Johnson awoke to erroneous press reports that the Viet Cong were actually inside the Embassy building, Westmoreland ordered units from the 101st Airborne Division to retake the compound. Six hours after the attack began, the PLAF sapper team had been either killed or captured.

General Westmoreland arrived at the Embassy with Ambassador Ellsworth Bunker at 9:30 a.m. in starched and pristine fatigues. With the destruction of the battle and enemy corpses around him, Westmoreland proceeded to tell reporters that the Embassy attack had been a minor incident, that the attacks around Saigon and South Vietnam had failed, and that everything was under control. While he may have been right, it did not look as though he was giving an accurate assessment of the situation. In November he had told the nation that progress was being made in Vietnam —if progress was being made, how then could the North Vietnamese stage the most dramatic offensive of the entire war?

Historiographic point

What was the impact of the attack on the U.S. Embassy?

Historians and writers generally agree that the PLAF sapper attack on the Embassy in Saigon had a significant impact on public perceptions of the war back in the United States and was representative of the disconnect between MACV's priorities during the early hours of the Tet Offensive versus priorities back in Washington. Militarily, the Embassy battle was one of hundreds of fights that erupted during the morning of January 31. In Washington, however, the press and the Johnson administration became narrowly focused on the American Embassy in Saigon.

An historian of the North Vietnamese side of the Vietnam War, William Duiker notes that the mere sight of PLAF sappers in the Embassy compound "shook the confidence of many Americans in the prospects for final victory in South Vietnam" and severely undermined Westmoreland's credibility.[33] Don Oberdorfer suggests that at first the Embassy attack did not receive much attention by the North Vietnamese and the assault itself was even ridiculed by People's Liberation Front commander General Tran Do for being so poorly planned and executed. Only later, as the failure of the Tet attacks became clearer and positive propaganda became more of an imperative, did North Vietnamese propagandists capitalize upon the Embassy attack, claiming the assault had resulted in over two hundred American dead and proclaiming the sappers heroes of the revolution. Like Duiker, Oberdorfer agrees that Westmoreland's credibility with the press was gravely undermined, and "many Americans sat up in their chairs" when they saw the dramatic footage of the Embassy battle on network television news. Headlines back in the United States, according to Oberdorfer, focused on the erroneous report that the

Viet Cong had actually penetrated the Embassy building, followed by editorials wondering how this could be after Westmoreland and the Johnson administration had said progress was being made.[34]

Historian George Donelson Moss contends that "Americans were shocked to learn that an enemy supposedly on its last legs could bring the war to the symbolic heart of American power" in South Vietnam.[35] William Hammond also notes the shock of the Embassy attack. He suggests that one of the main reasons the Embassy attack received so much media attention and thus had such an impact in the United States was that in the early hours of the Tet Offensive the Saigon press corps had nowhere else to go to cover the fighting except the Embassy, which was just blocks from many reporters' hotels. For the reporters at the Embassy, Westmoreland's impromptu assurance that everything was under control did not mesh well with what they saw around them, not to mention with what Westmoreland had told them over the previous months.[36]

Ronnie Ford is critical of the Viet Cong's failure to reinforce the sappers who penetrated the Embassy compound, which was a symbolic target. Armed with only personal weapons and grenades, it was impossible for the sapper unit to hold their objective for long without reinforcement.[37] James Arnold is most critical of the sapper attack on the American Embassy, suggesting that the Communists never fully appreciated the "potential psychological impact" of the operation. Not until the North Vietnamese realized the impact the Embassy assault was having in the United States did they begin to utilize the attack in their propaganda. Arnold goes further, stating, "Here was the paradox of the war: a small, ill-conceived, tactically flawed attack against an insignificant military objective, designed to impress the South Vietnamese, proved the decisive action of the war because of its impact on the American public."[38] Journalist Stanley Karnow agrees with Arnold, implying that the attack on the Embassy was calculated to "demonstrate to the South Vietnamese people that the United States was vulnerable despite its immense power."[39]

Tet across South Vietnam

The Tet Offensive, of course, was much more than just the attack on Saigon and the Battle for Khe Sanh. PLAF and PAVN units staged assaults across South Vietnam and, other than the spectacular capture of Hue, met costly defeat in every instance. In many cases, defenders were caught in at least partial surprise. Enemy units had orders to hold captured objectives and to stand and fight, and few had contingency plans for any sort of strategic withdrawal or retreat. Thus, American firepower was able to catch concentrations of Viet Cong and PAVN units in the open, with lethal results.

In the north, PLAF sappers attacked the South Vietnamese I Corps headquarters at Da Nang, but were beaten back by ARVN units and very close bombing strikes from American warplanes. Quang Tri was also attacked. In II CTZ, the battle for Nha Trang lasted almost twelve hours before ARVN and Army Ranger units defeated enemy forces. At Qui Nhon in the Central Highlands, ARVN intelligence actually knew of attack plans from captured Viet Cong agents. Nonetheless, the attackers were able to seize numerous objectives, at least temporarily. At Ban Me Thuot, the fighting raged for nine days with the city center changing hands at least four times during the battle. The ARVN commander at Ban Me Thuot, Colonel Dao Quang An, had cancelled holiday leaves and sent out preemptive ambush patrols based upon intelligence from captured NLF agents. The American advisor to Colonel An's command praised the colonel for his tactical leadership in the battle.

In the Mekong River Delta, PLAF units staged several attacks that involved almost every enemy unit American intelligence had listed in its order of battle. The American Mobile Riverine Force (MRF) played a key role in repelling these attacks, most notably at My Tho, where heavy house-to-house fighting placed MRF forces in an unfamiliar combat environment. The river city of Ben Tre was nearly destroyed in the fight to oust Viet Cong forces; supposedly an officer told a reporter that "It became necessary to destroy the town in order to save it," a phrase which, real or not, became part of the vernacular of the war. Unlike Colonel An at Ban Me Thuot, some ARVN commanders failed in the heat of battle. One major general reportedly did not leave his command bunker for over four days, and a colonel at Vinh Long had a complete physical and mental breakdown. One commander allegedly wore civilian clothing under his uniform in order to escape with refugees. ARVN forces generally performed well in response to the Tet attacks, but some units and commanders cracked under the extreme pressure.

The battle for Hue

By late February, North Vietnamese commanders issued orders to halt any attacks in the cities and instead to retreat back to the countryside. Assaults on static fortified positions were forbidden. Those Viet Cong units that could muster the strength returned to pre-Tet ambush and hit-and-run tactics. Hue, however, was the exception. Units in the imperial city received orders to hold their ground. For American and ARVN forces, retaking Hue became the longest and bloodiest battle of the war.

Hue was the old imperial city and home of elite preparatory schools and a university, which had educated many of Vietnam's political and military leaders, including Diem and Giap. A beautiful city that represented the cultural heritage of Vietnam, Hue served as the imperial seat of the Annamese emperors of the Nguyen Dynasty from 1802 to 1945. Many considered Hue Vietnam's most beautiful city. Gardens, pagodas, and beautiful buildings and homes could be found within the walls of the very formidable Citadel, a nineteenth-century fortification which covered over three square miles, including the Ay Loc Airfield, and was surrounded by huge walls and large moats. Located on the north side of Song Hu'ong, or the Perfume River, the Citadel area and the residential district of Gia Hoi was known as the Old City and accounted for two-thirds of the 140,000 people living in Hue in 1968. In the northeast corner of the Citadel, the ARVN 1st Division had its headquarters, which was defended by the elite Hac Bao Company, nicknamed the Black Panthers. Most 1st Division units were deployed in the countryside just outside the city.

On the south side of the river was the New City, built more recently and home to the remaining third of the city's population. The New City included government buildings, Hue University, the hospital, and the cathedral. In 1968, a small MACV advisory headquarters of about two hundred American and Australian personnel was also located in the New City, just south of the six-span Nguyen Hoang Bridge, which served as the Perfume River crossing for Highway 1, the main supply artery from Da Nang to Quang Tri and posts near the DMZ. The nearest major American presence was the Marine base eight miles south at Phu Bai, which was home to Task Force X-Ray of the 1st Marine Division. Commanded by Brigadier General

Foster C. LaHue, Task Force X-Ray included two regimental headquarters and three battalions of Marines.

Up to 1968, Hue enjoyed an informal open-city status, as neither side staged significant military operations in and near the city. Many intellectuals, academics, and political conservatives who strongly opposed Communism and Ho Chi Minh resided in the city. For the North Vietnamese and in particular the regional Viet Cong, Hue was indeed a strategic but also symbolic target for the Tet Offensive. Capturing and holding Hue would disrupt American and ARVN operations in the I CTZ, would demonstrate the weakness of the South Vietnamese government, and would give the Communists control of the cultural and intellectual center of Vietnam.

The fighting at Hue would be unlike previous fighting in the Vietnam War, in which rural operations were the norm. Hue, however, was a tight urban environment, with narrow, twisty streets, thousands of alleyways, and dense structures (Figure 15). The battle to come would resemble the fight for Manila in the Philippines during World War II rather than any battle that had taken place in the Vietnam War to that point. American and ARVN units had little training and still less experience fighting in such an environment, while Viet Cong and PAVN forces lacked experience but had trained in urban warfare tactics in specific preparation for the assault on Hue.

Viet Cong forces around Hue included six main-force battalions, while two PAVN regiments operated in the area. As the battle unfolded, three more PAVN regiments redeployed from Khe Sanh arrived as reinforcements. The North Vietnamese plan of attack on Hue involved intensive preparation and reconnaissance. Over 190 targets, including every government and military installation on both sides of the river would be hit on January 31 by a force of five thousand. Other forces would block American and ARVN reinforcement routes, mainly Highway 1. Over half of the ARVN 1st Division was on holiday leave and PAVN commanders believed the population of Hue would join the fight as part of the General Uprising. Additionally, North Vietnamese intelligence agents had drawn up lengthy lists of South Vietnamese government and military officials, intellectuals, foreigners, and reactionaries who had assisted the Americans or spoke out against the Communists, to be arrested and executed. This aspect of the Hue fight would produce one of the worst atrocities of the war (Figure 16).

On January 30, ARVN 1st Division commander General Ngo Quang Truong learned of the premature Tet attacks in the region and quickly placed his division on full alert. Truong was considered one of the best ARVN commanders by his American colleagues. While the Black Panther Company arranged for the defense of the headquarters compound in the Citadel, Truong deployed his remaining units outside the city, wrongly believing that as Hue was an open city, the North Vietnamese would

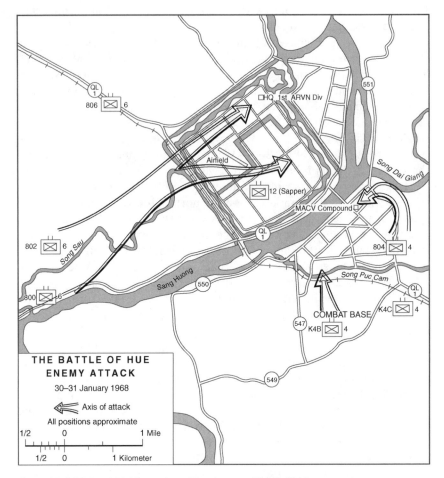

Figure 15 PAVN and PLAF attack on Hue, January 30–31, 1968.

Source: Willard Pearson, *The War in the Northern Provinces, 1966–1968* (Washington, D.C.: Department of the Army, 1975), 39.

not attack it directly. In one of the many intelligence failures of the Tet Offensive, an American military listening post at Phu Bai intercepted Communist orders for the attack on Hue, but by the time the intercept made its way up the chain of command for analysis, the attack had already begun. At the MACV compound in the New City, the Americans were caught completely by surprise.

As in Saigon, NLF agents were already inside the city, ready to assist the attacking forces when they arrived. The attack began at about 3:40 a.m. with mortar and rocket barrages on both sides of the river. Viet Cong

Figure 16 City officials of Hue who are responsible for identifying the victims of the Tet offensive of 1968 arrange the coffins before mass funeral services, 1969.

Source: National Archives.

and PAVN units poured through the city gates, quickly taking control of government buildings, the police station, and most of the Citadel, except for General Truong's headquarters. Attacked by rockets and then a delayed infantry assault, the defenders of the MACV compound held their ground at great cost. By daylight, other than the MACV compound and the ARVN 1st Division headquarters, PAVN and PLAF forces controlled the city of Hue. They immediately set up revolutionary committees to govern sections of the city. On loudspeakers intelligence agents read aloud the names of reactionaries and intellectuals, hoping neighbors would turn the suspects in to Viet Cong authorities. Thousands were arrested and most were never heard from again.

General Truong ordered reinforcements from outside the city to fight their way through Hue to his position in the Citadel, which two airborne battalions and an armored unit managed to do by late afternoon on January 31. The MACV compound also called for reinforcements. The situation all across the I CTZ was still confused, however, and the request for help lost its imperative among the numerous other calls for reinforcements in the I CTZ area. Even when I CTZ commanders ordered reinforcements from Task Force X-Ray to relieve the defenders at the MACV compound, no one realized the magnitude of the attack on Hue. General LaHue sent only a company of Marines from Task Force X-Ray up Highway 1 to Hue. Meeting unusually stiff resistance just outside the city, the company was reinforced when a larger reaction force arrived with armor and self-propelled guns. The Marines were able to finally secure the compound late in the afternoon at the cost of ten dead and thirty wounded. The Marines then attempted to cross the Nguyen Hoang Bridge, but were forced back to the south side of the Perfume River.

By the night of January 31, the situation at Hue had become clearer. At I CTZ headquarters, American and ARVN commanders agreed to divide responsibilities for retaking Hue. The Marines would assault the New City, while ARVN forces would retake the Citadel. At first, restrictions limited firepower in the Old City in a vain attempt not to destroy the historic landmark. However, as the fight intensified, these restrictions were lifted to allow artillery and close-air support to root out PLAF and PAVN defenders, thus resulting in the unfortunate destruction of much of Hue.

Progress was slow. The Marines had to clear out entrenched PAVN and PLAF forces in well-fortified positions, literally building by building, street by street. The fighting was brutally intense and bloody. PAVN and PLAF forces fired upon the Marines from rooftops, apartment buildings, houses, and businesses, from every direction, with rifle, machine guns, and rocket-propelled grenades. Marine tanks had difficulty maneuvering on the tight streets, and the poor weather made close-air support difficult during the first days of the battle. Marines with non-debilitating wounds were patched up and put back in the line (Figure 17). It took two weeks to gain moderate control of the southern part of Hue, and another twelve days to finally secure it.

Meanwhile, the ARVN attack on the Citadel had stalled by February 4. A PAVN counter-attack during the next two days forced ARVN troops to sacrifice much of the precious little ground they had gained. Both sides reinforced but the stalemate continued. On February 10, General Truong had to ask General LaHue for Marine assistance. LaHue sent in a Marine battalion, which assaulted the east wall of the Citadel. It took a week of exhaustive fighting to secure the wall at the cost of forty-seven killed and 240 wounded. On the west side of the Citadel, the Army's 1st Cavalry Division prevented PAVN reinforcement and re-supply. PAVN forces in the Citadel were now trapped near the old Imperial Palace. On the night of February 23, an ARVN battalion attacked toward the Palace, pushing the now poorly supplied and exhausted PAVN units out of their positions. Over the next few days, remaining PAVN and PLAF units retreated out of the city.

Over the course of the twenty-six-day battle, an estimated five thousand PAVN and Viet Cong forces had been killed in the battle. ARVN losses amounted to 384 killed and more than eighteen hundred wounded, while the United States Army suffered seventy-four killed and over five hundred wounded. Among the three Marine regiments involved in the battle, 142 Marines were killed and over 850 wounded. Of all the Tet attacks, the Hue battle may have been the most damaging for the Americans and South Vietnamese. Despite the heroic and costly success in retaking the city from PAVN and PLAF forces, the fact that the enemy had taken and occupied such a symbolic city was a shock to commanders in Vietnam as well as to the American public, who watched the progress of the battle daily on television news. Even Walter Cronkite went to Hue, filing special reports on the tough fighting and the sacrifice of the Marines (Figure 18).

At battle's end, Hue had been reduced to rubble. Forty percent of the city had been destroyed and over 100,000 of Hue's 140,000 inhabitants were now homeless. Over 5,800 civilians had been killed. As many as three thousand died in the fighting, caught in crossfire or killed by deadly artillery fire. The remaining 2,800 came from the lists, and were detained, convicted and sentenced by kangaroo courts, taken to various locations inside as

Figure 17 D. R. Howe (Glencoe, MN) treats the wounds of Private First Class D. A. Crum (New Brighton, PA), "H" Company, 2nd Battalion, Fifth Marine Regiment, during Operation Hue City.

Source: National Archives.

Figure 18 CBS News anchor Walter Cronkite interviews Hue University Professor Mai in Hue City, February 20, 1968.

Source: National Archives.

well as outside the city, then executed. A lucky few were sent to special camps for reeducation. As mass shallow graves began to be discovered in late February, the scope of the atrocity became evident. Many bodies were bound and had a single shot to the back of the skull, while others had apparently been buried alive.

The aftermath of Tet

The initial phase of the Tet Offensive ended with the battle for Hue, but despite the severe cost in casualties the North Vietnamese pressed on with subsequent phases of the offensive in May and later in the summer of 1968. PAVN replacements filled out or replaced shattered PLAF units and on May 5 struck 119 targets that included attacks in Saigon. Unlike the January 31 offensive, the May 5 round of attacks was anticipated. American and ARVN units were ready and in many cases preemptively attacked PAVN forces before they could launch their assaults. Hue was spared another massive battle, but the Cholon district in Saigon was again the scene of heavy fighting from May 5 through May 13 and again in late May and early June, and Saigon received enemy rocket attacks almost daily throughout June. Despite being prepared and quickly repelling the so-called Mini-Tet assaults in May, American forces paid a dear price. Over 550 American troops died in the fighting during the week of May 4 through May 11, contributing to the loss of almost two thousand dead for the month of May, the costliest month for the United States during the entire war. PLAF attacks in the Mekong River Delta in August and PAVN attacks near Saigon in September were both repelled at great cost to Viet Cong and PAVN forces. Afterwards, North Vietnamese commanders terminated the offensive and ordered remaining main-force units to withdraw to sanctuaries, most of which were located in nearby Cambodia and Laos.

The Tet battles from January through February 1968 cost American, South Vietnamese, Australian, and South Korean forces almost five thousand killed and over sixteen thousand wounded. American estimates placed PAVN and PLAF at between forty and fifty thousand killed and thousands more wounded. Although the estimate may be high, PLAF units seemed to have borne the brunt of the casualties. In a purely military sense, Tet appeared to be a resounding victory for American and South Vietnamese forces, as the Communist gamble to concentrate forces for mass assaults against defensible positions allowed American firepower to lay waste to thousands of the PLAF's most experienced forces. Yet, the political fallout in the United States indicated that something less than a victorious military feat had occurred.

To the American public, Tet was a shock. Westmoreland and the Johnson administration had been telling them that there was "light at the end of the tunnel" in November 1967 and that the strategy of attrition was working. How, then, could the North Vietnamese stage such a country-wide assault on so many targets, attack what had been well-defended cities that had previously been untouched by the war, keep thousands of Marines pinned down at Khe Sanh, and actually get inside the American Embassy compound in Saigon? The images of dead enemy sappers littered about the Embassy grounds, General Loan's execution of an NLF officer, and the dark grainy news footage of the combat at Khe Sanh and Hue were indeed compelling if not disturbing. Newspapers and politicians, including an increasing number of Democrats who had supported the war, began asking such questions. The Johnson administration seemed incapable of explaining the military significance of Tet. The horrific images of combat, destruction, and casualties that appeared on the nightly news seemed to indicate something other than what Westmoreland and Johnson had been telling the public over the previous months.

On February 27, Walter Cronkite hosted a special edition of the *CBS Evening News* on Vietnam. Cronkite, perhaps the most trusted news voice in America, had been in Hue conducting interviews with Marines and civilians amid the fighting. A veteran war reporter, Cronkite had been shocked by the scope of the Tet Offensive and the intensity of the fighting. Heretofore Cronkite had resisted editorializing in his newscasts, but his feelings about Vietnam had become so strong that he felt compelled to speak out. At the end of the broadcast, Cronkite told millions of viewers that Vietnam had become an unwinnable stalemate. In so many words, he said the United States should get out. President Johnson allegedly said, upon watching the broadcast, that if he had lost Cronkite, he had lost the support of mainstream America.

Public support of the war had been gradually eroding well before the Tet Offensive, and the offensive itself had little appreciable impact upon public opinion except to confirm the doubts of those who were reevaluating their positions on the war. Polls indicated a slight bump in support for the war as a result of the Success Campaign of November and December 1967. Tet simply restored the steady decline of support for the conflict that had been apparent since early 1967.

The request for more troops

One of the curious effects of the Tet Offensive was the disconnect it exposed between Washington and Saigon. General Westmoreland's controversial request for more troops for Vietnam highlighted this disconnect. In early February, General Earle Wheeler, the Chairman of the Joint Chiefs of Staff, cabled Westmoreland to ask if he needed reinforcements. President Johnson's fixation on the battle at Khe Sanh, brought on in part by Westmoreland's insistence that Khe Sanh was the principal objective of the Tet Offensive, probably led Wheeler to ask. Westmoreland responded that Khe Sanh was under control and that he wanted only the additional forces, some ten thousand, which had already been approved and mobilized.

From Washington, Westmoreland was receiving signals that President Johnson was considering expanding operations in the northern sector of South Vietnam, perhaps even into Laos, where many NLF and PAVN sanctuaries were located. Westmoreland had long advocated such an expansion of the war, and had earlier suggested operations across the DMZ into the southern part of North Vietnam. Westmoreland cabled Wheeler to ask for an additional division if such operations were authorized. It seems that Johnson was concerned about the current situation at Khe Sanh, while Westmoreland was not and was instead considering future needs.

To add to the problem of forces in Vietnam, American forces worldwide were stretched very thin, dangerously so in Wheeler's opinion. With commitments and possible threats in Western Europe, Korea (which at this time was in a heightened state of alert because of the *Pueblo* crisis), and the Middle East, Vietnam was draining American manpower resources as well as equipment. Options to rectify this situation basically boiled down to expanding the draft or calling up the reserves. Both had domestic political implications for the Johnson administration and would involve massive additional financial costs; calling up the reserves seemed to be the less politically costly. For Wheeler, the broader strategic picture demanded additional forces. The problem was how to convince Johnson to mobilize the reserves.

Whether or not Wheeler set up Westmorland to achieve the reserve call-up, Westmoreland made an additional troop request. According to Westmoreland, although American and ARVN forces were beating back the Tet attacks, North Vietnam was replenishing depleted forces at an accelerated rate. Westmoreland reasoned that this period of replenishment presented an opportunity to strike a decisive blow against PAVN and PLAF forces in South Vietnam. To strike this blow, Westmoreland quickly needed more troops.

Having previously told General Wheeler and President Johnson that his troop needs were adequate, Westmoreland's sudden change in force needs confused Johnson. General Wheeler came to Vietnam to confer with Westmoreland in February, while the battle at Khe Sanh still raged. Wheeler reported to Johnson that a troop increase was needed to offset losses during the Tet Offensive and to decisively defeat another mass offensive, which Wheeler was certain would come. Wheeler was perhaps using his meeting with Westmoreland to persuade Johnson to call up the reserves, and thus meet Wheeler's troop needs for American forces world-wide as well as in Vietnam. Westmoreland and Wheeler somehow decided upon 206,000 addition troops needed for Vietnam, with the first increment of 108,000 arriving in Vietnam by May 1. The remaining ninety-eight thousand would be held in reserve depending upon changing conditions in Vietnam.

Not surprisingly, the troop request did not go over well back in Washington. Johnson tasked incoming Secretary of Defense Clark Clifford to form a committee to evaluate Westmoreland's request. Clifford, an advisor to every president since Franklin Roosevelt and long-time Washington insider, had supported the war in Vietnam since the Kennedy years but had started to change his mind. Clifford's study group concluded that the current strategy of attrition was failing and additional troops would not bring the war's end any closer, and recommended an escalation of twenty-two thousand troops and mobilizing 245,000 reservists. The call-up would not be open-ended; rather, future escalation would depend upon the stability of the South Vietnamese government. Clifford, once a supporter of the war, now began to privately convince Johnson he needed to find a way out.

On March 10, news of the request for 206,000 more troops leaked to the press. News reports made it appear as though the entire 206,000 would be sent to Vietnam as opposed to Wheeler's hope to use some of the troops to augment the strategic reserve. Nonetheless, a mixed message had been sent to the American people. Westmoreland and the Johnson administration had told the public that Tet had been a major victory over the Communists, yet Westmoreland now needed more troops. How could that be?

Public opinion

Table 1 Tet in context, August 1965–May 1971: In view of the developments since we entered the fighting in Vietnam, do you think the United States has made a mistake sending troops to fight in Vietnam?

Date	Yes	No	Don't know
August 1965	24%	60%	16%
March 1966	25%	59%	16%
May 1966	36%	49%	15%
September 1966	35%	48%	17%
November 1966	31%	51%	18%
January 1967	32%	52%	16%
April 1967	37%	50%	13%
July 1967	41%	48%	11%
October 1967	47%	44%	10%
December 1967	45%	46%	9%
Early February 1968	45%	43%	12%
Late February 1968	50%	42%	8%
April 1968	49%	40%	11%
August 1968	53%	36%	11%
September 1969	58%	32%	10%
January 1970	57%	33%	10%
April 1970	51%	34%	15%
May 1970	57%	35%	8%
June 1970	56%	36%	8%
January 1971	59%	31%	10%
May 1971	62%	28%	10%

Source: Gallup Opinion Index, Report 54 (December 1969), 7–8.

Table 2 Tet in context, July 1965–April 1968: Do you approve or disapprove of the way President Johnson is handling the situation in Vietnam?

Date	Approve	Disapprove	No opinion
July 1965	56%	26%	22%
August 1965	56%	25%	20%
January 1966	57%	27%	15%
April 1966	47%	35%	18%
June 1966	38%	44%	18%
August 1966	43%	41%	17%
October 1966	43%	37%	19%
January 1967	38%	43%	19%
March 1967	41%	45%	13%
May 1967	37%	46%	17%
August 1967	32%	54%	13%
December 1967	38%	49%	12%
January 1968	39%	47%	14%
Early February 1968	35%	53%	13%
Late February 1968	32%	58%	10%
Late March 1968	26%	62%	11%
April 1968	42%	48%	11%

Source: Gallup Opinion Index, Report 35 (May 1968), 17.

Table 3 Tet in context, November 1967–February 1968: Just your impression, do you think the United States and its allies are losing ground in Vietnam, standing still, or making progress?

Date	Losing ground	Standing still	Making progress	No opinion
November 1967	8%	33%	51%	8%
Late February 1968	21%	42%	32%	6%

Source: Gallup Opinion Index, Report 34 (April 1968), 12.

Table 4 Tet in context, December 1967–November 1969: People are called "hawks" if they want to step up our military effort in Vietnam. They are called "doves" if they want to reduce our military effort in Vietnam. How would you describe yourself—as a "hawk" or a "dove"?

Date	Hawk	Dove	No opinion
December 1967	53%	25%	13%
January 1968	56%	27%	17%
Early February 1968	61%	23%	16%
Late February 1968	58%	27%	15%
April 1968	42%	40%	18%
September 1968	45%	40%	16%
November 1969	31%	55%	14%

Source: Gallup Opinion Index, Report 54 (December 1969), 7–8.

Table 5 Tet in context, December 1966–March 1969: In terms of time—months or years—how long do you think the fighting in Vietnam will last?

Date	2 years or less	Over 2 years	Uncertain, no opinion
December 1966	39%	42%	19%
June 1967	27%	41%	32%
November 1967	48%	32%	20%
Late February 1968	35%	30%	35%
March 1969	27%	49%	24%

Source: Gallup Opinion Index, Report 46 (April 1969), 15–16.

A change in policy

By early March, congressional support for the war in Vietnam was eroding. In the House of Representatives, 139 members publicly signed a petition calling for a reevaluation of the president's Vietnam policies. In the Senate, Arkansas Democrat J. William Fulbright began hearings in the Senate Foreign Relations Committee on Vietnam. Administration officials came under intense questioning on how they could rectify claims of progress against the apparent shock of the Tet Offensive, and now the troop request.

The first primary of the 1968 presidential election campaign was held, as had become traditional, in New Hampshire on March 12. Democrat Eugene McCarthy, a senator from Minnesota, had announced his candidacy in November 1967, calling himself the "Peace Candidate." In January, McCarthy had been polling in single digits. Tet boosted his numbers to near 20 percent in February. Remarkably, and surprisingly to many, McCarthy captured 42 percent of the vote in New Hampshire, but more importantly he won twenty of the twenty-four available delegates. Johnson had escaped defeat by a mere 230 votes. McCarthy's strong showing shocked Johnson's campaign team and was attributed to dissatisfaction with Johnson's handling of the war and increasing strains on the economy. On March 14, the growing gold crisis and increasing inflation forced the Department of the Treasury to close the gold market after a stunning $372 million loss and a fear that over $1 billion could be lost if the market was open on the 15th. On March 16, Robert Kennedy announced his bid for the Democratic Party's nomination, running on an anti-war platform. On March 18, Johnson delivered an address in Minneapolis that featured his standard anti-appeasement and "we will persevere" rhetoric.

With his own party dramatically rebuffing his policies and an inflationary financial crisis becoming more severe each passing day, Johnson was increasingly politically isolated. He also began having doubts about the war and his own political viability. On March 25 and 26, Johnson again called together the Wise Men to give him counsel. Where in November the group had advised staying the course, after numerous briefings and much intense discussion the Wise Men now advised President Johnson that the war could not be won, and that the United States should begin turning over responsibility for fighting the war to the South Vietnamese and withdrawing American troops as soon as possible. Some of the Wise Men thought the United States was not doing enough to try to win, while most of the group had concluded victory was hopeless. This dichotomy reflected what many in America felt about the lack of progress; "hawks" wanted to do more, "doves" wanted to get out. Johnson was getting hammered from both sides. The group further recommended a halt to the bombing of North Vietnam in the hope of beginning meaningful negotiations with the North Vietnamese.

On March 27, Johnson met with the National Security Council at the White House. Johnson expressed his discouragement that the South Vietnamese government was helpless as a result of the Tet attacks. With the Viet Cong isolating the cities, NLF influence had grown in the countryside at the expense of years of pacification efforts. Defeat did not seem likely, yet neither did victory. Johnson decided not to grant Westmoreland's and Wheeler's request for additional forces. Instead, the National Security Council agreed to a troop ceiling of 549,500, which gave Westmoreland only 13,500 troops in addition to the eleven thousand already en route to Vietnam. Granting the troops request would have placed over 700,000 American troops in Vietnam with no foreseeable guarantee of progress toward winning the war.

On March 31, 1968, Johnson addressed the nation on national television. This had originally been a speech reassuring the public about the war in the midst of the Tet Offensive while reminding of the need for sacrifice and perseverance, but leaders in the Johnson administration, such as new Secretary of Defense Clark Clifford, Secretary of State Dean Rusk, and Special Counsel to the President Harry McPherson, had convinced Johnson to rewrite the speech to signal a new direction for the United States in Vietnam. Johnson began with a review of previous offers to begin negotiations with North Vietnam and defended the American and South Vietnamese victory over PAVN and NLF forces in the Tet Offensive. He then revealed he was ordering a bombing halt over much of North Vietnam in the hope of persuading the North Vietnamese to begin substantive peace talks, and further shocked the nation by announcing he would not seek reelection in 1968. In April, ARVN units began the gradual take-over of combat operations. In May, American and North Vietnamese representatives had begun formal talks in Paris, which would last four and a half years through the first term of the next president, Republican Richard Nixon. In June, General William Westmoreland became Army Chief of Staff. General Creighton Abrams replaced Westmoreland as MACV commander after four and half years of command in Vietnam.

Historiographic point

What was the role of the media in the Tet Offensive?

One of the most controversial aspects of the Vietnam War is the role of the media. In the first "television war," news reporters could file reports for national television network news programs via satellite on the same day, an advancement that represented a revolution in war reporting. Interpretations fluctuate: some believe that the reporting on Tet influenced public opinion, which in turn forced a change in American strategy in the war, while others argue that media reporting on the war was balanced and did little to influence opinion. The role of the media in the Vietnam War is a contentious problem; Tet represents a microcosm of this historiographic issue.

Chester Pach argues that news reports on the Tet Offensive were "spectacular and unsettling, both for viewers who had become accustomed to the misleading optimism of the Progress Campaign and for top government officials, who recognized the damage to their credibility." Pach claims that the Johnson administration "shaped policies to counteract what they considered to be critical, unfair, and sensational reporting." The effect, if any, reporting had because of Tet was to expose the credibility gap between what the Johnson administration had told the public before Tet and what the public saw on their television during Tet.[40] Still, Pach warns against attributing "too much power" to the television reports during Tet, as Johnson's advisors were more influenced by their own sense of what was happening in Vietnam than by the media.[41]

Journalist Don Oberdorfer writes that "For the American press, the combination of high drama and low national understanding created a monumental challenge in Vietnam—and the press, like the government, was ill-equipped to meet it." Oberdorfer claims that, well before Tet, journalists sensed the government was not telling the whole story about Vietnam, and because they were "unrestrained by censorship and goaded by competition, much of the press leaped to stark conclusions when sudden events in the previously untouched cities seemed to prove its theories right." With satellite technology and instant communications, reporters became less inclined to offer thoughtful analysis due to the pressure of the moment: "Instant analysis was often faulty analysis." Oberdorfer implies this was the case with Tet. Still, Oberdorfer believes American reporters as a whole represented and reflected American society, and thus "the view of the public, in turn, influenced the mood of the press."[42]

In her study of media coverage of the Vietnam War during the Johnson administration, Kathleen J. Turner suggests that the Tet Offensive gave many reporters their first "extended view of the enemy" because of the fighting taking place in Saigon. Generally, according to Turner, reporters had little familiarity with Vietnamese culture and language, which, combined with the difficult transportation problems, "hampered both the ability and the inclination of many reporters to see the wider context of the offensive." Over 90 percent of news stories during the Tet Offensive centered on Saigon, Hue, and Khe Sanh. Thus, reporting during Tet

> depicted an opponent not only willing to continue the battle but also capable of inflicting major losses on both South Vietnamese and American troops, contrary to the image of an enemy whose spirit and military machine were almost broken by bombing raids and American might.

According to Turner, what journalists reported to the American public about Tet did not match what the American public had been told before Tet.[43]

Turner's interpretation matches that of Peter Braestrup, a journalist who reported from Vietnam. Braestrup offers this post-mortem on Tet reporting:

> The net result, in terms of media treatment, was that the fighting in Saigon, Hue, and Khe Sanh became the whole war, a war in which, seemingly, no or few ARVN forces fought, and U.S. forces were particularly

hard pressed. The overall—and inaccurate—impression given, especially on film, was that, well in to March, the outcome on the Vietnam battlefield was very much in doubt.[44]

In his work on the media and the Vietnam War, historian William M. Hammond argues that the increasingly stark assessments of the Tet fighting probably did not have a great impact on public opinion, as polls show. However, according to Hammond, such reporting "nonetheless reinforced doubts already circulating within the Johnson administration."[45] Daniel Hallin also contends that reporting during Tet had little influence on public opinion other than to highlight what some critics of the war had already been arguing. According to Hallin, Tet reporting contributed to a "crossover point, a moment when trends that had been in motion for some time reached a balance and began to tip the other way."[46]

Historian David Schmitz suggests the focus on the influence of the media during Tet is perhaps misplaced. Press coverage of Tet, Schmitz maintains, "was not a factor in the decisive decisions made by the Johnson administration after Tet." Officials in the Johnson administration were not "directly influenced by public opinion and certainly not by television's coverage of the war." Instead, the political elite in Washington and members of the Johnson administration who changed their stand on the war during this period were influenced by "the reports they received and their own calculations."[47]

Historian James Willbanks supports the idea that Tet reporting "only served to add velocity to a situation made bad by the credibility gap that had begun to develop well before the Communists launched their offensive in 1968." News reports during Tet may have indeed occasionally been "biased and erroneous," but the "earlier bursts of optimism" stemming from the Progress Campaign of late 1967 that did not square with the "stunning surprise" of the attacks probably had the greater impact.[48] Historian David Culbert supports the idea that the reporting on Tet, especially the visual images, confirmed the suspicions of those who already doubted the optimism of the Progress Campaign and stirred suspicions among some of those who believed what the Johnson administration had said about the war in the fall of 1967. Culbert argues further:

> In a time of uncertainty, compelling visual evidence has a power denied it in ordinary circumstances. This is why Tet was a military disaster for the North Vietnamese, though it ended up as a psychological victory in terms of its effect on public opinion in the USA.[49]

George Herring admits that "it is difficult to measure the impact of television coverage on public attitudes," but argues that "the idea that a hypocritical media undercut" public attitudes "just at that point when the war could have been won is suspect" when discussing the media coverage of the Tet Offensive.[50] Author Michael Lind argues that the perception of Tet as a defeat for the United States grew from negative press reporting during and after the offensive. Admitting that the offensive did discredit Westmoreland's optimistic reports in the fall of 1967, Lind lays significant blame on "the sensationalism of western journalists, who gave the American public a misleading impression of the power and popularity" of the enemy.[51]

The impact of Tet

The impact of the Tet offensive is complex and varied. It assuredly was a pivotal moment in the American war in Vietnam. In less than three months, the Johnson administration had gone from expressing optimism for progress and victory to a complete change in policy that began the process of the ultimate American withdrawal in January 1973.

On the NLF/PLAF

The NLF had hoped the Tet Offensive would strengthen its position in the South, perhaps even at the expense of the North Vietnamese government. A negotiated settlement with a new government dominated by the NLF would have placed the NLF in a very formidable position in post-war Vietnam. After years of very difficult fighting and hardship, the NLF had high expectations for the Tet Offensive. Yet, because of the way the offensive was planned, PLAF forces bore the brunt of the fighting in the cities and sacrificed many of their best political and military leaders. Moreover, as the NLF was largely responsible for the General Uprising in the cities, the perceived manifest failure of this part of the offensive reflected poorly on the NLF. Supporters in North Vietnam had less faith in NLF capabilities, while the NLF's influence among the South Vietnamese came under intense scrutiny. Initial gains in the countryside made in the first days of the offensive had been possible because many American and ARVN units were redeployed to the cities, thus it appeared early that NLF influence had increased. Yet, because many PLAF main-force units remained deployed in forward attacks throughout the spring and early summer of 1968 they suffered high casualties from American firepower. Arguably the initial phase did not destroy the NLF, but the subsequent phases dramatically worsened and lengthened the recovery.

The PLAF played a decreasingly less military role after 1968. Many PLAF main-force units had been destroyed in the fighting and were not reconstructed afterwards. By 1972, almost 90 percent of the war was being fought by PAVN regulars rather than the Viet Cong. Whether by design or consequence, by 1969 the war became more of a conventional conflict with fewer guerilla operations. PAVN forces took over the bulk of the fighting while the PLAF performed more routine military duties. Whether the North Vietnamese intended to sacrifice as much of the NLF and PLAF as possible for political and military reasons or welcomed the decline of both as an unintended consequence of the Tet Offensive, the fact remains that the NLF did not wield the same power after Tet as it had before the offensive.

On North Vietnam

The North Vietnamese had held high hopes for the Tet Offensive. Of these hopes, the grand General Uprising was perhaps the most significant part of the Tet plan. As the offensive unfolded, it became starkly apparent to North Vietnamese leaders that the uprising would not occur. Moreover, the tremendous losses among the NLF infrastructure, especially in the cities, had not been anticipated. Rebuilding this infrastructure became a priority in 1968 through a united-front strategy, which emphasized cooperation between the NLF and the ruling Lao Dong Party in Hanoi. Alternatively, the united-front approach could also be interpreted as a subversive effort to further weaken the NLF so that the South Vietnamese insurgents would play less of a role in a post-war government.

The Lao Dong Party Politburo praised PAVN and NLF forces for what it considered the successful undermining of the South Vietnamese government and destruction of ARVN forces. The Politburo also comprehended the modest but unintentional gains made in the countryside at the expense of American and South Vietnamese pacification programs. Still, casualties had been unacceptably high, though not as high as American estimates. Thousands of PAVN soldiers made their way south to reconstitute many Viet Cong main-force units that had been destroyed during February and March. In the short term, this move weakened PAVN regular forces, but manpower shortages were overcome, as they had been for much of the war. The high losses in 1968 made 1969 and 1970 very lean and difficult years for PAVN and Viet Cong forces. Conserving manpower rather than expending it became a principal part of North Vietnamese strategy in the war. Tet, in other words, would not be repeated.

The North Vietnamese had hoped the offensive would have an adverse effect on the American will to continue the war. The extent of the impact on domestic politics in the United States, however, was unforeseen and yet another unintended consequence. North Vietnamese leaders were elated at the defeatism that seemed to take hold in Washington by spring 1968. Thus, even though the offensive had been costly and the General Uprising had failed, the extreme impact on the political will of the United States changed the war. North Vietnam could carry on the war indefinitely if the United States began to pull back. In this light, for the North Vietnamese the Tet Offensive could be considered decisive.

On South Vietnam

South Vietnam suffered appalling destruction from the Tet battles, especially in the cities, and the offensive left a perhaps permanent psychological scar on the Vietnamese consciousness. Both the Cholon district in Saigon and Hue lay in ruins. Hundreds of thousands of Vietnamese were homeless; many had become refugees, flocking to cities like Da Nang and Saigon for relief.

For the South Vietnamese military Tet had been a mixed experience. Many ARVN units fought surprisingly well, notably in Saigon and Hue, but others exposed their ineffectiveness in combat. Morale among the South Vietnamese military, which was never great to begin with, plummeted. ARVN desertion rates increased from 10.5 per thousand in late 1967 to 16.5 per thousand in July 1968, which translated to over ten thousand deserters per month. Pacification programs suffered, as ARVN pacification teams abandoned villages they considered no longer secure. Ironically, the ARVN units that fought the best typically suffered more costly casualties, which weakened the long-term combat effectiveness of these better units.

Perhaps the greatest impact had been the realization among the Vietnamese people that the South Vietnamese government, with all the backing provided by the powerful United States, could not consistently provide respect for the rule of law and civil rights, basic services, and most importantly security. Tet caused grave doubts among the Vietnamese people as to the viability and legitimacy of the South Vietnamese government. After Tet, the government would struggle even more with corruption, its inability to govern, and its legitimacy.

On the United States

American forces, along with their ARVN and Free World allies, had militarily defeated the Tet Offensive. Yet, the domestic impact in the United States of the offensive and the cost of defeating it contributed to a radical change in American strategy in Vietnam. The Tet Offensive made the tactical military successes from 1965 through 1967 relatively meaningless. The United States now had to accept that the North Vietnamese could carry on the war indefinitely. The worsening American economic crisis made continuing the war under pre-Tet conditions untenable and increasing the American presence in Vietnam impossible. The shock of the attacks and the economic situation had weakened American political will to achieve victory in Vietnam.

Regardless of whether it was true, the perception was that Tet undermined the military's credibility in its claims of progress and the success of the strategy of attrition. If American forces were winning, many political elites concluded, then they were winning badly. In the absence of any viable alternative offered by the American military, continuing to win badly was no longer an option after Tet. Despite overwhelming superiority in firepower, air power, logistical capabilities, and other resources brought to bear against the enemy in Vietnam since 1965, there was no guarantee of victory in the near future. Still, the American military remained convinced that Tet was an Allied victory and thus did little to reevaluate its strategy in Vietnam.

Perhaps the greatest impact of the Tet Offensive on the United States was the full realization that military force alone could not solve a political problem. Without a legitimate client state, the United States could never win the hearts and minds of the Vietnamese people to support an independent South Vietnam. The North Vietnamese apparently understood this concept, while the United States did not, at least up to the Tet Offensive.

Tet, of course, marked the beginning of an *annus horribilis* for the American people. The year 1968 would see the murders of Martin Luther King, Jr, and Robert Kennedy, the bloody riots at the Democratic National Convention in Chicago, and the dramatic growth of a hodge-podge of movements that protested the war and authority in general. The massacre of hundreds of South Vietnamese civilians at a small village called My Lai in March 1968 by American soldiers would be revealed to the American public the next year, giving the anti-war movement more fuel for its protest against the war and broadening discontent with Vietnam altogether. Richard Nixon, a Republican from California who had been a staunch anti-Communist vice-president under President Dwight Eisenhower, won the presidential election in November. Under Nixon's presidency, the process of getting out of Vietnam that began under President Johnson after the Tet Offensive would ultimately, though slowly, be achieved.

After Tet, the United States reluctantly welcomed negotiations with the North Vietnamese and began the process of turning the war over to the South Vietnamese government and military—a process that came to be called "Vietnamization." As American forces performed fewer combat duties in 1970 and 1971, tedious logistical and support duties contributed to a crisis in discipline that infected American forces worldwide. The anti-war movement intensified across a broader segment of the American public, moving beyond college campuses. With deteriorating conditions in American society at home, and concluding that all that could be reasonably done had been done in South Vietnam, the Nixon administration stepped up negotiations with North Vietnam in late 1972. In January 1973, the United States and North Vietnam reached a peace settlement without the blessing of the South Vietnamese government. In April 1975, South Vietnam fell to North Vietnamese forces. North and South Vietnam were united under a Communist government.

Historiographic point

Was Tet the turning point of the Vietnam War?

There is general consensus among historians and other writers that the 1968 Tet Offensive was the turning point, or at least the pivotal moment, in the Vietnam War for both North Vietnam and the United States. Gabriel Kolko calls Tet the "most important and complicated event of the war," arguing that for the North Vietnamese Tet "was the threshold in the war's development, a major turning point guaranteeing that the Revolution would not be defeated."[52] Historian Ronald Spector contends that although the Tet battles proved militarily indecisive, the overall Tet Offensive, from January through August 1968, proved a political success for the North Vietnamese. Nonetheless, even though Tet convinced "almost all influential Americans that the war could not be won at an acceptable price or in an acceptable time," the military "deadlock" in South Vietnam "doomed" the Communists to a continued four and a half more years of war with the United States. For Spector, the war remained a stalemate despite "the drama of the Tet attacks, the ruin of the Johnson administration, the agonizing attempts at peace negotiations, and the sanguinary trials on the battlefield."[53]

General Tran Van Tra concludes that the Tet Offensive was a definitive turning point in the war. He calls Tet a "tremendous victory, that . . . ushered us into a decisive phase of our road to victory," though the North Vietnamese "paid a high price." For Tra, Tet was "the most strategic turning point of the war, eventually leading us to total victory."[54] In his biography of General Giap, Cecil Curry focuses on Tet as a decisive moment for the North Vietnamese and praises Giap for "accomplishing a military stalemate in the face of overwhelming American military technology." Curry notes that although Giap's offensive was a "tactical disaster," the Tet Offensive had "persuaded a massively growing number of Americans to look for a way out as well," just as Giap had done to French domestic support at Dien Bien Phu in 1954.[55] In Peter MacDonald's biography of the North Vietnamese general, Giap himself assessed the significance of Tet as a turning point in the war:

And that was our great victory: to change the ideas of the United States.

The Tet Offensive had been directed primarily at the people of South Vietnam, but as it turned out it affected the people of the United States more. Until Tet they had thought they could win the war, but now they knew that they could not. Johnson was forced to decrease military activity and start to discuss with us around the table how to end the war.[56]

In his memoir, General Westmoreland portrays the Tet Offensive as an opportunity lost. He claims the offensive was a "galvanizing event" for the South Vietnamese, and contends that the impact of the offensive on the South Vietnamese people was that of a "unifying catalyst," similar to Pearl Harbor's impact upon the American people. In the United States, however,

> the enemy scored . . . the psychological victory that eluded him in Vietnam, so influencing President Johnson and his civilian advisers that they ignored the maxim that when the enemy is hurting, you don't diminish the pressure, you increase it.[57]

William Duiker agrees with observers in 1968 who saw Tet as a crucial turning point in the war and contends that this view still holds. For Duiker, assessing the impact of the Tet Offensive is more complex than simply assigning victory or defeat to either side. Nonetheless, after the Tet Offensive the United States gave up trying to win the war and realized there would have to be limitations placed on the American commitment to South Vietnam. According to Duiker, "The dynamics of the war had been changed, and the stage was set for new initiatives" to bring the war to an end.[58] Historian David Schmitz goes further, concluding that "Tet had opened the door to new questions, attitudes, and answers about the war in Vietnam and America's role in the world." Schmitz downplays the influence of public opinion, and instead sees the change in attitudes among the establishment and elite from supporting the war, and the escalation needed to fight it, to concluding the war could not be won without grave costs to the economy, America's standing in the world, and American society. Tet convinced elites in the United States that domestic issues and other international concerns now outweighed victory over Communists in Southeast Asia.[59]

Historian James Willbanks sees Tet as a definite point where the tide turned in favor of an eventual North Vietnamese victory. Tet, according to Willbanks, had been a "calculated campaign" with broad objectives that ultimately "proved to the United States that the war was unwinnable, effectively toppled a president, convinced the new president to Vietnamize the war, and paved the way for the ultimate triumph of Communist forces in 1975."[60] For Larry Berman, an historian of the Johnson presidency and the Vietnam War, Tet was the turning point that allowed the doubters in the Johnson administration to convince Johnson that his Vietnam policy was flawed. In so doing, the American strategy in the war changed from continued escalation to de-escalation and withdrawal. Tet made it possible to disengage.[61] Historian David Barrett would agree with Berman, explaining that Tet was the catalyst for a change in direction of American policy in Vietnam.[62]

George Herring sees Tet as the moment when a major review of American military strategy should have occurred, but he contends that, "Not until the shock of the 1968 Tet Offensive compelled it were the basic issues of how the war was being fought even raised. Even then, they were quickly dropped and left largely unresolved." Tet had convinced Johnson to pursue a fighting-while-negotiating posture, similar to that of the North Vietnamese, but according to Herring, the Johnson administration's hard-line post-Tet approach to negotiations only served to deepen the stalemate. Johnson failed to give the North Vietnamese a real incentive to reach a settlement.[63] Lloyd Gardner argues that Tet was the moment that "demonstrated the war could not be won with 500,000 Americans in Vietnam, that the bombing campaign could not interdict supplies to the enemy, and that the costs of continuing at current levels, let alone new escalations, were prohibitive." With Tet, President Johnson had simply run out of arguments to convince the American people that Communist aggression in Southeast Asia was a threat to the United States. The Munich analogy no longer held.[64]

Historian Victor Davis Hansen maintains that Tet was one of the American military's "most impressive" victories of the war. However, "the disaster in the narrow tactical sense," according to Hansen, "was that in the wake of victory the Americans failed to capitalize on the Communist disarray but instead halted the bombing and began a radical retrenchment." Tet had been a "clear military victory that had dashed those pretensions" of optimism voiced in 1967.[65] Journalist Don Oberdorfer offered, in the foreword of a new edition of his book on Tet in 1983, the view that as more time passed since 1968, "it seems clearer than ever that the 1968 Tet Offensive was the turning point in the ill-fated U.S. military effort in Vietnam, and thus a historic junction in contemporary history."[66]

Finally, historian Robert Buzzanco argues that the most controversial impact of the Tet Offensive was the troop request made by Generals Westmoreland and Wheeler. As a turning point, the military recognized that civilian leaders in the United States were not going to dramatically escalate the war before Tet, and certainly not after the offensive. Both the military and the civilian leadership, according to Buzzanco, knew after Tet that neither was willing to "win" in Vietnam. By requesting 206,000 additional troops, the military transferred the burden of the conduct of the war to President Johnson, and thus shifted whatever blame there was for losing the war onto the civilian leadership as well.[67]

Part II

Documents

Document I

JUSPAO Field Memorandum Number 31

A Vietnamese looks at Tet,
November 28, 1966

Tet in Vietnam

Chuong Dac Long

The custom of celebrating Tet goes back to remote antiquity. Like many other Vietnamese traditions it was imported from China, probably by the Chinese tribe of the Yueh, which came 4,000 years ago from the banks of the Yang-Tse-Kiang to settle the land of the Giao-Chi (now North Viet Nam). The essence of this custom has been maintained throughout the ages. But, as with rites in other societies, its original significance gradually was lost or deformed so that later generations often came to repeat words and gestures that were so transformed they had lost all meaning. Certain old books on magic sometimes give an idea of what was in the mind of our ancestors who devised and imposed such or such a rite. But, more often, one can only conjecture.

One of the best-preserved rites of Tet is the celebration of the feast of Jinni of the Home, on the 23rd day of the 12th month. This feast gradually lost its original meaning, even in China, and when it was imported to Viet Nam, it underwent a profound change in the mind of the people and became simply a sentimental story.

The same may be said of nearly all the customs concerning Tet. Originally they were imbued with lofty and precise philosophical significance, although usually disguised under a poetic parable. The incomprehension of the later ages brought about profound transformation and alteration, and the customs became largely folk beliefs. They should be examined in this light, rather than rejected outright as beliefs of no value, unworthy of consideration. Nothing is more moving to Vietnamese than the permanence of these rites, they are like messages addressed to us by our ancestors from the distances of time.

One of the most characteristic customs of Tet consists in buying a flowering peach-tree branch that is placed in a vase for the duration of Tet.

Certain villages in the North specialize in the cultivation of peach trees for this purpose, especially on the Great Lake, near the village of Chem. Many people imagine that these branches have no further purpose than to add a graceful decoration to Vietnamese homes, and today, in fact, they have no other significance. Originally, however, they had the same effect as the *cay-neu* (a tall decorated pole erected before the house during Tet) and were used like them, to protect oneself from the visit of demons. An old Chinese book, the *Kinh-so tue thon-ky*, prescribes that two boards made of peach wood covered with terrifying drawings of the Jinnis, Than-do and Uat-luy, should be leaned against the door of every house. These boards were called *dao phu* (the talisman in peach wood). The first Emperor of the Ming Chinese dynasty had the boards replaced by bands of red paper, covered with the same drawings. At the same period, these boards were replaced by the graceful branches of the flowering peach tree we know today. As for the Jinnis, Than-do and Uat-luy, the old book *Phong Tuc Thong* tells the following story about them:

"There were two brothers who possessed the marvelous power of seeing demons, even in full daylight, and of exterminating them. Heaven thus entrusted them with the mission of posting themselves in front of houses, chiefly during Tet, to bar the way to any demons who might make their appearance. They were so feared that it was enough to draw their pictures, with grimacing faces, on sheets of red paper, to frighten away the evil demons forever."

According to the Chinese astrological calendar, time is circumscribed in revolutions of 60 years, divided into cycles of 12 years, each cycle containing 12 months, etc. Years and months thus have the same names: there is the year *thin* (Dragon), just as there is the month *thin*; the year *ty* (Serpent), the month *ty*, the day *ty*, the hour *ty*, etc.

A cycle of twelve years is placed under the sign of twelve supernatural powers (*hanh-khien*), some of whom are well disposed and others hard and cruel. On the last night of the year, this power passes to the new power, the passing of service that is known as *giao-thua*.

In town and countryside, the head of each family; each mayor (*ly-truong*), each mandarin governing a province, the Emperor in his capital and all the pagodas, would offer a token sacrifice at the same moment to thank the old power, *hanh-khien*, and to welcome the new. This ceremony of *giao-thua* is performed in homes at midnight, the moment when the hour of the Pig (*gio hoi*) changes to that of the Rat (*gio ty*). It is carried out with great solemnity. In the old days it used to be accompanied by noisy and interminable fireworks and the beating of drums. This has given rise to the expression *Trong keu ran nhu trong giao-thua* ("A rolling of drums comparable to those of the *giao-thua*").

It is the custom at *giao-thua* for everyone to stay awake till morning so as to be prepared to welcome in the New Year. It is often amusing to see parents, as soon as the drums of the pagoda announce the arrival of the New Year, rush to wake up all the sleepy children in the house, sitting them up by force if necessary and in spite of their cries and grumblings, so they too will not tempt fate by failing to observe this custom.

It is strictly forbidden to sweep the house (after *giao-thua*) during the first day of Tet. During the days that follow sweeping is allowed but it is absolutely forbidden to gather up rubbish and throw it away. This custom also comes from China. Phong Tho Ky tells the following story:

"There lived in Heaven a young housewife named Bi-Tieu, whose duty it was to cook the celestial food (*thien-tao, thien-tru*). She was extremely greedy and often took copious samplings of all the dishes she prepared for the Master of the Universe. One day the latter, in a rage, exiled her to Earth, where she was forced to take the form of a broom (*than-choi*) so that in the future she would pick up only rubbish instead of the delicacies of the Heavens.

She was ashamed and unhappy in this existence. Much later she sent up a prayer, explaining that as a broom she worked unceasingly and never had a day of rest. Heaven was touched and granted her one day of rest, each New Year's Day."

For this reason it is forbidden to touch a broom on this Tet day. Vietnamese children recited the following riddle: *Trong nha co mot ba hay la liem*, which means: "What person in the house scrounges all she wants?" The answer, of course, is "The broom," it picks things up wherever it passes.

The origin of the prohibition on removing household refuse is found in another Chinese legend. The book *Suu Than Ky* relates how a poor wretch of a Chinese named Au-Minh was sitting one day near the lake Than-Thao, meditating bitterly on his poverty. The Jinni of the Lake was moved to pity and made him a present of a tiny charm, in the form of an animal named Hau. Au-Minh soon became extremely rich. One day—it happened exactly on New Year's Day—he fell into a temper and stepped on the little charm. It disappeared into a heap of rubbish lying in the corner of the house. His owner becoming worried sought the charm everywhere but never thought of looking in the rubbish pile. The rubbish was thrown out and the little charm went with it. Following this, Au-Minh soon became as poor as he had been before. Since then, it has become a custom never to throw away household rubbish during the first days of the year, for it would mean, symbolically, throwing away one's most precious possession.

One of the customs concerning Tet has a curious resemblance to a practice taught by the Druids of ancient Gaul, who used to lead the people into the forest on the first day of the year seeking lucky branches of mistletoe they would keep the following twelve months. The Chinese and Vietnamese are also expected to bring home from their first walk of the New Year a leafy branch, if possible covered with fruit and flowers (*canh-loc*). The heavier the branch, the greater will be the riches (*loc*) earned during the coming year. Today this belief has become a reason for people to go for walks in public gardens or the Vietnamese countryside.

The great chief Nguyen-Hue, enthroned under the name of Quang-Trung, defied the Chinese of the first Ts'ing dynasty in the Hanoi plain, during the first day of the Tet in the year Ky-Dau (1789).

The *Dao khe nhan toai* explains that King Quang-Trung was able to enter so easily into Thang-Long (Hanoi) thanks to a *banh chung* (rice cake specially made for the Tet). The occupying Chinese, to gain the confidence of the Vietnamese population, had given important posts to Vietnamese who had taken their side or appeared to do so. Important Chinese army stores had been entrusted to a Vietnamese named Dinh, who was in reality an ardent patriot. King Quang-Trung planned that the liberation of Hanoi should be brought about with a simultaneous attack by his troops outside and by an uprising within. The problem was, how to inform Dinh and his men in Hanoi of the day on which the attack was to take place?

Tet had just begun. King Quang-Trung gave a few *banh chung* to an old *ong do* (school teacher) named Nguyen-Thiep. A message was hidden in one of the branches, marked by the King's seal and addressed to Dinh, chief of the resistants. Dinh was thus notified. The result was that, at the moment when Quang-Trung's troops attacked the gates of Thang-Long—engaging the Chinese garrison under Marshal Ton-Si-Nghi in battle—a tremendous fire broke out in the Army storehouse, set alight by Dinh and his men. Marshal Ton-Si Nghi, confused, thought that the fire meant Quang Trung's troops had breached the capital walls. In a panic, he ordered his men to abandon the town and make for the opposite bank of the Red River, so that they would not have their line of retreat cut off. So great was his haste that he even forgot his personal papers and his Commander's seal, which fell into the hands of King Quang-Trung.

It is generally supposed that Tet in Viet Nam begins on the first day of the first month of the lunar New Year. This is true in general, but there is an exception in certain provinces (Hadong, Son Tay and Thai Nguyen), where Tet is celebrated later, during the first month.

Source: JUSPAO Field Memorandum Number 31 A Vietnamese Looks at Tet, 28 November 1966, Folder 09, Box 13, Douglas Pike Collection: Unit 03—Insurgency Warfare, The Vietnam Archive, Texas Tech University

Document 2

Memorandum from the Special Assistant for Counterinsurgency and Special Activities (DePuy) to the Director, Joint Staff (Goodpaster)

September 8, 1967

Subject: The end of the war in Vietnam and its aftermath

1   Without debating the desirability of the matter I am convinced that the war in Vietnam will be brought to a close at U.S. initiative sometime within the next 18 months. I am further convinced that a major effort in this direction will be mounted no later than the traditional Christmas cease-fire in December of this year.

2   The Joint Chiefs of Staff and the military services, and the country as a whole, should be greatly concerned about the after-taste. If U.S. disengagement has the flavor of a military defeat, or even military frustration, it will take years to repair the damage to morale, the traditions, and even the concept for employment of military forces in the national defense.

3   We have lived through one such experience in the case of Korea. Without reopening the details of the debate which took place at the end of the Korean war, it can be said that public attention was not focused on the successful defense of South Korea but instead was focused on the restrictions and inhibitions of the use of military force. The after-taste which persists to this day was that the military operations had been frustrated and were therefore not successful. However, for reasons political and psychological, the war was terminated by the highest authorities in the land.

4   It is not difficult to visualize a similar denouement in Vietnam. The fact is, that the North Vietnamese have been clearly and unmistakably prevented from taking over South Vietnam by military force. We are now faced with the choice of describing this as a military success or a military failure. This is not an easy choice to make and it may even be impossible to make such a choice, but there are some powerful reasons why the matter should be addressed and carefully thought out. By the Joint Chiefs of Staff themselves and by the services individually and collectively:

(a) Many brave lives have been spent and the families of those soldiers, sailors, air men and marines deserve to be told that these lives were not spent in vain—that they were spent in the process of achieving a very important national military objective—the very objective we set out to attain in the first place.

(b) If the after-taste is not one of success from a military standpoint, one can foresee enormous problems in the post-war period in connection with the rationale for military forces. In short, there will be many who say that military forces are not able to cope with wars of national liberation and that therefore, such forces need not be maintained.

(c) The organization, tactics and techniques of the military forces will be thrown open to question and doubt as a part of the same reaction which pertains to paragraph 4b above.

(d) American military forces have a tradition of success on the battlefield from which stems much of their strength, discipline, and effectiveness. It would be tragic if this tradition were to be sacrificed through a misinterpretation of the military outcome of the war in Vietnam.

5   It is already clear that the pressures of an election year will cause partisans of various kinds to accentuate any differences, real or imagined, between the Joint Chiefs of Staff and the Administration on the conduct of the war. However well-meaning these attempts may be, and disregarding the substance of the issues, there is a very real danger that the net effect will suggest a military failure where in fact there has been none.

6   What I am suggesting is that the Joint Chiefs of Staff might find it highly desirable in the long range interests of the United States and the armed forces to accentuate the positive in their discussions and testimony, not so much in terms of future prospects but in terms of concrete accomplishments already evident from both a strategic and tactical standpoint in Vietnam. In short, and given the limited nature of the war, the main military objective has already been accomplished.

7   I recommend that you discuss this with the Chairman so that he may, if he sees any merit in the proposal, in turn discuss it with the other members of the Joint Chiefs of Staff.

W. E. DePuy
Major General, USA

Source: *Foreign Relations of the United States, 1964–1968, Volume V, Vietnam, 1967* (Washington, D.C.: Government Printing Office, 2002), 762–63

Address on Vietnam before the National Legislative Conference, San Antonio, Texas

September 29, 1967

I deeply appreciate this opportunity to appear before an organization whose members contribute every day such important work to the public affairs of our State and of our country.

This evening I came here to speak to you about Vietnam.

I do not have to tell you that our people are profoundly concerned about that struggle.

There are passionate convictions about the wisest course for our Nation to follow. There are many sincere and patriotic Americans who harbor doubts about sustaining the commitment that three Presidents and a half a million of our young men have made.

Doubt and debate are enlarged because the problems of Vietnam are quite complex. They are a mixture of political turmoil—of poverty—of religious and factional strife—of ancient servitude and modern longing for freedom. Vietnam is all of these things.

Vietnam is also the scene of a powerful aggression that is spurred by an appetite for conquest.

It is the arena where Communist expansionism is most aggressively at work in the world today—where it is crossing international frontiers in violation of international agreements; where it is killing and kidnapping; where it is ruthlessly attempting to bend free people to its will.

Into this mixture of subversion and war, of terror and hope, America has entered—with its material power and with its moral commitment.

Why?

Why should three Presidents and the elected representatives of our people have chosen to defend this Asian nation more than 10,000 miles from American shores?

We cherish freedom—yes. We cherish self-determination for all people— yes. We abhor the political murder of any state by another, and the bodily murder of any state by another, and the bodily murder of any people by gangsters of whatever ideology. And for 27 years—since the days of lend-lease—we have sought to strengthen free people against domination by aggressive foreign powers.

But the key to all that we have done is really our own security. At times of crisis—before asking Americans to fight and die to resist aggression in a foreign land—every American President has finally had to answer this question:

Is the aggression a threat—not only to the immediate victim—but to the United States of America and to the peace and security of the entire world of which we in America are a vital part?

That is the question which Dwight Eisenhower and John Kennedy and Lyndon Johnson had to answer in facing the issue in Vietnam.

That is the question that the Senate of the United States answered by a vote of 82 to 1 when it ratified and approved the SEATO treaty in 1955, and to which the Members of the United States Congress responded in a resolution that it passed in 1964 by a vote of 504 to 2, "the United States is, therefore, prepared, as the President determines, to take all necessary steps, including the use of armed force, to assist any member or protocol state of the Southeast Asia Collective Defense Treaty requesting assistance in defense of its freedom."

Those who tell us now that we should abandon our commitment—that securing South Vietnam from armed domination is not worth the price we are paying—must also answer this question. And the test they must meet is this: What would be the consequences of letting armed aggression against South Vietnam succeed? What would follow in the time ahead? What kind of world are they prepared to live in 5 months or 5 years from tonight?

For those who have borne the responsibility for decision during these past 10 years, the stakes to us have seemed clear—and have seemed high.

President Dwight Eisenhower said in 1959:

"Strategically, South Vietnam's capture by the Communists would bring their power several hundred miles into a hitherto free region. The remaining countries in Southeast Asia would be menaced by a great flanking movement. The freedom of 12 million people would be lost immediately, and that of 150 million in adjacent lands would be seriously endangered. The loss of South Vietnam would set in motion a crumbling process that could, as it progressed, have grave consequences for us and for freedom."

And President John F. Kennedy said in 1962:

"withdrawal in the case of Vietnam and the case of Thailand might mean a collapse of the entire area."

A year later, he reaffirmed that:

"We are not going to withdraw from that effort. In my opinion, for us to withdraw from that effort would mean a collapse not only of South Vietnam, but Southeast Asia. So we are going to stay there," said President Kennedy.

This is not simply an American viewpoint, I would have you legislative leaders know. I am going to call the roll now of those who live in that part of the world—in the great arc of Asian and Pacific nations—and who bear the responsibility for leading their people, and the responsibility for the fate of their people.

The President of the Philippines had this to say:

"Vietnam is the focus of attention now. . . . It may happen to Thailand or the Philippines, or anywhere, wherever there is misery, disease, ignorance. . . . For you to renounce your position of leadership in Asia is to allow the Red Chinese to gobble up all of Asia."

The Foreign Minister of Thailand said:

"[The American] decision will go down in history as the move that prevented the world from having to face another major conflagration."

The Prime Minister of Australia said: "We are there because while Communist aggression persists the whole of Southeast Asia is threatened."

President Park of Korea said:

"For the first time in our history, we decided to dispatch our combat troops overseas . . . because in our belief any aggression against the Republic of Vietnam represented a direct and grave menace against the security and peace of free Asia, and therefore directly jeopardized the very security and freedom of our own people."

The Prime Minister of Malaysia warned his people that if the United States pulled out of South Vietnam, it would go to the Communists, and after that, it would be only a matter of time until they moved against neighboring states.

The Prime Minister of New Zealand said: "We can thank God that America at least regards aggression in Asia with the same concern as it regards aggression in Europe—and is prepared to back up its concern with action."

The Prime Minister of Singapore said:

"I feel the fate of Asia—South and Southeast Asia—will be decided in the next few years by what happens in Vietnam."

I cannot tell you tonight as your President—with certainty—that a Communist conquest of South Vietnam would be followed by a Communist conquest of Southeast Asia. But I do know there are North Vietnamese troops in Laos. I do know that there are North Vietnamese trained guerrillas tonight in northeast Thailand. I do know that there are Communist-supported guerrilla forces operating in Burma. And a Communist coup was barely averted in Indonesia, the fifth largest nation in the world.

So your American President cannot tell you—with certainty—that a Southeast Asia dominated by Communist power would bring a third world war much closer to terrible reality. One could hope that this would not be so.

But all that we have learned in this tragic century strongly suggests to me that it would be so. As President of the United States, I am not prepared to gamble on the chance that it is not so. I am not prepared to risk the security—indeed, the survival—of this American Nation on mere hope and wishful thinking. I am convinced that by seeing this struggle through now, we are greatly reducing the chances of a much larger war—perhaps a nuclear war. I would rather stand in Vietnam, in our time, and, by meeting this danger now, and facing up to it, thereby reduce the danger for our children and for our grandchildren.

I want now to turn to the struggle in Vietnam itself.

There are questions about this difficult war that must trouble every really thoughtful person. I am going to put some of these questions. And I am going to give you the very best answers I can give you.

First, are the Vietnamese—with our help and that of their other allies—really making any progress? Is there a forward movement? The reports I see make it clear that there is. Certainly there is a positive movement toward constitutional government. Thus far the Vietnamese have met the political schedule that they laid down in January 1966.

The people wanted an elected, responsive government. They wanted it strongly enough to brave a vicious campaign of Communist terror and assassination to vote for it. It has been said that they killed more civilians in four weeks trying to keep them from voting before the election than our American bombers have killed in the big cities of North Vietnam in bombing military targets.

On November 1, subject to the action, of course, of the Constituent Assembly, an elected government will be inaugurated and an elected Senate and Legislature will be installed. Their responsibility is clear: To answer the desires of the South Vietnamese people for self-determination, and for peace, for an attack on corruption, for economic development, and for social justice.

There is progress in the war itself, steady progress considering the war that we are fighting; rather dramatic progress considering the situation that actually prevailed when we sent our troops there in 1965; when we intervened to prevent the dismemberment of the country by the Vietcong and the North Vietnamese.

The campaign of the last year drove the enemy from many of their major interior bases. The military victory almost within Hanoi's grasp in 1965 has now been denied them. The grip of the Vietcong on the people is being broken.

Since our commitment of major forces in July 1965 the proportion of the population living under Communist control has been reduced to well under 20 percent. Tonight the secure proportion of the population has grown from about 45 percent to 65 percent—and in contested areas, the tide continues to run with us.

But the struggle remains hard. The South Vietnamese have suffered severely, as have we—particularly in the First Corps area in the north, where the enemy has mounted his heaviest attacks, and where his lines of communication to North Vietnam are shortest. Our casualties in the war have reached about 13,500 killed in action, and about 85,000 wounded. Of those 85,000 wounded, we thank God that 79,000 of the 85,000 have been returned, or will return, to duty shortly. Thanks to our great American medical science and the helicopter.

I know there are other questions on your minds, and on the minds of many sincere, troubled Americans: "Why not negotiate now?" so many ask me. The answer is that we and our South Vietnamese allies are wholly prepared to negotiate tonight.

I am ready to talk with Ho Chi Minh, and other chiefs of state concerned, tomorrow.

I am ready to have Secretary Rusk meet with their foreign minister tomorrow.

I am ready to send a trusted representative of America to any spot on this earth to talk in public or private with a spokesman of Hanoi.

We have twice sought to have the issue of Vietnam dealt with by the United Nations—and twice Hanoi has refused.

Our desire to negotiate peace—through the United Nations or out—has been made very, very clear to Hanoi—directly and many times through third parties.

As we have told Hanoi time and time and time again, the heart of the matter is really this: the United States is willing to stop all aerial and naval bombardment of North Vietnam when this will lead promptly to productive discussions. We, of course, assume that while discussions proceed, North Vietnam would not take advantage of the bombing cessation or limitation.

But Hanoi has not accepted any of these proposals.

So it is by Hanoi's choice—and not ours, and not the rest of the world's—that the war continues.

Why, in the face of military and political progress in the South, and the burden of our bombing in the North, do they insist and persist with war?

From many sources the answer is the same. They still hope that the people of the United States will not see this struggle through to the very end. As one Western diplomat reported to me only this week—he had just been in Hanoi—"They believe their staying power is greater than ours and that they can't lose." A visitor from a Communist capital had this to say: "They expect the war to be long, and that the Americans in the end will be defeated by a breakdown in morale, fatigue, and psychological factors." The Premier of North Vietnam said as far back as 1962: "Americans do not like long, inconclusive war. . . . Thus we are sure to win in the end."

Are the North Vietnamese right about us? I think not. No. I think they are wrong. I think it is the common failing of totalitarian regimes that they cannot really understand the nature of our democracy:

- They mistake dissent for disloyalty.
- They mistake restlessness for a rejection of policy.
- They misjudge individual speeches for public policy.

They are no better suited to judge the strength and perseverance of America than the Nazi and the Stalinist propagandists were able to judge it. It is a tragedy that they must discover these qualities in the American people, and discover them through a bloody war.

And, soon or late, they will discover them.

In the meantime, it shall be our policy to continue to seek negotiations—confident that reason will some day prevail; that Hanoi will realize that it just can never win; that it will turn away from fighting and start building for its own people.

Since World War II, this Nation has met and mastered many challenges—challenges in Greece and Turkey, in Berlin, in Korea, in Cuba.

We met them because brave men were willing to risk their lives for their nation's security. And braver men have never lived than those who carry our colors in Vietnam at this very hour.

The price of these efforts, of course, has been heavy. But the price of not having made them at all, not having seen them through, in my judgment would have been vastly greater.

Our goal has been the same—in Europe, in Asia, in our own hemisphere. It has been—and it is now—peace.

And peace cannot be secured by wishes; peace cannot be preserved by noble words and pure intentions. "Enduring peace," Franklin D. Roosevelt said, "cannot be bought at the cost of other people's freedom." The late President Kennedy put it precisely in November 1961, when he said: "We are neither war mongers nor appeasers, neither hard nor soft. We are Americans determined to defend the frontiers of freedom by an honorable peace if possible but by arms if arms are used against us."

The true peace-keepers in the world tonight are not those who urge us to retire from the field in Vietnam—who tell us to try to find the quickest, cheapest exit from that tormented land, no matter what the consequences to us may be.

The true peace-keepers are those men who stand out there on the DMZ at this very hour, taking the worst that the enemy can give. The true peace-keepers are the soldiers who are breaking the terrorist's grip around the villages of Vietnam—the civilians who are bringing medical care and food and education to people who have already suffered a generation of war.

And so I report to you that we are going to continue to press forward. Two things we must do. Two things we shall do.

First, we must not mislead the enemy. Let him not think that debate and dissent will produce wavering and withdrawal. For I can assure you they won't. Let him not think that protests will produce surrender. Because they won't. Let him not think that he will wait us out. For he won't.

Second, we will provide all that our brave men require to do the job that must be done. And that job is going to be done.

These gallant men have our prayers—have our thanks—have our heartfelt praise—our deepest gratitude.

Let the world know that the keepers of peace will endure through every trial—and that with the full backing of their countrymen, they are going to prevail.

Source: *Public Papers of the Presidents, Lyndon B. Johnson, 1967, Book II: July 1–December 31, 1967* (Washington, D.C.: Government Printing Office, 1968), 876–81

Document 4

Memorandum from the President's Assistant (Jones) to President Johnson

Meeting of the Wise Men, November 2, 1967

Subject: Meeting with foreign policy Advisors, Thursday, November 2, 1967

Meeting convened—10:42 a.m.

Meeting adjourned following luncheon at 2:15 p.m.

Attending were: Clark Clifford, George Ball, McGeorge Bundy, Maxwell Taylor, General Omar Bradley, Robert Murphy, Henry Cabot Lodge, Secretary Dean Rusk, Secretary Nick Katzenbach, Governor Averell Harriman, Assistant Secretary William Bundy, Secretary Robert McNamara, CIA Director Richard Helms, Dean Acheson, Justice Abe Fortas, Arthur Dean, Douglas Dillon, Walt Rostow, George Christian and Jim Jones.

The President greeted the group around the Cabinet table and pointed out that he did know the details of what had been accomplished in their discussions to this point. He said he did want to raise some questions that concerned him. "I have a peculiar confidence in you as patriots and that is why I have picked you," the President said. He said he wanted to know if our course in Vietnam was right. If not, how should it be modified? He said he is deeply concerned about the deterioration of public support and the lack of editorial support for our policies. He pointed out that if a bomb accidentally kills two civilians in North Vietnam, it makes banner headlines. However, they can lob mortar shells into the Palace grounds in Saigon and there are no editorial complaints against it.

The President said he watched General Norstad on television Thursday morning. He found it interesting. "I agreed with almost all he said up to the point of bombing." The President said that Norstad did not say yes or no on the bombing issue. He (Norstad) did point out that the Administration has not unified the nation because we have never told the country that we are really willing to negotiate. The President said Norstad commented that he did not believe the credibility of the argument, but merely ended up saying the government has failed to communicate with the nation about our willingness to negotiate.

The President said he thought that "when we sent men to nearly every capital that this would dramatize our willingness, but apparently the people have forgotten this. So the question is how do we unite the country?"

The President said: "I would like to consider the following five questions and get your advice: (1) What could we do that we are not doing in South Vietnam? (2) Concerning the North, should we continue what we are doing, or should we mine the ports and take out the dikes, or should we eliminate the bombing of the North? (3) On negotiations—should we adopt a passive policy of willingness to negotiate, or should we be more aggressive, or should we bow out? (4) Should we get out of Vietnam? (At this point the President noted a poll from a Congressional district in Iowa which had 11,000 responses. The poll showed that 34 percent favored pulling out; 20 percent approved of present policies and 40 percent thought we should do more. The President also said some other polls have been taken in some larger states. These show that about 30 percent favor either a pull in or pull out of Vietnam. Those who want to do more comprise about 35–40 percent and those who approve of what we are doing now about 30 percent. "So it's about 70–30," the President said, "but that 30 has grown from 15 percent.") (5) What positive steps should the Administration take to unite the people and to communicate with the nation better?"

The President then called on Secretary Rusk.

Secretary Rusk reported that the group started their meetings yesterday with briefings by George Carver of the CIA and General Wheeler. Rusk then read from a letter marked personal and confidential from U.S. Ambassador Ellsworth Bunker which reflected on his first six months in Saigon. In general, the letter noted that there has been improvement in the past six months. The military has established a base which has allowed us to go on the offensive. The training of the Vietnamese units has improved considerably. The civil side of the war is proceeding well with the constitutional process and the pacification success equaling in importance the military improvements. The village and the hamlet programs are going well and the Chie Hoi program is expanding. Bunker's letter points out that last year the revolutionary development program really got underway. The newly elected government, especially Thieu and Ky, know that they must show progress in order to gain support of the people. Steady progress is being made. Much still needs to be done, however, such as a vigorous processing of the war, elimination of corruption, improvement of the standard of living, especially in rural areas. Bunker wrote that in the past we have been overly optimistic and have become prisoners of this optimism. However, he is enthusiastic about the progress being made.

Rusk then reported that the group talked about the bombing program, although no consensus was reached, nor was a consensus requested. Rusk said the views ranged widely. Rusk said it was a good evening. Rusk declined to speak for the group because there was no consensus.

The President said "I have met with the Leadership of the Republican Party in Congress and all the Democratic Members of Congress. I have received no alternatives from Congress on the course we are taking. One of the things that divides us is that a great number of the hawks want to do more, but the other side is more vociferous."

The President then called on Former Secretary of State Dean Acheson.

Acheson addressed himself to each of the five questions posed by the President. "In the South, I was very impressed by George Carver's restatement of what we are doing there. This is the heart of the matter. I agree that this should be pressed just as fast as possible, and as fast as South Vietnam will permit. I am encouraged by the ground fighting in the South and that we are taking the initiative. I got the impression this is a matter we can and will win. So on the first question, I think this is going well," Acheson said.

On the second question concerning the North, Acheson said his view is different than some others. He agrees with the view of the Secretary of Defense and would not stop the bombing. Acheson regards this, however, as a purely marginal operation as far as the fighting in the South is concerned. He said the bombing in the North is not the essential point.

On negotiations, Acheson said, "We must understand that we are not going to have negotiations. The bombing has no effect on negotiations. When these fellows decide they can't defeat the South, then they will give up. This is the way it was in Korea. This is the way the Communists operate."

"The importance of bombing in the North is not that it is important militarily," Acheson said. "It could be used as a signal, however, not that it is a solution to the stopping of the fighting across the demilitarized zone."

Acheson said it is possible that they will not reduce the fighting until the 1968 election is resolved. "Until that is resolved they may say let's see it out," Acheson added. "I would not talk about negotiations any more. You have made it clear where you stand. This isn't the Communist method. If they can't win they just quit after a while." Acheson suggested that we put the bombing in a position where it could be stopped and/or started. In other words play it down. The targets must become less dramatic.

The President replied that we don't play it either up or down. However, it is front page news. The President pointed out that the dramatic impact of the bombing traces to Secretary McNamara's testimony before Senator Stuart Symington's Committee. That generated both the hawks and the doves talking about bombing.

The President said "I am like the steering wheel of a car without any control. The Senate won't let us play down the bombing issue."

Acheson replied "The cross you have to bear is a lousy Senate Foreign Relations Committee. You have a dilettante fool at the head of the Committee."

About reaching the people, Acheson said, "If you agree to the policy I have outlined, then get everyone in the government to agree on it and talk along these policy lines."

Acheson added "We certainly should not get out of Vietnam." He noted that General Bradley remembers after General MacArthur took his licking at Yalu in the Korean War there was a great outcry to get out. On December 4, however, Acheson had Dean Rusk and George Kennan into his office and told them to see Secretary George Marshall. "We want less Goddamn analysis and more fighting spirit." Acheson said that the President had a good commander who takes orders in General Westmoreland. Acheson said that he spoke to about 21 Supreme Court law clerks and they were all amazed that I thought we should not get out of Vietnam. Acheson suggested a program be adopted similar to the Citizens' Committee on the Marshall Plan and he said perhaps the Paul Douglas group would be the proper vehicle. He noted that the Citizens' Committee on the Marshall Plan organized a group in every city over 150,000 population; got money mostly from private groups and got several readable pamphlets that were used as speech material. Acheson also said that the President, the Secretary of State and the Secretary of Defense have taken the whole burden of the Vietnam issue. The people know what these three stand for. What is needed now is several thousand new speakers to support our policy in every city in the nation. Acheson pointed out the main thing is that the President should not worry about this. He said he was pleased to read in Scotty Reston's column that the President gave up whiskey and took up golf.

The President interjected that "he was wrong on both counts. When Mac Bundy walked out of Washington, so did Scotty Reston and he doesn't know what is going on."

In summary on bombing, Acheson believes we should play down its importance. When the Communists ease the pressure off the DMZ, we can reduce the bombing in the North. However, we should not give advance notice of these bombing pauses.

McGeorge Bundy said he agreed with nearly everything Acheson said. He said the bombing in the North is out of proportion to its importance. Bundy said to go after the dikes or Haiphong would not be a net gain and would unnecessarily worry the moderate to dovish population.

Bundy said that the South is the focus. He thinks that it is right that the President continues to have the Medal of Honor winners presented in the Rose Garden. He thinks a great deal has been done in the provinces and these people should be honored and publicized. Bundy said "We have done a remarkable job in the last two years in getting work in the provinces organized. We have a wonderful first team in there. Vietnam will have to do more. Anything that shows that Vietnam is doing more will be helpful over here."

Bundy said he shares Acheson's opinion that there will not be negotiations. "I suppose we cannot say that publicly because the judges of public opinion in the nation won't believe it. But I think it is logical to say that we in the Administration do not expect negotiations in the next year," Bundy said.

Bundy said, "Getting out of Vietnam is as impossible and [as?] it is undesirable." He pointed out that there is an enormous difference in Asia as it is now and what it might have been because of what the President did in 1965. He said this point should be emphasized.

As to how to pull the nation together—Bundy said the communication people who are centered in New York cannot be allowed to set the tone of the debate. "Your (the President's) sense of where you are going is very important here."

"One must also ask," Bundy added, "that what is eroding public support are the battles and deaths and dangers to the sons of mothers and fathers with no picture of a result in sight. If we can permeate to the public that we are seeing results and the end of the road, this will be helpful."

Former Secretary of the Treasury Douglas Dillon said he "agrees with a great deal of what has been said. There is nothing additional in the South that we can do that is not being done now." He pointed out however that the South Vietnamese must be expected to do more.

"In the North, it is just about right and we should continue as we are doing. I would not think of going further and bombing the dikes and harbors. This is different than the way I thought two years ago," Dillon said.

On negotiations Dillon agreed with Acheson. The trade suggested by Acheson is excellent.

Dillon said we must not get out of Vietnam.

On how to better communicate—Dillon said "Our major emphasis should be shifted to the position that we are in rather than why or how we got there. We should clarify what we are doing. There is a lot of misunderstanding about what we are doing. The subject that McGeorge Bundy discussed is most important. That is the feeling on both sides, including both doves and hawks, that the situation over there is hopeless. We must show some progress. To talk of 15 years seems like forever. I was surprised last night, things were better than I had expected," Dillon said.

"The revolutionary development program should be emphasized. Perhaps Bunker could come back and make report to the nation. But we must give some hope that there is a possibility in the next two or three years of seeing light at the end of the tunnel. If the people thought that this could end at some time, we would gain a lot more support," Dillon said.

Dillon suggested one group to talk to are the top educators, and the heads of colleges and the deans. He noted that much of the trouble is coming largely from the younger professors and students. Those college presidents whom Dillon knows, sympathize with the students' dovish views. Dillon believes a good briefing to these top educators who are responsible people would be very helpful.

Arthur Dean said the country as a whole is confused. "Very few people have read the Geneva Accords of 1954. It calls for a single election in the North and the South. Then we have said that we will not let the people of South Vietnam down and not let them be incorporated into the North. This is inconsistent with our profession of belief in the Geneva Accords of '54."

Dean said there is also a feeling that Ambassador Arthur Goldberg is willing to negotiate on less honorous terms that Washington. If South Vietnam is as important, then why are we willing to say that we will abide by the majority vote? This means all our sacrifice will have been in vain.

Dean said there is a strong feeling among the hawks especially that the President and Secretary McNamara are vetoing the recommendations of the Joint Chiefs. Dean suggested that someone pull together everything there is on why we are in Vietnam. If the majority of the people are satisfied based on the national interest, they would support us. Dean said the people are puzzled. They are puzzled about the value of bombing. He said he agrees generally with Secretary Acheson. Rusk worried that if we get them to the conference table, they will do the same thing they did in the Korean War by demanding that we get out before any other points of negotiation are taken up.

Henry Cabot Lodge said he had three suggestions for the South: "(1) There should be an independent audit of how the revamping of the ARVN is going; or those training the ARVN; and how the local police technique is improving. Do the trainees understand the significance of the ARVN thing itself? (2) Public opinion is more concerned with U.S. casualties than with our bombing program. If the casualties go down, nothing else matters so much. An exclusive military victory is not conceivable to me."

Lodge suggested a "split up and keep off balance" military policy rather than a "seek out and destroy" policy. "I would take a look at this policy because it utilizes the smaller units and means less casualties. This also diminishes the number of refugees." (3) Lodge pointed out that when he went to Saigon in 1965 he talked about true revolution to win over the people. "In Vietnam, this means non-government activity. However, the government must give the green light, and the U.S. must help but it must be way in the background." Lodge recommended the use of the Tenant Farmers Union, etc., to develop farm credit, rice milling, and marketing programs. He pointed out that six months ago, fertilizers were piped in through the Tenant

Farmers Union, and now the Union has tripled. "But you must stimulate and agitate them. This will be visual proof of a true revolution to win over the people. This may take the French and Chinese to the wall, but it will point out a true revolution to the Vietnamese. As this program succeeds, you can cut down on U.S. involvement, and thereby cut down on U.S. casualties." Lodge said it is better to work through the unions, and organizations such as this as opposed to the local governments because you do not have competent local governments as such in Vietnam yet.

Lodge agreed with Acheson about the bombing, and the negotiations. Lodge also added it would be unthinkable about getting out of Vietnam. "In this war we are trying to divert a change in the balance of power."

Lodge said he is working with the Citizens' Committee. "They are planning a series of brochures to discuss why we are in Vietnam, what we have accomplished, what needs to be done, a history of the people and the trouble there."

Lodge suggested that Bunker should be given lots of publicity when he gets back to report.

At this point, the President invited all of the group to lunch. Everyone accepted except Douglas Dillon who had a previous commitment and would have to leave.

Robert Murphy said it is best to focus on what might be done. We don't know whether there will be negotiations or not. Murphy pointed out that he works with Norstad and Norstad has strange illusions on negotiations. Murphy suggested that the bombing be left in the hands of the Joint Chiefs as much as possible. He said it is effective. Murphy noted that there is no hate complex like there was against Hitler. He said that Ho Chi Minh is not regarded as evil in many places in the United States and in Europe he is regarded as a kindly hero. There should also be a better fixation on the small group of men who are responsible in the North. This should be a priority of the 303 Committee. The President should not personally be involved. He said he has been told that this not possible, but an intensive study should be given to the elimination of the group of men responsible in the North.

Governor Averell Harriman said he wished Dean Acheson would say publicly what he said about the character of the Foreign Relations Committee Chairman. Harriman added that he "had tremendous respect for Senator Gale McGee and they threw him off the committee." Harriman said the difference between Senator Vandenberg and his Committee and the present committee is as great as black and white.

The President pointed out that even then, Vandenberg and the Foreign Relations Committee made it miserable for the Secretary of State.

General Omar Bradley said in general he agrees with the comments that have been made. "The military services, both ours and the Vietnamese, are improving, and we are making progress. It is difficult for the American people to understand why we cannot draw a line and push this line up and back. There is confusion among the people because they cannot view Vietnam in the same way they did in World War II. The enemy may be 10 or 15 feet away from you and you cannot see him. The improvement in the local forces are beginning to be played up in the last few days. Some of the units are very good. They are training them well," Bradley said.

"On bombing, we should stick to military targets. They do affect the North Vietnamese ability to fight in the South. We must keep up the bombing." Bradley said military targets are sometimes questionable. "Whether the dikes will become military targets, I do not know."

"On negotiations there should not be so much talk. The more we talk about negotiations, this is a sign of weakness to them. If we stop the bombing, we don't need to tell them in advance," Bradley said.

The President noted that when we had told them in advance about our bombing pauses, it has not worked in the past.

Concerning the troubles at home, Bradley said our means of communications are largely responsible. "For example, the *Washington Post* used three pages to describe the 35,000 or so peace marchers who converged on the Pentagon recently. However, there were 180,000 in New York and New Jersey who demonstrated in support of our men in Vietnam, and this played on page 17 of the *Post*."

Bradley said "we've got to arouse patriotism somehow. We've never had a war without patriotic slogans. Perhaps the slogan in this would be 'Patience,' 100 years means nothing to a Chinaman, but we do not have their same patience. The Korean troops in Vietnam have more patience. They'll sit in front of a tunnel until the North Vietnamese come out." Bradley said he believes if it wasn't for all the protesters, the North Vietnamese would give up. He said that captured prisoners have told him they (North Vietnam) would win the war, not in Vietnam but back in the States, as they did with the French. "We are winning, but we must have patience," Bradley concluded.

The President asked General Bradley to tell the group about the competence of the South Vietnamese, the Korean, and the United States men in Vietnam.

Bradley said "I have never seen better morale or better fed troops. They get ice cream about three times a week. Only two out of the thousand that I and my wife visited disliked being there or did not understand why they were there. These were two colored soldiers from Detroit who were more interested in the riots in Detroit than in Vietnam. As for the Vietnamese, all are enthusiastic, they still have some leaders that should not be there, but they are trying to get them out. I was impressed with the popular forces in the villages. We must do something to get the hearts of the Vietnamese people. They want to be let alone and grow their rice more than anything else. They probably feel a little more secure with the government of South Vietnam than the Viet Cong. Two captured Viet Cong were about 12 or 13 years old and they said they had to go fight for the Viet Cong or their families would be killed," Bradley said.

General Maxwell Taylor said that in the South, things are going well. He made two points. (1) He questions the close defense of the frontier on the DMZ and in the highland area, and (2) he believes that we have never decided on what we are going to offer the Viet Cong and this is a problem.

Taylor said the bombing is an essential part of our strategy, and to give it up without clearly getting something in return would be wrong.

The President asked him if he was talking about quid pro quo or the Acheson program.

Taylor said he prefers the first but would go along with the latter.

On negotiations, Taylor agrees that a subsiding solution is more likely than negotiations. He pointed out that if he were Ho Chi Minh, he would stay with what the North Vietnamese are doing, at least through the elections in 1968.

On the home front, Taylor said that he has made more speeches than anyone, having completed his 126th last night. "The people still are asking why they are not being told all the facts on Vietnam. We should organize a nationwide campaign that will be continuous. Television is our best weapon as it is with the opposition. Every week we should have a program either sponsored by public or private in which the people can ask their government questions. We can also bring personalities—returning veterans, diplomats, etc.—to discuss Vietnam."

George Ball said that no one in the group thinks we should get out of Vietnam, and no one gives propriety to the Gavin or Galbraith enclave theory.

"In the South, the report we received was very reassuring. The war of attrition and civil action is in competent hands and we are doing very well there. We should focus on the conditions that will lead the other side to stop the fighting. We must look and see how the war looks to them. These are two wars in the eyes of Hanoi. First the war in the South. This one they can afford to lose or withdraw from. Second is the war in the North which is viewed as a war by the greatest imperialist force against a sister socialist state. Can they afford to lose that one, we must ask," Ball said.

"In light of that then, is the bombing useful in the North? Bombing in the North won't limit the flow of supplies to the South significantly. On the other hand, it will make it almost impossible for them to stop the war." Ball recommended a change of tactics, that is, shifting of the bombing away from the harbor and dikes to the bombing of the DMZ as an interdiction of men and supplies. "This would clearly show the other side that we are creating conditions to let them stop the fighting," Ball said.

As far as persuading the U.S. to support our efforts there, Ball pointed out that a double standard is implicit in our presence in Vietnam. He said there is a great disparity in size and strength between the United States and the Viet Cong and North Vietnam. He also pointed out that many students can't understand why we are using our air power against a primitive people that has no air power.

Ball said very few Americans really see a political solution as another Munich. We don't talk about getting out. He said he has had a bad reaction to Goldberg's statement that six months after the war, we'll get out. People don't really believe this, because they look at Korea and see we've been there 17 years. Furthermore, if they do believe we are telling the truth, they think we should have our heads examined because we would be throwing away everything we fought for. Ball said we should consider all these in terms of the American national interest. We are in a position now instead of arguing how we got there as to what we do about it now that we're there.

Following Ball's statement the group adjourned to wash up before lunch.

Lunch convened at 1:03 p.m.

The President called on Justice Fortas.

Fortas said there was a remarkable presentation by George Carver of the CIA last night. Fortas said the country should hear the presentation made by Carver. He said the nation is totally unaware of this side of the Vietnam conflict. He said Carver told the story with complete conviction and great sophistication. Fortas suggested that the press might be told that Carver briefed the Cabinet and he would be available to brief the press in a low-key way. Following this, Fortas recommended a repeat performance by Carver for Members of Congress and later for other opinion makers. He said these briefings would be contrary to the opinion of the country that there are no improvements. Fortas then suggested that later on Ambassador Bunker return and report.

Fortas expressed his gratitude to the Paul Douglas Committee participants. He said at last some leaders and people of the country are beginning to speak out. "I believe there is a good deal of over-reaction to what appears to be the public attitude in the United States. This opposition exists in only a small group of the community, primarily the intellectuals or so-called intellectuals and the press. The opposition is not as widespread as we think. Public opinion is a fickle thing and a changeable thing. The American people are committed to a few propositions that are contrary to the rash of opposition. The public would be outraged if we withdrew. We are not now prepared for a 'Fortress America,' nor are we for the foreseeable future. It is very important to separate superficialities of expression from the fundamentals of American belief."

Negotiations are symbolic rather than a real thing, Fortas said. This could be an ingenious trap to trap us into negotiations on terms or at a time when they can be corrosive to us. "We've been fortunate so far that North Vietnam has rejected our offer. When the time comes what will happen will be the cessation of hostilities, not negotiations. The American people are not interested in negotiations. That is merely a symbol. That is why the people don't understand you when you say you're willing to negotiate, because American people really don't believe in negotiations. It would serve no purpose to continue to emphasize our willingness to negotiate. You have already stated your position. Don't repudiate what you have done but tone down on it in the future. To continue to talk about negotiations only signals to the Communists that they are succeeding in winning over American public opinion," Fortas said.

On the bombing, Fortas said in reference to George Ball's comments, that he admires the ingenuity in the proposal but rejects the logic for stopping the bombing in the North: "I don't believe North Vietnam thinks we are out to overthrow their government, and I don't believe it would have any effect if we shifted our bombing. The bombing of the North is not the way to end the war but a way to make cessation of the hostilities on a basis acceptable to us a possibility."

The President asked Dick Helms what the minimum and maximum figures of people who are being tied up in the North to repair the damage done by U.S. bombing.

Helms replied about 500,000.

Fortas continued saying he was interested in Lodge's proposal. "I wonder if all questions have been asked about the nature of our military action in the South. I think we should explore a greater use of the small military units in the South."

The President said he has asked the Secretary how we could speed up winning the war. "The Joint Chiefs came up with 10 proposals, all of which involved the North. I sent it back to them to focus on the South and they reported that we can't do anything more than we are doing in the South now," the President said.

Dean Acheson commented on the Fortas' idea of having Carver brief the press, saying "neither George (Christian) nor the CIA should brief the press."

Fortas said he was very impressed by what he (Carver) said and how he said it. He realizes, of course, that anything anyone in Government says will be denounced by the Fulbrights.

The President asked the group to give any suggestion on Vietnam or any danger signals they see in any other part of the world. He said he did not want this group to confine itself totally to Vietnam. He asked them to want to and to feel obligated to tell him personally for his eyes only about any of these subjects, even his own competence or that of the Secretary of State or Defense in handling matters of world affairs. He then introduced Clark Clifford as one of his most valued advisors who is most generous with his time.

Clifford said that the President was aware of his stand on the questions posed, and thus he would confine his comments to one subject—the attitude of the American people. "An effort must be made to explain and to educate the American people. There is another area which we have not discussed today—namely that American people will react to hearing from those individuals who live in Southeast Asia who can give a better color of the conditions there. For example, President Thieu should visit the United States if the protocol can be worked out. He could address a Joint Session of Congress, he could be invited to the Press Club and I am certain he could get prime time on television some evening where he could explain the nature of the problem there. He is an intelligent and reasonable fellow, and more balanced than Ky. He could go through the background of the conflict, the importance of the conflict, and I think this would be very helpful. Colonel Robin Olds, who is our only air ace, could be assigned to speak to large audiences. Selected officials from other Southeast Asian nations and Ambassadors from Southeast Asian nations could visit the United States to make appearances," Clifford suggested.

"The thing to keep in mind however is that no matter what this accomplishes, this will not be a popular war. No wars have been popular. In the Revolutionary War there was an enormous body who felt this was a tragic mistake. The same was true in the Civil War where President Lincoln was beleaguered day after day with people who thought he should get out. The First World War was enormously unpopular with many of the American people. In the Korean War, it was popular in 1950, and in 1951 more than 60 percent thought we were wrong," Clifford said.

The President interjected at this time to point out that the Korean War at the time of our entering was favored 83–7 percent and 6 months later the balance had shifted to 66–24 against.

Clifford continued saying that he remembers well Senator Taft calling the Korean Conflict "Truman's War." One possible exception is World War II. "But wars will be unpopular and we won't be able to sell it to everyone. But we must go on because what we are doing is right. But recognizing this fact, I hope we won't get frustrated."

"Last night was an enormously interesting experience. Secretary McNamara said that perhaps he and Rusk's efforts since 1961 have been a failure. But this is not true. Their efforts have constituted an enormous success. One of the measures of success that history will look very favorably upon is that both Presidents Kennedy and Johnson didn't wait for public opinion to catch up with them. They went ahead with what was right, and because of that the war is a success today. You can look around and find that the other nations say we have provided them with a shield. They cannot depend upon the British or the French. This has been an enormous success but we won't be able to convince the American people of that as long as it is going on. So we should go right on doing what we're going to do. It is important that we do so," Clifford continued.

"Any cessation in the South or the North will be interpreted as a sign of weakness of the American people. If we keep up the pressure on them, gradually the will of the Viet Cong and the North Vietnamese will wear down," Clifford concluded.

At 1:45 p.m. Lynda Bird brought Patrick Lyndon Nugent in to the President. Lyn stayed in the President's arms for most of the remainder of the luncheon.

The President then briefly summarized the consensus of opinions given today. Generally everyone agrees with our present course in the South. The Lodge proposal is generally agreed upon. In the North, there is general agreement that we should not extend the bombing any further. There is some sentiment for moderating the bombing. We have moved far along on the bombing. We've hit all but 24 out of the 9,000 targets or the 5,000 military targets. The President then called on McGeorge Bundy to summarize the feelings of the group and asked Bundy to put on paper his summary.

Bundy suggested two things. First, he said no one has said anything about China because no one really believes that the President will do anything that will start trouble with China. Most people understand that. Although there are many in Bundy's circle of moderate to dovish people who do not understand that and he will go about to make this clear. Also, there is a sense of clarity and calmness among the group with a heavy majority agreed about what we should or should not do. Bundy pointed out that this unity of agreement is not reported in the Press and is a popular misconception. He said an endless many hours have been spent pointing out how we got to where we are now. Instead, the emphasis should be what do we do now. He said there is agreement that the bombing is important but is over-emphasized. He pointed out that the group has not given detailed attention to a pause or refusal of a pause, but there is some agreement that it is not a critical point.

The President asked that all of the group try to give their views to the public, and he asked that when they make speeches that they provide him a copy of what they said so he will know.

Walt Rostow addressed himself to Hanoi's mind which must concern itself with the rate of erosion of their manpower base against the erosion of the American political base. He pointed out that at least half of the job must be done by the South Vietnamese government. They must show improved administration. They must make a bold, bloody attack on corruption and the ARVN must be more aggressive in pacification.

Rostow agrees that this will not be a popular war but he points out that the progress taking place will help win support. He said that there are ways of guiding the press to show light at the end of the tunnel.

On negotiations, Rostow said the normal way for the Communists is to pack up and cease aggression rather than negotiate. He pointed out however that Vietnam may be different in that Hanoi will not want the NLF destroyed as it was in Indonesia and they may want to negotiate on this point. Secondly, Hanoi may want to negotiate about bases in South Vietnam. So negotiations are not out of the realm of possibility.

The President called on Under Secretary Nicholas Katzenbach who chided that if President Thieu and Ambassador Bunker are brought back to the United States, "that leaves Vietnam under Locke and Ky!"

Secretary McNamara expressed his personal appreciation to the group.

The President said that no nation has been more enlightenedly serviced than under Secretaries Rusk and McNamara. He pointed out that these two are the highest type of manhood that this nation can produce. Their working relationship is good and they have had no petty jealousies or quarrels. "Their only test is what is good for the country," the President said.

Secretary Rusk said that the deliberations in the past two days have been thoughtful, imaginative and responsible. He expressed his personal appreciation. He agreed that this was not a popular war but one of the problems in polling of public opinion on the popularity of the war is the way the questions are phrased. He said that he is sure that if the President were asked by a pollster, "are you happy about Vietnam," the President would reply "hell no."

On negotiations, Rusk said we don't expect Hanoi to come to the negotiating table very soon.

In bombing, he pointed out what it does for the morale of our men. So when we consider a shifting or a stopping of the bombing on a geography basis, we must consider the morale of the men.

The President said that we are studying what essential targets remain. There will have to be some restrikes and we are studying when and where. The President then called on Secretary McNamara to discuss the so-called barrier.

McNamara said first of all it is not a barrier. For five or six years we have been studying how to interdict men and materials. We've considered many things from the use of divisions to an actual Maginot Line, but none merited being put into play. About a year and a half ago, we got our scientists and engineers to analyze the situation, and they improved the effectiveness of our air campaign in Laos, including laying seismic sensors on the ground and acoustical sensors in the trees to detect equipment and men.

The principle is that once these sensors detect movement they transmit to a base in Thailand and from there planes are dispatched. We start the operation against vehicles on December 1 and against men on January 1. We don't know how effective it's going to be, but we are hopeful. There are also obstacle defenses in which we have a cleared area with mines and other obstacles and fixed fire positions in the north of South Vietnam.

McNamara revealed that captured documents showed about 20 percent of those who leave the North do not reach the South. About 2 percent of these are because of air casualties. Our scientists and engineers hope this new system will increase the air casualties by 15 fold, in other words, up to 30 percent. They think the destruction of the trucks by air casualties will increase 200–300 percent. McNamara points out that we haven't discussed this program because it is so complex that with some ingenuity by the enemy it can be detected and destroyed. Therefore, I have put a flat barrier that there will be no discussions. McNamara said he does not want to overstate its effectiveness, but if it improves the casualty ration by even a few percent it will have been worth the effort.

Secretary Rusk addressed himself briefly to the Goldberg–Mansfield Resolution on bringing the Vietnam issue to the United Nations. He pointed out that several efforts in the past to do this have not worked. It is both an illusion and sophistication. In the Security Council we do not have the nine votes necessary. The Soviet Union does not want it brought up. They do not want to heat up any issues between them and the United States at this time. Other nations oppose it for different reasons. Denmark doesn't want it brought up because to vote with us would probably mean the downfall of their government. Paul Martin of Canada is against it because he wants to be Prime Minister more than anything else, and his statements are for pure domestic consumption. Hanoi and Peking say that it does not belong in the United Nations. If we don't get the nine votes or if we get an adverse vote, it's going to be interpreted as a repudiation of our policy. In the General Assembly the situation is much the same way. The difference between the public view and the private statements of these world leaders is enormous. For example, there is no more of a hawk than Ne Win of Burma, yet if it were brought before the UN, he would probably vote against it. We have tried to make clear to these Senators that they are not on a realistic path. We have a resolution pending now which no one wants to vote on.

The President pointed out that the United States' presence in Southeast Asia has had its effect. It has hampered China's policy and caused reversals against China in Indonesia and other parts of the world. Practically all the leaders in Asia are in deep sympathy with us. Prime Minister Lee of Singapore said he came to the United States to find out if the American people would hold out. He knew that the President, Secretary Rusk and Secretary McNamara would, but he didn't know about the resoluteness of the American people. The President pointed out that General Taylor and Clark Clifford did a marvelous job on their trip to Southeast Asia. As a result, the Thais have brought up their troop strength to 10,000. The Koreans, Australians, New Zealanders are all going to send more troops. The South Vietnamese are increasing their troop strength by 60 or 65,000.

The President adjourned the group at 2:15 p.m.

Source: *Foreign Relations of the United States, 1964–1968, Volume V, Vietnam, 1967* (Washington, D.C.: Government Printing Office, 2002), 954–70

Document 5

Telegram from the Embassy in Vietnam to the Department of State

November 22, 1967

1   I saw President Thieu afternoon November 22 to discuss holiday cease-fire. I outlined our position as contained para 1 and 2 of reftel, pointing out that we agreed with the times proposed by the GVN, namely 24 hours for Christmas, 24 hours for New Year, and 48 hours for Tet.

2   Thieu said that in his public comment he had been mistaken about the number of hours proposed for each holiday ceasefire and had stated they should be same number of times used last year, incorrectly stating this was 24–24–48 hours. These periods were respectively 48–48–96 hours. Thieu said he had just been discussing this matter with Generals Cao Van Vien and Def Min Vy who wished to shorten these hours. They had therefore agreed on the following possible schedule: From 7 am December 24 to 7 pm December 25 (36 hours); from 7 am December 31 to 7 pm January 1 (36 hours); from 7 am January 29 to 7 am February 1 (72 hours). In addition they had agreed that New Year and Tet standdown would be contingent on NVN/VC "performance" in complying with Christmas standdown. He mentioned the large number of NVN/VC violations of past standdowns.

Source: *Foreign Relations of the United States, 1964–1968, Volume V, Vietnam, 1967* (Washington, D.C.: Government Printing Office, 2002), 1064

Telegram from the Commander, Military Assistance Command, Vietnam (Westmoreland) to the Deputy Commander, Military Assistance Command, Vietnam (Abrams)

November 25, 1967

Subject: Concept of situation portrayed during recent visit to Washington

1   During my recent visit to Washington, I was required to present my views on the situation in Vietnam to Highest Authority, Secretary of Defense, Joint Chiefs of Staff, Senate Armed Services Committee, and the House Armed Services Committee. In addition, I appeared on several nationwide television programs, addressed the National Press Club, and held an on-the-record press conference in the Pentagon. On each occasion, I presented in full or in part the following concept: we are grinding down the Communist enemy in South Vietnam, and there is evidence that manpower problems are emerging in North Vietnam. Our forces are growing stronger and becoming more proficient in the environment. The Vietnamese armed forces are getting stronger and becoming more effective on the battlefield. The Vietnamese armed forces are being provided with more modern equipment. These trends should continue, with the enemy becoming weaker and the GVN becoming stronger to the point where conceivably in two years or less the Vietnamese can shoulder a larger share of the war and thereby permit the U.S. to begin phasing down the level of its commitment. This phasedown will probably be token at first.

2   On my own initiative, I took this position after considerable thought, based on the following consideration: I believe the concept and objective plan for our forces, as well as those of the Vietnamese, is practical and as such it should serve as an incentive. The concept is compatible with the evolution of the war since our initial commitment and portrays to the American people "some light at the end of the tunnel." The concept justifies the augmentation of troops I've asked for based on the principle of reinforcing success and also supports an increase in the strength of Vietnamese forces and their modernization. The concept

straddles the Presidential election of November 1968, implying that the election is not a benchmark from a military point of view. Finally, it puts emphasis on the essential role of the Vietnamese in carrying a major burden of their war against the Communists but also suggests that we must be prepared for a protracted commitment.

3   The concept lends itself to a programmatic approach, and I would like the staff to proceed with studying the specific areas and time frames in which responsibility might be transferred from the U.S. to the Vietnamese. Based on these studies, I visualize a program that would initiate and manage the multiple actions necessary to put the Vietnamese in a posture to make possible some transfer of responsibility at the earliest practical time.

4   Please have the staff come to grips with this matter. We will explore it in depth following analysis and upon my return.

Source: *Foreign Relations of the United States, 1964–1968, Volume V, Vietnam, 1967* (Washington, D.C.: Government Printing Office, 2002), 1071–72

Telegram from General Westmoreland, COMUSMACV, to General Wheeler, CJCS

December 10, 1967

1   I have received your message which raises the old specter of "why do we fight the enemy near the borders?" I welcome the opportunity to state my views again on the subject, because it gets at the basic issues of how this war must be fought.

2   The enemy has chosen to concentrate major elements of his NVA forces along the borders in Quang Tri, Kontum/Pleiku, and Northwestern III CTZ so that he can launch major attacks against SVN to gain a psychological and political victory, while at the same time retaining the best hope of disengaging when defeated. He has demonstrated this strategy by his recent incursions near Conthien, Dak To, and in the Con Ninh/Song Be areas. In each of these battles, the targets of the enemy attacks, and the big chance for an exploitable psychological victory, were the closest major GVN/U.S. positions to the border and the populated areas surrounding them. In the north his targets were marine and ARVN positions at Con Thien, Gio Linh and Dong Ha and the populated areas of Quang Tri. In Kontum it was the position at Dak To and the whole of the populated valleys along Route 14. At Loc Ninh and Song Be it was the district and province headquarters and the population centers nearby—as graphically demonstrated by the grisly attack on the village of Dak Son where the murder of civilians was abominable.

3   When the enemy moves across the borders we must strike him as soon as he is within reach, and before he can gain a victory or tyrannize the local population. We cannot permit him to strike the confidence of the SVN people in ultimate victory or to bolster his own morale with success. To do otherwise would be to deliver to him without contest, the very objectives which he seeks. However, we do not stand along the border and catch the enemy as he enters. Rather, we take every step to meet him and stop him before he reaches his objectives. The recent battle of Dak To is a good example. We knew the enemy was on the move towards Dak To and Highway 14. We moved forces, not to the

border, but to Dak To, from which we could base our operations so that the enemy could not overrun any portion of the populated areas of Kontum, and at the same time maneuver against him. It is important to realize that our most recent hamlet evaluation survey shows that 84.3 percent of the population of Kontum Province is under GVN control. If we intentionally let the enemy deep into Kontum Province, we would be taking a major step backwards. Time people (in that province) could feel, justifiably, that they had been let down, the refugee program would be enormous and the first step in total erosion of our posture in this country would have begun.

4   In addition to the psychological, political and economic impact of a withdrawal policy, it is also unsound from a military standpoint. If we let the enemy into such places as Kontum, he will be in a position to isolate GVN positions (which must be maintained to protect the people and their land), interdict the roads and forces us deploy and support our forces entirely by air. This is a very difficult task, as was proven in 1965 in the highlands when the enemy succeeded in cutting all roads and isolating all towns. Also, once the enemy gets established in SVN proper, he is not necessarily an easier target to destroy. In fact, the opposite is the case. If, for example, we had to engage the enemy along the populated valleys of Kontum, rather than in the difficult (but unpopulated) terrain southwest of Dak To, we would have a much more serious proposition. We cannot apply our firepower with as much freedom, we permit him to get at potential sources of food to sustain his forces and we give him more maneuver room, also I am certain that, if we did not fight the enemy at Con Thien or near Dak To, it would have cost us at least twice as much in military casualties (not to mention civilian casualties) and would have taken at least twice as long to do the job. We have had plenty of experience in fighting NVA divisions that have gotten adrift deep within SVN and it is not an attractive proposition. To surround and destroy such an enemy is most difficult. The 2D NVA Division got into Quang Tin province last year and we have been fighting it ever since. We have had an almost uninterrupted battle in that area since May of this year, in which we have inflicted approximately 7,000 casualties on the enemy, and have suffered nearly 1,000 KIA on our part. The 3D NVA Division has been in southern Quang Nghai and northern Binh Dinh for over a year. And, the 1st Cav. Div. has had its hands full in searching them out and destroying them in that highly populated area. In addition to fighting NVA Divisions in the populated areas we have plenty of evidence that fighting combinations of local forces, main forces and guerrillas in such places as Hau Nghia and Tay Ninh is not a fast, cheap road to victory. Since May 1967 the 25th U.S. Division has been devoted entirely to this task in operation

Kole Kole, Barking Sands and Diamond Head. During the period 11 May–7 Dec the Division has suffered 324 KIA, while killing 1,686 enemy. These figures are remarkably comparable to the Dak To fighting —except that the Hau Nghia–Tay Ninh fight kept a whole division tied down for seven months whereas Dak To took three weeks.

5   If we do not violently contest every attempt to get NVA units into SVN, we permit him to expand his system of bases in-country. He is in a better position to support the local forces and the guerrillas in the vital battle for the people. Conversely, the main forces are in a better position to levy taxes on the people, to get their rice and prove to the people, visibly, that the NVA is very much alive in SVN. When we engage the enemy near the borders we often preempt his plans and force him to fight before he is fully organized and before he can do his damage. Although such fighting gets high visibility in the press, it has low visibility to the people of South Vietnam since it is not being fought in their front yard. This how they would like it to continue.

6   The idea that we can't fight the enemy along the borders without seriously diverting forces from the populated areas is not entirely sound. Again, let's look at Dak To. When the battle started to shape up we had one battalion in Kontum. As the enemy moved, we took advantage of our mobility and rapidly built up our U.S. forces to nine battalions, drawing down from selected areas for minimum periods of time. We have already returned the two 1st Cav. Battalions to Binh Dinh. One was away for about ten days, the other for about one month. Temporary drawdowns of this nature do not raise havoc with the pacification process, but they do contribute enormously to the defeat of the enemy in the areas where he elects to concentrate. In general, I keep my reserves in populated areas (along the coast in II Corps) where they can be productively employed to grind down the enemy while awaiting other missions.

7   As to the idea that fighting near the borders creates pressures for escalatory action against the out-of-country sanctuaries, I find this reverse reasoning. The fact that the enemy is gainfully using these sanctuaries from which to mount his attacks is what stimulates our desire to strike them. If we elect not to protect the border provinces, the enemy would still use these sanctuaries to avoid the attacks by fire that we can apply to in-country bases. We would still be faced with the decision of attacking or granting immunity to these bases. By contacting him at the borders and thereby exposing the fact that he is making tactical use of these sanctuaries as part of the border battlefields, we are simply putting the spotlight on the hard fact of life which cannot be ignored by the tactical commander, despite a full realization of the political implications. We have had a hard time in the past convincing the world that this

war was an invasion. By forcing the enemy to fight on the borders, from his sanctuaries, we bring frontier defense into sharp and realistic focus.

8   I can see absolutely no psychological or military advantage to a strategy that would intentionally invite the war east towards the coast. It would be retrogressive, costly in casualties and refugees, and almost certainly prolong the war.

Source: MAC 11956, December 10, 1967, Tet Offensive Official History Files, U.S. Army Center of Military History

Document 8

Information memorandum from the President's Special Assistant (Rostow) to President Johnson

December 16, 1967

Subject: Are the next four months decisive?

I asked Saigon to collect and analyze all the captured documents they have on the present winter–spring offensive and negotiations, including the coalition government.

They did a good, long paper.

I then asked CIA to reproduce it and comment on it. The comment and the Saigon paper are attached.

Taken together, they reveal an interesting difference of emphasis and judgment between Saigon and CIA Washington.

The Saigon people read these documents as saying (see p. II, 5–8, paper clipped):

- the Communists are simultaneously making a maximum military effort and preparing their people for an early negotiation;
- if they achieve some tactical success, they are likely to negotiate in the late winter or spring;
- if they do not, they are likely to scale down the war;
- "the war is probably nearing a turning point and the outcome of the 1967–68 winter–spring campaign will in all likelihood determine the future direction of the war."

Our CIA people (as you can see in the marked passages of the covering note) are inclined to believe the present military campaign, combined with emphasis on a negotiated coalition government, is less "decisive" than Saigon. They see the war going for several years.

At the end, however, they accept an important point: having gotten the Viet Cong to accept these months as "decisive" and moving towards peace and victory "this situation could have serious effects on Viet Cong morale and lead to a substantial increase in defections" if the campaign fails.

In any case, I thought you'd like to know the terms in which experts are debating the present evidence.

Walt

Source: *Foreign Relations of the United States, 1964–1968, Volume V, Vietnam, 1967* (Washington, D.C.: Government Printing Office, 2002), 1117–18

Document 9

U.S., puppets, to sabotage holiday cease-fire on Liberation Radio in Vietnamese to South Vietnam

December 18, 1967

According to Saigon Radio, in compliance with his U.S. masters' order, on 14 December Nguyen Cao Ky, the Vietnamese traitor who once claimed to be a disciple of Hitler, declared that the Republic of Vietnamese and Allied forces—that is, the U.S., puppet, and satellite troops—will cease fire for one day on Christmas, one day on New Year's Day, and two days on Tet. This constitutes an open and flagrant challenge of the U.S.–Thieu–Ky clique to all the South Vietnamese people.

It is recalled that on 18 November 1967, the NLFSV Central Committee Presidium issued a statement, and on 19 November the South Vietnamese People's Liberation Armed Forces Command issued an order on the cessation of military attacks for three days, on Christmas, from 0000 Indochina time on 24 December 1967 (?) until 0000 Indochina time on 27 December 1967; for three days over the new year from 0000 Indochina time on 30 December 1967 until 0000 Indochina time on 2 January 1968; for seven days over Tet, from 0000 Indochina time on 27 January 1968, that is 28 December, lunar calendar, to 0000 on 3 February 1968, that is, 5 January on the lunar calendar.

This is a humanitarian and completely correct policy of the Front. It fully meets the aspirations of our compatriots, the American people, and the peoples of many other countries. At the same time, it fulfills the legitimate hope of members of the puppet army and administration, and of the U.S. and satellite troops to have a family reunion on these sacred days in order to celebrate Tet and to greet the new year and the birth of Christ.

The South Vietnamese people and their Liberation Armed Forces, under the NLFSV's leadership, have welcomed the Front's order with overwhelming joy. They are ready to generously welcome those in the enemy's ranks who want to have the opportunity to enjoy springtime and the holidays, to move about when they can rid themselves of the miserable and tense life in the U.S.–puppet bonds, which is menaced by death, and to have a reunion with their kith and kin.

Throughout the past 13 years, especially during the past year, the U.S., puppet, and satellite troops have led a miserable existence in their outposts, bases, and fortifications all over the south. In the face of the resolute and increasingly vigorous offensive thrust of the Liberation Armed Forces, the U.S., puppet, and satellite troops have suffered serious casualties. They have lived in a state of moral tension and in a precarious situation. Everywhere in the south, from the well-fortified [?outposts] such as the U.S. marine base at Con Pien and the remote mountainous areas such as Dakto, to the puppet administration's Independence Palace in Saigon, the surging flames of the Liberation Armed Forces' attacks can engulf and destroy the enemy at any moment. Therefore, [? during] these holidays the front [words indistinct] the members of the puppet army and administration and the U.S. and satellite troops create favorable conditions for them to find the way to live and to extricate themselves from their dark and ignominious situation.

At a time when the South Vietnamese people, the American people, the peoples of many other countries, and the U.S., puppet, and satellite troops have welcomed the South Vietnam People's Liberation Armed Forces Command's order on the cessation of military attacks, carrying out his U.S. masters' order, the traitor Nguyen Cao Ky announced the above-mentioned reactionary policy. It is obvious that the U.S.–Thieu–Ky clique does not abide by the Liberation Armed Forces Command's order. Therefore, the U.S.–Thieu–Ky clique has ruthlessly trampled on the dearest aspirations and the sacred rights of the U.S., puppet, and satellite troops. This is tantamount to a crime for which the U.S.–Thieu–Ky clique must be severely punished.

The U.S.–Thieu–Ky clique was compelled to announce a short cease-fire, which does not jibe with the length of the cease-fire announced by the front. Yes, even during the short cease-fire, which it has announced with a view to coping with public opinion, the U.S.–puppet clique will seek by all means to sabotage it. This is not the first time it has acted thus. In previous years, on the occasion of the major holidays and Tet, the U.S.–Thieu–Ky clique also announced a cease-fire. Yet, throughout the cease-fire period it had announced the U.S.–puppet clique sent aircraft, warships, and tanks to open relentless fire on our compatriots and recklessly directed their artillery fire at our people's villages and hamlets. Even worse, the U.S.–puppet clique also conducted large-scale mopup operations during the cease-fire, such as operation Junction City, the biggest mopup operation, which was conducted throughout the Tet holidays. In this operation, the Americans and puppets razed many villages and hamlets and continuously caused disaster to our compatriots. The U.S.–Thieu–Ky clique ruthlessly repressed and prevented many members of the puppet army and administration and U.S. and satellite troops from enjoying the holidays during which the Front ceased military attacks.

The U.S.–Thieu–Ky clique's new criminal act has further exposed its insidious and warlike nature and its bloody hands. Once again, the U.S. imperialists and their lackeys have aroused hatred of the South Vietnamese people and of mankind and have stirred the indignation of the U.S.–puppet troops and personnel.

He who sows wind will certainly reap the whirlwind. Thieu and Ky, who carried out their U.S. masters' order to stifle the aspirations of the U.S., puppet, and satellite troops, can by no means ward off a situation in which the U.S., puppet, and satellite troops will turn their indignation into action by directing their fire at the heads of the tyrants and will punish the U.S.–Thieu–Ky clique for all its obstructive acts, in order to enjoy the pleasant holidays in accordance with the Front's order. As for the southern people and their Liberation Armed Forces, they are aware of the Front's decision on the cessation of military attacks and will fully carry out the Front's order. The southern people and Liberation Armed Forces are prepared to intercept and to direct appropriate counterblows at the enemy and to punish the U.S.–Thieu–Ky clique for all its schemes and its violations and sabotage of the Front's decision to cease military attacks for three days on the occasion of Christmas, for three days on the occasion of New Year's Day, and for seven days on the occasion of Tet. The southern armed forces and people are prepared to crush all gross violations of the Front's order on the cessation of military attacks on these holidays and will take advantage of their victories to surge forward to achieve even greater successes.

Source: "U.S., puppets to sabotage holiday cease-fire," Liberation Radio, 19 December 1967, Folder 03, Box 10, Douglas Pike Collection: Unit 02—Military Operations, The Vietnam Archive, Texas Tech University

Memorandum from the Chairman of the Joint Chiefs of Staff (Wheeler) to Secretary of Defense McNamara

January 20, 1968

Subject: Tet stand down

1   This responds to a request from Mr. Walt W. Rostow for General Westmoreland's rationale behind his recommendation for a 36-hour Tet stand down. In requesting General Westmoreland's views, I provided to him a summary of the rationale which the Joint Staff prepared for me on this question. This was provided to Mr. Steadman, OSD (ISA), and Department of State on 18 January. General Westmoreland agreed with that rationale and the logistical data therein. His comments are reflected below:

(a)   Holiday ceasefires have been unilaterally established, together with rules of conduct, by both the enemy and ourselves. However, our respective objectives are unrelated. The record is replete with documented evidence that the enemy's intent and actions have been consistently contrary to any peaceful objectives. Hanoi has directed the truce periods be fully exploited for improving the communist military posture.

(b)   Free World casualties sustained during truce periods are but slightly less than during non-truce conflict. Hence, there can be no sense of security or safety for the people of the Republic of Vietnam (RVN) for the enjoyment of holidays, whether ceasefire periods are established or not. On the other hand, the aggressor in this conflict and his people suffer no similar limitations while pursuing their mockery of our concessions.

(c)   For so long as Hanoi persists in its direction and support of the war in RVN, our air interdiction efforts in North Vietnam (NVN) are indispensable to both the defense of RVN and the achievement of an early and acceptable negotiations posture. The expense in men and planes has fallen very heavily on the United States. Bombing pauses, however brief, are capitalized on fully to rebuild the essential elements of the NVN logistics system which we have so painstakingly disrupted. It would be unfortunate if our costly, necessary, and yet restrained air interdiction program were nullified by the concession of unilateral privileges which can be accurately forecast as being unproductive.

(d) The enemy is presently developing a threatening posture in several areas in order to seek victories essential to achieving prestige and bargaining power. He may exercise his initiatives prior to, during or after Tet. It is altogether possible that he has planned to complete his offensive preparations during the Free World ceasefire. He has used past truce periods for this purpose and can be expected to do so again. We shall do all possible to restrict the movement of men and materials by the enemy in RVN during the ceasefire through advance positioning of our forces.

(e) President Thieu and General Vien do not question the advisability of keeping ceasefires to the shortest possible time periods, and they recognize the wholly unilateral aspect of the holiday truces. They do, nevertheless, feel bound to at least a token observance of this most important of Vietnam holidays. However, they do not propose standing down the war for the full run of the traditional Tet celebration; this out of frank recognition of the severe penalties of imposing unwarranted trust in an enemy whose duplicity in such actions is so well established.

(f) In summary, the longer the truce the greater the cost to us and to our Allies in lives, material and probably the duration of the war. It has been conclusively demonstrated that holiday truces of whatever length will not have any mollifying effect upon the enemy. The additional 12 hours (to 48 hours) will offer the Vietnamese people nothing in the form of safety or respite from the communists. It would seem that the additional 12 hours will serve only the purpose of the enemy, with no reciprocal benefits to us.

2   Admiral Sharp, in response to my request for his views on this matter, strongly recommended that the Tet ceasefire period be of the shortest possible duration, no more than 36 hours, to permit the enemy the shortest possible period to refurbish and reposition his forces. The additional 12 hours permitted by a 48 hour stand down would allow a very considerable increase in supply movement south and can only result in additional casualties to friendly forces.

Earle G. Wheeler

Source: *Foreign Relations of the United States, 1964–1968, Volume VI, Vietnam, January–August 1968* (Washington, D.C.: Government Printing Office, 2002), 55–56

Memorandum from the Joint Chiefs of Staff to President Johnson

January 29, 1968

Subject: The situation at Khe Sanh

1   You will recall that on 12 January 1968 General Westmoreland informed me that the Khe Sanh position is important to us for the following reasons: (a) it is the western anchor of our defense of the DMZ area against enemy incursions into the northern portion of South Vietnam; (b) its abandonment would bring enemy forces into areas contiguous to the heavily populated and important coastal area; and (c) its abandonment would constitute a major propaganda victory for the enemy which would seriously affect Vietnamese and U.S. morale. In summary, General Westmoreland declared that withdrawal from Khe Sanh would be a tremendous step backwards.

2   At 0910 hours this morning, I discussed the Khe Sanh situation by telephone with General Westmoreland. He had just returned from a visit to northern I Corps Area during which he conferred with senior commanders, personally surveyed the situation, and finalized contingency plans. General Westmoreland made the following points:

    (a) The Khe Sanh garrison now consists of 5,000 U.S. and ARVN troops. They have more than a battalion of U.S. artillery supporting them, and 16 175 MM guns which can fire from easterly positions in support of the Khe Sanh force.

    (b) Among other reinforcing actions, he has moved a full U.S. Army Division into northern I Corps. Within a few days the equivalent of an ARVN airborne division will also reinforce this area.

    (c) He has established a Field Army Headquarters in the Hue/Phu Bai area to control all forces, both U.S. and ARVN, in northern I Corps. This headquarters is commanded by General Abrams.

    (d) General Momyer, Commander 7th Air Force, is coordinating all supporting air strikes in the Niagara area which constitutes the locale of enemy buildup around Khe Sanh.

    (e) Air action since 17 January has been remunerative. About 40 B-52 sorties per day and some 500 tactical air sorties per day are being conducted in the Niagara area. There have been numerous secondary explosions. It appears that air strikes and our artillery fire have disrupted the enemy's logistic buildup and troop concentration.

3   General Westmoreland stated to me that, in his judgment, we can hold Khe Sanh and we should hold Khe Sanh. He reports that everyone is confident. He believes that this is an opportunity to inflict a severe defeat upon the enemy. Further, General Westmoreland considers that all preparatory and precautionary measures have been taken, both in South Vietnam and here, to conduct a successful defense in the Khe Sanh area.

4   The Joint Chiefs of Staff have reviewed the situation at Khe Sanh and concur with General Westmoreland's assessment of the situation. They recommend that we maintain our position at Khe Sanh.

For the Joint Chiefs of Staff:

Earle G. Wheeler

Chairman, Joint Chiefs of Staff

Source: *Foreign Relations of the United States, 1964–1968, Volume VI, Vietnam, January–August 1968* (Washington, D.C.: Government Printing Office, 2002), 69–70

Document 12

Telegram from the Commander of the Military Assistance Command, Vietnam (Westmoreland) to the Commander in Chief, Pacific Forces (Sharp) and the Chairman of the Joint Chiefs of Staff (Wheeler)

January 30, 1968

The events of the past 18 hours have been replete with enemy attacks against certain of our key installations in the I and II CTZs. The heaviest attacks were launched against Danang, Kontum, Pleiku, Nha Trang, Ban Me Thuot, and Can Canh in the Dak To area. Lesser attacks were made on Qui Nhon and Tuy Hoa. Although enemy activity in III and IV CTZs was comparatively light during this period, we are alert to attempts by the enemy to attack significant targets in these areas. Repeated attempts can also be expected in the I and II CTZs. While our operations reports to your headquarters have covered these attacks in some detail, I felt it would be helpful to give you a wrap-up on the situation as it stands now.

It is significant that in I CTZ none of these attacks were directed against our installations north of the Ai Van Pass, perhaps because of the thickening of U.S. forces in that area. Danang was the prime target and was attacked beginning at 20 minutes past midnight. The facilities at Marble Mountain and the Danang air base were mortared and rocketed with a number of aircraft receiving damage, to include five jet aircraft destroyed. The rocket site was immediately located and brought under fire with unknown results at this time. Simultaneously, the ARVN Corps Headquarters came under enemy mortar and ground attack by an estimated reinforced enemy company. An attempt was made against the Danang bridge by underwater swimmers. It was thwarted with three enemy KIA and one captured. Timely warning of the attacks plus rapid reaction by U.S./ARVN/ROK forces has brought the situation in the Danang area under control at this time. Casualties so far list 89 enemy KIA and 7 friendly KIA. Noteworthy among the counteractions launched in the early morning hours was that of the ROK Marines, who, in response to an enemy ground attack in the Hoi An area, inserted a force by helicopter, engaged the enemy, killing 21 with no friendly casualties.

The II CTZ received the bulk and intensity of the enemy attacks. In the Kontum area, in excess of 500 enemy attacked from the north in the vicinity of the airfield, and were engaged by elements of the 4th U.S. Division and assorted Vietnamese units. The area is now under control with artillery and air strikes being employed against an estimated two enemy battalions. Seven U.S. were killed in this action, with 165 NVA KIA. Vietnamese casualties are unknown. In Tan Canh of Kontum Province, contact is sporadic with elements of the 3/42 ARVN regiment opposing an unknown size enemy force. Four friendly have been killed and five NVA. In Pleiku, contact continues with an enemy of unknown size in the city, with friendly forces attempting to cut off the enemy forces trying to escape. The 4th Inf. Div. captured 220 enemy in the vicinity of Pleiku. Of these, 20 had North Vietnamese money on their person. The vast majority are Montagnards believed to be pressed into service. Average age appears to be 18 to 30. Fifty-eight claim to be Hoi Chanhs. ARVN forces are in the city (Pleiku). Seven friendly have been killed as against 103 enemy. In Nha Trang, sporadic fighting continues in the city. Friendly lost 21 KIA; enemy 60 KIA. Fighting continues against the enemy attempting to withdraw. City fighting continues in Ban Me Thuot with enemy still in the vicinity. Casualties are reported to be 7 friendly KIA and 131 enemy KIA. In addition, 36 enemy have been killed in the Tuy Hoa area and 11 NVA KIA in the Ninh Hoa area. In Qui Nhon, the enemy holds the radio station and the maintenance area but has lost 50 KIA. The ROKs have the radio station surrounded but have not attacked, since the enemy is holding three hostages.

In II CTZ in Binh Dinh Duong Province, southwest of Ben Cat, units of the 25th U.S. Division made a significant contact with an enemy force, resulting in 66 enemy killed, with eight friendly killed and 14 wounded. IV CTZ had one significant encounter in the Vinh Long area, where gunships and tactical support aircraft engaged a cleared target of sampans in a canal area, killing 80 enemy, destroying 124 sampans, with three secondary explosions.

During the course of the day, we had a maximum air effort, which was reported to be extremely effective.

The current outlook depicts a situation similar to my foregoing account.

In summary, the enemy has displayed what appears to be desperation tactics, using NVA troops to terrorize populated areas. He attempted to achieve surprise by attacking during the truce period. The reaction of Vietnamese, U.S. and free world forces to the situation has been generally good. Since the enemy has exposed himself, he has suffered many casualties. As of now, they add up to almost 700. When the dust settles, there will probably be more. All my subordinate commanders report the situation well in hand.

Source: *Foreign Relations of the United States, 1964–1968, Volume VI, Vietnam, January–August 1968* (Washington, D.C.: Government Printing Office, 2002), 75–77

Notes of meeting

January 30, 1968

THOSE ATTENDING THE MEETING WERE

Secretary Rusk
Secretary McNamara
Clark Clifford
CIA Director Helms
Walt Rostow
George Christian
Tom Johnson

[Omitted here is discussion of the *Pueblo* crisis.]

The President: What about Buttercup?

Secretary Rusk: The last Buttercup messenger turned around because of particularly heavy activity around Hanoi. On his last report the message was not very clear. Ambassador Bunker wants it authenticated. Their people think we should release four additional prisoners. I think we should leave the details of this with Ambassador Bunker to work out with Thieu.

The President: What about Packers?

Secretary Rusk: Our man is expected in Bucharest on February 1. I think Hanoi is waiting to see how they come out in this offensive.

The President: General Wheeler, will you give us the most up to date information about Khe Sanh.

General Wheeler: First reports indicate 700 enemy killed. U.S. and Vietnamese casualties are light. There have been rockets and mortars hit Da Nang. The city of Da Nang was also attacked. Pleiku was attacked by a couple of hundred men. They terrorized the city and struck at the Pleiku air base. There have been at least two other acts, one against the 4th Infantry and one at Nha Trong and Kontum.

At Khe Sanh the situation is quiet and the weather is good. At 9:00 am today EST General Westmoreland said that he had talked with his Commander at Khe Sanh and the situation is well in hand. At Tet it is customary for many people from the countryside to come into town. It is easy for the Viet Cong to infiltrate these groups. They can bring in a mortar and a rocket easily. They assemble it at a pre-arranged time and attack these installations. We caught four trying to blow up a bridge. The enemy has lost quite heavily. The 4th Infantry captured 200 Viet Cong, most of whom were Montagnard Tribesmen. Twenty of them had North Vietnamese money.

Secretary McNamara: There are three military actions we would like to bring up at this time. Two of them will require the President's approval, and one is for the President's information.

General Wheeler: We would like approval of the Talos anti-aircraft missile for use south of the 20 degree south latitude. We have noticed recently that the MiGs are carrying wing tanks which give them greater range. They will be going after the B-52s in South Vietnam. They have been trying to shoot down a B-52 for psychological purposes for some time. (The President approved this action upon the recommendation of General Wheeler, Secretary Rusk and Secretary McNamara.)

The second item on which the President's approval is requested is the use of patrols in the DMZ. These patrols would be used to check on the disposition of supplies, troops and other developments inside the DMZ. Intelligence indicates a thickening of forces around Khe Sanh with a thinning in the Eastern end of the DMZ. As an alternative to use of U.S. patrols, we would suggest use of ARVN patrols with U.S. advisers.

Secretary Rusk: We will lose some men this way, but there is no political problem.

Secretary McNamara: I have no problem because of the Khe Sanh build-up. It is natural that we will want to know what is going on in the DMZ, particularly with Khe Sanh shaping up the way it is.

Secretary McNamara: The third action we proposed is to organize and mount a feint of a full scale landing above the DMZ. This would involve mounting naval gun fire, making air strikes along the coast and moving amphibious shipping north into the area.

The President: Is this about the same as the proposal I have heard once before?

General Wheeler: Yes, sir. There are some disadvantages. If we made such a feint, North Vietnam would claim a victory, but we request the President's approval to go ahead and prepare a plan. This plan would be submitted to the Joint Chiefs of Staff and to the President for approval. We would pretend we were going to make a landing and we would let it leak to the South Vietnamese to make sure that the North Vietnamese would learn of it. We would use naval gunfire and marshal the shipping as though we were going to load troops. The objective of this would be to make them believe that we were about to have a major landing. This would, if its purpose is realized, get them to move troops and lessen the pressure in the Khe Sanh area.

One advantage of this is that if it does break publicly, we have never made such a move.

Secretary McNamara: We would plan this on the basis that it would be brought to the attention of the North Vietnamese and not to the American public.

CIA Director Helms: It is a great thing if you can keep it out of the hands of the press.

Secretary McNamara: I agree.

Walt Rostow: I would not leak it to the ARVN. Once you do it will become known to the press. I would make the cover through the use of the most sophisticated electronic equipment we have.

Clark Clifford: Here is my uninformed reaction. If we go ahead and plan on this and it should become known, people would say we used this as an excuse for the real thing.

The President: Go ahead and plan it. I want to give weight to the Field Commander's recommendation in this case.

[Omitted here is continuing discussion of the *Pueblo* crisis.]

Walt Rostow: What are we going to do about Ted Kennedy's report?

Secretary Rusk: He has used figures we cannot legitimately attack. Corruption is a tough one to deal with.

Secretary McNamara: There is no excuse for the Vietnamese not lowering their draft age to below 20.

The President: We should sit down with these people who have been to Vietnam and talk to them before they are turned loose on an unsuspecting public.

(At 2:35 Walt Rostow returned from a call he had taken from Bromley Smith. He reported to the meeting that "we have just been informed we are being heavily mortared in Saigon. The Presidential Palace, our BOQs, the Embassy and the city itself have been hit. This flash was just received from the NMCC.")

The President: This could be very bad.

Secretary Rusk: Yes, I hope it is not Ambassador Bunker's residence.

The President: What can we do to shake them from this?

This looks like where we came in. Remember it was at Pleiku that they hit our barracks and that we began to strike them in the north.

What comes to mind in the way of retaliation?

General Wheeler: It was the same type of thing before. You will remember that during the inauguration that the MACV headquarters was hit. In a city like Saigon people can infiltrate easily. They carry in rounds of ammunition and mortars. They fire and run.

It is impossible to stop this in its entirety. This is about as tough to stop as it is to protect against an individual mugging in Washington, D.C.

We have got to pacify all of this area and get rid of the Viet Cong infrastructure.

They are making a major effort to mount a series of these actions to make a big splurge at Tet.

Secretary McNamara: I have two recommendations. This is a public relations problem not a military one. We need to keep General Loan in charge of the Saigon police. He should not be removed as some of our people in the State Department are suggesting. At least not until we find somebody better.

CIA Director Helms: I agree completely.

Secretary McNamara: He is the best security chief since Diem's time. He has cleaned up Saigon well.

Secretary Rusk: He is a good police chief, but he has been rather uncooperative with some of our people.

Secretary McNamara: The answer to the mortar attacks is success at Khe Sanh. We must get our story across. Phil Goulding called General Sidle this morning in Saigon. We are inflicting very heavy casualties on the enemy and we are not unprepared for the encounter.

[Omitted here is discussion of clearing the Suez Canal]

Source: *Foreign Relations of the United States, 1964–1968, Volume VI, Vietnam, January–August 1968* (Washington, D.C.: Government Printing Office, 2002), 79–82

Document 14

Intelligence memorandum

January 31, 1968

The Communist Tet Offensive

Summary

The current series of coordinated enemy attacks in South Vietnam appears designed for maximum psychological impact and to demonstrate the Communists' continued power despite the presence of strong U.S. forces. The Communists clearly have made careful preparations for the offensive. These preparations point to a major assault in the Khe Sanh area possibly in conjunction with a drive throughout the northern I corps area, and widespread attacks against U.S. installations may be preparatory to or in support of such action. The enemy probably hopes to score some major battlefield successes during their campaign. Their military actions appear related to Hanoi's recent offer to open talks, but it is questionable that the Communists are making a final desperate bid before suing for peace.

1   The current coordinated series of enemy attacks in South Vietnam, so far targeted primarily against population centers and U.S. installations from I Corps to the delta, appears primarily designed for maximum psychological impact. The Communists appear to be trying to demonstrate to the South Vietnamese, to U.S. and world opinion and probably to their own forces that, almost three years after the intervention of U.S. forces, they can still enter major towns and bases, threaten the U.S. Embassy itself, and seriously disrupt the country, if only temporarily.

2   Extensive harassment of U.S. airfields, logistical centers, and command and communications centers appears—in addition to its shock effect—partly designed to inhibit immediate allied reaction and retaliation. It may be preparatory to or intended to support further impending enemy actions in the Khe Sanh/DMZ/northern Quang Tri area. So far this area has been relatively quiet during the latest round of attacks, but the enemy concentration in this area remains the most ominous in the country.

3   Evidence has been building up for the past several weeks that the Communists intended a major nationwide offensive in connection with the Tet season. Enemy propaganda, however, has stressed an intention to honor a seven-day cease-fire regardless of the period of the allied standdown. This line may have been intended to enhance the surprise factor of attacks on the day of Tet itself. It may also be that the Communist timetable—in past years calling for stepped up action just prior to and immediately following the Tet truce—was sufficiently flexible to call for action during the Tet if the allies could be put in the position of apparently bearing the onus. In any event, Communist propagandists were clearly ready with the line that the enemy attacks were "punishment" for allied violations.

4   It is clear that the Communists made careful and, most recently, urgent preparations for the current offensive. These preparations seem to point, in coming days or weeks, to a major assault around Khe Sanh, possibly in conjunction with a campaign throughout the northern I Corps area. The Communists probably hope, in addition to psychological gains, to score some dramatic battlefield successes, ideally (from their standpoint) the overrunning of Khe Sanh or a U.S. withdrawal from this or some other key garrison. In launching a series of bold actions, they incur the risk of serious defeats or retaliation, with possible repercussions on their own forces. Nonetheless, they probably hope to gain the strategic initiative and to pin down substantial numbers of allied troops over wide areas in which the Communists hold some military advantages. A major objective of the entire Communist "winter–spring" campaign since autumn appears to be to draw off U.S. forces while the VC attempt to erode the pacification effort through guerrilla-type actions. Furthermore, the Communists certainly hope to make political mileage out of heightened U.S. casualty rates and a demonstration of continued VC strength.

5   There seems to be little question that the present Communist offensive activity bears a relation to Hanoi's recent offer to open talks. Foremost, the Communists probably hope to improve their political and military image in the event that any negotiations are initiated in coming months. Prior to the initiation of the "winter–spring" campaign, Communist forces throughout the country were intensively indoctrinated on the importance of the campaign. At least in some areas, the campaign itself was linked, directly or by implication, to the possibility of a political settlement. Some of this indoctrination may have been propaganda intended to instill a victory psychology among troops possibly discouraged by hardships and talk of "protracted war." Although the current surge of Communist activity involves both a military and political gamble, it is highly questionable that the Communists are making a

final desperate effort for a show of strength prior to suing for peace. Despite evident problems of manpower and supply, enemy forces continued to display improved fire-power, flexibility of tactics, and a considerable degree of resiliency. Their current offensive is probably intended to convey the impression that despite VC problems and despite half a million U.S. troops, the Communists are still powerful and capable of waging war.

Source: *Foreign Relations of the United States, 1964–1968, Volume VI, Vietnam, January–August 1968* (Washington, D.C.: Government Printing Office, 2002), 92–94

Document 15

Interrogation of Ngo Van Giang

January 28–January 31, 1968

COUNTRY: RVN
SUBJECT: Attack on U.S. Embassy
DATE OF INFORMATION: 28 Jan 68 to 31 Jan 68
PLACE OF ACQUISITION: CMIC, SAIGON
EVALUATION: Source B Information 2
SOURCE: Captive NGO VAN GIANG (NGOO, VEAN JANG), aka (BA, VEAN), aka BA DEN (BA, DEN), aka BA OM (BA, OOMS); CMIC #1890
REPORT NUMBER: U.S. 538–68
DATE OF REPORT: 12 Mar 68
NUMBER OF PAGES: Eight
REFERENCES: CMIC Interrogation Guide; MACV ICP; SICR G-FIR-20595
PREPARED BY: E. D. Gaskins, CPT, U.S. Army

1   Biographical Information:

   (a) Name: NGO VAN GIANG (NGOO, VEAN JANG), aka BA VAN (BA, VAAN), aka BA DEN (BA, DEN), aka BA OM (BA, OOMS).
   (b) Rank: VC equivalent of CPT.
   (c) Position: CO of J9 Special Action Unit, subordinate to T700 Unit (formerly the C-10 Sapper Bn).
   (d) DPOB: 1925, in HOA LUONG Vil, THUONG TIN Dist, HA DONG Prov, NVN.
   (e) Past Activities of Source:
      (i)   Dec 60: Joined the VC as a member of the TAN AN HOI Vil Guerrilla Unit in CU CHI Dist., HAU NGHIA Prov.
      (ii) May 62: Attended a course for six months at the cadre school in TAY NINH Prov.
      (iii) May 63: Served as Company XO in GIA DINH Prov.

    (iv) May 64: Served as PO of the 59th Activities Unit, CU CHI Dist.

    (v) Dec 64: Assigned as a commo-liason team leader of the T700 (C-10) Special Action Unit.

    (vi) Dec 65: Assigned as CO of J9 Unit operating in LONG AN and HAU NGHIA Provinces.

2   Attack on the U.S. Embassy:

    (a) First knowledge. At 2100 hours on 28 Jan 68, while located in TRANG DAU Ham, AN TINH Vil, TRAN BANG Dist, HAU NGHIA Prov., source was told by BA TAM (BA, TAM), CofS of T700 Unit, that within the next few days source would be sent to attack a target, and that Sr CPT BAY TUYEN (BAYS, TUYEENS) would be in charge of the mission, with CPT UT NHO (UTS, NHOR) and source as his assistants. No further details were specified at that time, but source was told that at a later date, BAY TUYEN, a training cadre of T700, would fully explain the mission.

    (b) Weapons. At 0200 hours on 28 Jan 68, CPT UT NHO arrived at the house where source was located in TRANG DAU HAM, AN TINH Vil. NHO brought with him the following weapons and munitions: Two x B-40 ATGLs, 20 x B-40 rounds, eight x AK SMGs, 1000 x AK rounds, three x K-54 pistols, and 20 kg of explosives. Source, UT NHO, TEO (TEOR), SAU (SAUS) (CMIC #1828), and two others concealed the weapons in bamboo mats and wicker baskets. The B-40 ATGLs and AKs were placed between bamboo mats and rolled up so that the weapons would not be detected. The remaining weapons and munitions were placed in the bottom of wicker baskets, on top of which were placed tomatoes, thereby concealing the contents. Source did not know at that time where these arms were being taken, or for what purpose they were to be used. Subsequently, he learned that the weapons were to be used in the attack on the U.S. Embassy.

    (c) Rendezvous in SAIGON:

        (i) Before he left with the weapons, UT NHO instructed source and four other men that in the morning a vehicle would be sent to pick them up. This vehicle would be driven by NGUYEN VAN BA (NGUYEENX, VEAN BA), a chauffeur for the U.S. Embassy. UT NHO gave source a piece of paper with an address written on it. He also gave a verbal description of the house located at that address. Source was instructed to go to this house and say he was a friend of BA (BA). He and the four others were to wait there until contacted by UT NHO. UT

NHO then left with the weapons. Source and the four others remained in TRANG DAU Ham.

(ii)   At approx 1300 hours on 29 Jan 68, a small truck of unknown make arrived, driven by BA. Source said the four other men got in the truck with BA and all six drove to SAIGON, arriving at approx 1600 hours. When they arrived in SAIGON, source discovered that he had lost the piece of paper with the address on it. He remembered only that the house was located on NGUYEN DINH CHIEU Street near the TAN DINH Market. They drove along this street looking for a house that fitted the description given by UT NHO. When they found the house they believed to be the right one, BA remained with the truck while the other five went to the door. When they knocked, a child came to the door and source said he was a friend of Mr. BA. A man and a woman then came to the door and asked all of them to come in. While the woman began to close the doors and shutters, the man left the room and source believed that he was to slip out of the house and go to the corner and inform a National Policeman of their presence. At that time all five of the men ran from the house. Source ran to the truck and told BA what had happened. The other four men ran down the street towards the TAN DINH Market. Source and BA rode around the block and came upon the other four men. They asked BA to tell UT NHO that they were going to SAU's friend's house where they knew they would be safe. Two of them flagged a taxi and drove away. A short time later the other two flagged a taxi and drove away. (See Enclosure 1.)

(iii)   Source and BA returned to TRANG DAU HAM, arriving at 1900 hours. BA left source there and went to an unknown destination.

(d) Second Rendezvous. Source spent the night in TRANG DAU HAM. At 1000 hours on 30 Jan 68, an unknown comm-liason agent arrived at source's house with a verbal message from UT NHO. Source was told to remain where he was and that he would be contacted by an unspecified individual who would conduct him back to SAIGON to meet UT NHO. At 1200 hours, BA arrived on a Honda motorcycle with instructions to take source to SAIGON. They arrived in SAIGON at approx 1500 hours, drove by the SAIGON Market and stopped at the CU Market. BA instructed source to wait there until he returned. Ten or 15 minutes later, BA returned driving a U.S. station wagon of unknown make. The upper part of the car was light yellow in color and the lower part was light blue. BA drove source down TONG NHAT Boulevard by the U.S. Embassy, and around the block and then let him out on the corner. Source was instructed that he would be picked up at the same corner at 2300 hours. Source walked by the U.S. Embassy to the corner, and took a taxi to the SAIGON Market, arriving at approx 1600 hours. (See Enclosure 2.) Then he bought some fire-crackers and walked to the BACH DANG River. He stopped at a sidewalk cafe and had several beers. He then took a taxi and drove down TRAN QUI CAP Street looking for the house where he had lived with his wife and children six years before. He then arrived at the SAIGON Market where he drank beer until approx 2200 hours. At that time he took a taxi to the corner of the Embassy, arriving at approx 2300 hours. He walked past the Embassy to the corner where he was to be picked up. (See Enclosure 2.)

(e) Final Briefing. At approx 2300 hours, UT NHO arrived in a truck and took source to a garage near ARVN compound in DA KAO, TAN DINH Area. (Interrogator's Note: Based on information provided by SAU, a raid was conducted on this garage by the National Police.) When he arrived at the garage the following people were present: Source, UT NHO, BAY TUYEN, SAU, VINH (VINH), MANG (MANG), TEO (TEOR), and eight or nine other men and one woman whom source didn't know. Source heard that this woman owned the garage. From 2400 hours to 0250 hours on 31 Jan 68, BAY TUYEN and UT NHO gave a briefing on the mission, and the weapons were distributed. Source recognized them as the same weapons that he had helped pack in the wicker baskets and reed mats in TRAN DAU Ham. He was told that the group would attack the U.S. Embassy at 0300 hours. BAY TUYEN was in charge of the operation. UT NHO would be in charge of a group of six or seven men who had the mission of penetrating the main gate. Once inside, they were told to hold the gate against anyone trying to enter. Source was in charge of a group of four men: SAU, VINH, MANG and TEO, whose mission was to enter the side gate and hold against attackers. No instructions were given as to what was to be done once inside the Embassy. They were not given an escape route, not told how long to hold the Embassy, and were not told if replacements would arrive to relieve them. Source assumed that BAY TUYEN knew this information and would give further direction once inside the Embassy. They were told to kill anyone who resisted, but if anyone attempted to surrender or was unarmed, they were instructed to take him prisoner.

(f) Conduct of Attack. (See Enclosure 3.) AT 0250 hours on 31 Jan 68, all the men left the garage in two small trucks. The first truck was driven by an unknown man and carried BAY TUYEN, UT NHO, and six or seven others. The second truck was driven by an unknown driver and carried source, SAU, VINH, MANG and TEO. The two trucks arrived at the Embassy 0300 hours. The first truck stopped in the front of the Embassy and the second pulled past it and stopped a short distance away. The men in both trucks jumped out and immediately began assaulting the Embassy. Source does not know what happened to the two trucks and the drivers. Source led his group to the side of the Embassy, but found the sentry post deserted and the side gate secured. Shortly thereafter, a man from the other group relayed an order from UT NHO that source was to lead his men through a hole which had been made in the front wall by UT NHO's group. Source did not know how the hole was made. As he entered the breach in the wall, he saw two dead VC and one dead U.S. military policeman. Shortly after he entered the wall, source was wounded. At 0350 hours, he was taken to the far side of the building and was placed next to a small rock. From then until 0730 hours the next morning when he was captured, source was in a semi-conscious state. A short time after source was wounded, BA, the Embassy driver, who was also wounded, was placed next to him. BA died before morning. Source also saw both BAY TUYEN and UT NHO hit by gunfire. He did not know what happened to them. He knew only that SAU was also captured because he saw him being taken away the next morning. He thought everyone else must have been killed.

3   Interrogator's comment: Source's version of the attack on the U.S. Embassy should be compared with that of NGUYEN VAN SAU (NGUYEENX, VEAN SAUS), aka CHUC (CHUWCS), CMIC #1828, as contained in CMIC Report No. U.S. 328–68. The two stories are similar in general outline, but contain many conflicts in details.

Source: Attack on U.S. Embassy, Tet Official History Files, U.S. Army Center of Military History, Fort McNair, Washington, D.C.

Interrogation of Nguyen Van Sau

January 28–January 31, 1968

Subject: VC attack on U.S. Embassy, Saigon (31 January 68)

DATE OF INFORMATION: CMIC, Saigon
EVALUATION: Source C Information
SOURCE: Captive NGUYEN VAN SAU (NGUYEENX, VEAN SAUS), aka CHUC (CHUWCS); CMIC # 1828
REPORT NUMBER: U.S. 382–68
DATE OF REPORT: 26 Feb 68
NUMBER OF PAGES: Five (5)
REFERENCES: MACV ICP; Map: VIETNAM, AMS Series L7014, Sheet 6231-II, Dtd 1965, Scale: 1:50,000
PREPARED BY: T. L. Moran, SSG, U.S. Army

1   Induction by the VC

In May 1964, a group of armed VC surrounded source's village, TAN HOA Ham, VINH LOC Vil, TAN Binh Dist, GIA DINH Prov, SVN and forced approx 20 young men in the village to accompany them. The 20 men, including source, did not want to go with the VC, but the VC tied their hands and kept them under armed guard. The men were taken to LOC THUAN Vil, TRANG BANG Dist, TAY NINH Prov, vic (XT420172). LOC THUAN Vil was a regrouping station for approx 150 VC inductees who were waiting to move to training areas.

2   Basic training

In July 1964, source and two other inductees traveled to PHU HOA Ham, MY HUNG Vil, CU CHI Dist GIA DINH Prov to receive basic military training (exact location unknown). At PHU HOA Ham source was a common soldier in the B-60 Unit (platoon size), which was comprised of approx 30 men. The B-60 Unit was directly subordinate to MR4.

3   Reasons for remaining with the VC
During Jul 64, source decided to remain with the VC and fight with them until the war was over. Living and fighting with the VC was much more difficult than the relatively easy life at home in his village. His major complaint about living with the VC was that he did not receive enough food. Despite these hardships, source remained with the VC because most of the other young men from his and nearby villages were VC members and endured their hardships. Nearly everyone in source's unit was of the same age and background as he, and this gave source a secure feeling that he was doing what was right.

4   Qualifications
There were no qualifications necessary to join the VC. The VC preferred, however, to recruit mostly young and healthy men. A minority of the men joined the VC voluntarily, but the majority of new members were forced to fight with the VC. Source was never told what his term of enlistment was, but he presumed it to be until the war was over. He did not sign enlistment papers and was given no VC identification. There were no women in the VC units in this area, and source had also never heard of the VC attempting to recruit ARVN prisoners. There were many regroupees in the source's units, and they were usually in positions of importance. He never came into contact with North Vietnamese soldiers.

5   Political training
Source received two or three days of political training every two or three months for the entire time he was with the VC. The only subject he was lectured on was the war in South VIETNAM. He was told that the VC would fight in South VIETNAM until they were victorious, regardless of how many of their men were killed. Before he was captured, source felt that the VC would win the war because, during the political lectures, he was told that the VC outnumbered the allies and could win. After he came to SAIGON and was captured, source thought that the political lectures were not true and that the allies had enough men to win the war. The VC objective in the fighting was to bring peace to South VIETNAM.

6   Sapper training
In Sep 65, source was transferred to the 4th Squad, 2d Platoon, 1st Company, C-10 Infantry Bn (Interrogator's comments: When asked if the C-10 was a Sapper Bn, source stated that they trained in many subjects, including sapper, but were known as the C-10 Infantry Bn) from Sep 65, source and 90 or 100 other men received sapper training while assigned to the C-10 Inf Bn at PHU HOA Ham. The training was conducted in an open area outside the hamlet by the assistant company commander, NAM VAN (NEAM VEAN). The training covered the following subjects:

(a) Crawling

Source was taught how to crawl over rocky and other difficult terrain without making any noise. This training prepared him for crawling up to the perimeter of an enemy post to plant explosive charges. He was trained to crawl on the ground and feel with his hands for grenades or trip wires. He also received practice in crawling under barbed wire.

(b) Explosives

Source received limited training with TNT and C-4 explosives. He learned how to attack [sic] the fuse to the parcel of explosives. No further details.

(c) Source was taught two methods of scaling a wall.

The first method was accomplished by one person standing on another's shoulders and climbing over the wall. If the wall were too high for this method, they would then use a rope with a three pronged hook at its end to snag the top of the wall.

(d) Miscellaneous

Source's unit received very limited training in swimming, construction of small wooden foot bridges and how to avoid flares.

7   From Jan 66 to Aug 66, source was assigned as a squad leader of the B-10 Unit (platoon size), C-10 Inf Bn, which was located at RANG Ham, Vil unknown, CU CHI Dist, GIA DINH Prov (exact location unknown). Source's job was to supervise the couriers in transporting of messages from B-10, which was redesignated J-6, to J-9, J-4, J-5 and other small units within the C-10 Bn. The messages were always sealed; source had no knowledge of their contents. The only mission of the B-10 was to construct its own living quarters. Source had no knowledge of the mission of the C-10 Inf Bn. Source was never engaged in combat while assigned to the B-10 Unit.

8   From Aug 66 to 27 Jan 68, source was in charge of delivering messages for the Finance Office of the C-10 Bn located at THANH AN Vil, DAU TIENG Dist, BINH DUONG Prov, SVN. Seven men worked for source delivering the messages. The contents were unknown, since messages were always sealed. The C-10 Inf Bn engaged in several small attacks and ambushes between Aug 66 and Jan 68, but source was unable to provide details.

9   Attack on United States Embassy, SAIGON

(a) Personnel involved

On 28 Jan 68, source was told by his section leader, BA SUONG (BA SUOWNG) to go on an unknown mission with his Company Commander, BA DAN (BA ZAN), aka BA DEN (BA DEN), and five other men: DUC (DUWC), GIANG (JANG), TEO (TEOL),

VAN (VAANS) and VINH (VINH). Source was given no other details at this time. He had known all the previously mentioned individuals for approx one year since they were all members of the C-10 Inf Bn. BA DAN, GIANG, TEO, VAN and source had all received at least three months of sapper training but DUC and VINH were office workers and had had no sapper training.

(b) Transportation

On 28 Jan 68, the seven men left THANH AN Vil for SAIGON in a civilian truck which BA DAN had borrowed from an unknown source. The men carried with them only extra civilian clothing. They did not stop along the way to pick up or drop anyone off, nor did they stop to spend the night anywhere.

(c) Staging area

At 2000 hours, on 29 Jan 68, the group arrived in SAIGON. They drove directly to a house in DAKAO, SAIGON. Source entered and left the house when it was dark, so he did not know the house number. He was not allowed to go outside while he stayed at the house. He would not be able to find the house again, and this was the first time he had ever been to SAIGON. The house next door was occupied by Koreans (further details unknown). BA DAN knew the house number and the location of the house. South Vietnamese civilian family of unknown size lived in the house. The husband was gone from the house for the entire time source was there, so they never saw each other. The children were kept in a different room. The wife was 40 years old, 40 to 45 kilo in weight, light complexion, 1.58m tall, and long curly hair. Source was forbidden to talk to her, and did not know the names of any of the occupants of the house. At 2200 hours on 30 Jan 68, eight VC entered the house and stayed until time to depart for the attack. Their names were: BAY THIEN (BAYR TIEEN), CHINH (CHINHS), TAI (TAIL), BAY QUYEN (BAY QYEEN), DUONG (DUOWNG), THANH (THANHL), UT NHO (UTS NHOR), and the name of the eighth man was unknown. BAY THIEN and UT KNO were chief and asst chief, respectively of the Combat Section, C-10 Inf Bn. They were assistant chiefs of the embassy attack force. BA DAN was in charge of the attack. All of the eight men were sapper trained and were from the C-10 Inf Bn.

(d) Weapons

On the evening of 30 Jan 68, BA DAN left the house, picked up weapons for the entire group from an unknown source, and returned to the house in a civilian truck. The following weapons were used for the attack: seven AK-47s, six pistols of U.S. and North Vietnamese origin (caliber unknown), Two B-40 ATGLs, 30 kg of C-4 explosives,

120 rifle rounds per man, 10 B-40 rounds, and unknown number of pistol rounds. The AK-47s were relatively new; B-40s were old and well worn.

(e) Mission

Source did not know why he was told to come to SAIGON until 2400 hours on 30 Jan 68 when the weapons were passed out. He was then told that he was going to participate in the attack on the U.S. Embassy. The mission of the attack force was to overrun the embassy compound, enter the embassy building and hold it for 36 hours. After 36 hours, BA DAN was to order a withdrawal. Source did not know what the leaders of the attack force planned to accomplish after they entered the embassy building. Source did not know why they were to attack the embassy, and he considered that target to be unimportant. He did not know how many guards were at the embassy. His instructions were to shoot the embassy guards if they resisted the attack force, however, if the guards surrendered they were to be taken prisoner. Source did not expect to live through the attack, nor did he think that the attack force would overrun the embassy.

(f) At 0230 hours, 31 Jan 68, the 15-man attack force left the house. They were wearing white or blue shirts and black or blue trousers. Red armbands with no identifying numbers were worn on the left arm, and blue, white and yellow checked handkerchiefs were worn around their necks. They rode in one taxicab and one civilian truck to a spot approx 40 meters from the front of the embassy building. Source knew nothing of the drivers of the vehicles or where the vehicles were obtained. He saw no other VC, ARVN or U.S. soldiers positioned around the embassy.

(g) Attack

An electrically detonated charge of C-4 explosives was immediately set off against the embassy compound wall approx 120 meters to the right and front of the gate. The explosion knocked a hole in the wall large enough for a man to crawl through. Several B-40 rounds were fired by the attack squad from outside the wall to the upper floors of the embassy building. All 15 men entered the compound through the hole at 0300 hours. Source was the twelfth or thirteenth man to crawl through the hole. After they entered the compound, the members of the attack force crouched behind large shrubbery pots which were located throughout the compound. Within five minutes after the VC entered the compound, American MPs positioned themselves on rooftops of nearby houses and fired into the compound at the VC, killing an unknown number of them. This action lasted two or three hours. The VC were unable to enter the embassy building because it was impractical to use the B-40 ATGL, as the round would go through the door, but would not knock it down. The attack force theorized that the B-40 round, if used, would explode inside the embassy building, create a fire, and would burn the entire building down. Source did not know why BA DAN disapproved of burning the building, or what he planned to look for inside. American guards positioned on the second or higher floors of the embassy building shot four or five members of the attack force in the early stage of the battle. Source was wounded at approx 0310 hours on the morning of the attack. From the time he was wounded until 0700 that morning, he intermittently lapsed into states of unconsciousness, and could provide few details of what happened during this time. At 0700, source regained consciousness and found that he was lying next to a shrub pot. Source saw several Americans walking about the compound and noticed seven or eight dead VC lying on the ground around him. Source knew of two American Guards killed in the attack. Every member of the attack force was either killed or wounded. BA DAN was still alive after the attack, but source does not know what happened to his two assistants, BAY TIEN and UT NHO.

(Interrogator's comments: source received four wounds during the morning of the attack. One wound is on the left cheekbone and may have been caused by a fall or perhaps a round. He has several scratches on his right elbow, and a bullet wound on his left upper arm. Source and his interrogator are of the opinion that the slug is still lodged in his arm. The fourth wound was a round in his right buttocks. Source was quite certain that the leader or the attack force, BA DAN, lived through the attack, and was subsequently taken to CMIC, SAIGON. If BA DAN could be located and interrogated, he should be able to provide detailed information on the planning, staging area, and the mission of the 31 Jan 68 attack on the U.S. Embassy, SAIGON.)

Source: Attack on U.S. Embassy, Tet Offensive Official History File, U.S. Army Center of Military History, Fort McNair, Washington, D.C.

Document 17

Telegram from General Westmoreland, COMSUMACV to General Wheeler, CJCS

February 1, 1968

I assess the enemy situation as follows:

The enemy conducted simultaneous attacks against major cities and air facilities south of the DMZ area during the Tet holidays. His aim appears to be to cause movement of friendly units and to divert attention from what I believe will be his main effort, the Khe Sanh/DMZ area. Certainly he hoped to secure and hold a major city at least for a while. He sought also to obtain a favorable psychological effect on the SVN (and probably the U.S.) populace. His airfield attacks were aimed at the destruction of some portion of our air capability to prevent its use against him when he launches his major effort. His results were Pyrrhic, since enemy body count for the Tet holiday period will probably exceed 5,000.

Meanwhile, the enemy remains quiescent in the Khe Sanh/DMZ area, indicating he may be waiting to assess friendly reaction to his attacks farther south. It is too early to estimate the effect friendly air and artillery has had on the enemy. Certainly the air attack in his major HQs located west of the DMZ disrupted enemy control for probably several days . . .

. . . In summary, the enemy is capable of attacking in the Khe Sanh/DMZ area at any time with up to four divisions, though friendly air and artillery operations are causing him difficulties. I believe that the enemy will commence his major offensive in the near future. At this time indications point to the Khe Sanh combat base as his primary objective.

Source: Tet Offensive Official History Research Files, U.S. Army Center of Military History, Ft. McNair, Washington, D.C.

Telegram from the Commander, Military Assistance Command, Vietnam (Westmoreland) to the Chairman of the Joint Chiefs of Staff (Wheeler)

February 1, 1968

At 0545 hours, General Wheeler called me on the secure telephone and directed that I call Mr. Rostow at the White House and provide answers on behalf of Ambassador Bunker and myself to six questions. At 0650 hours, I contacted on the secure telephone General Binsberg [sic]. The following is a transcript of my oral report.

This is General Westmoreland speaking.

I was instructed by the Chairman of the Joint Chiefs of Staff to call the White House and ask for Mr. Rostow.

Six questions have been posed. I will read these as I interpret them and will give you our answers. I am speaking for Ambassador Bunker and myself—I have covered with Ambassador Bunker all these matters on the telephone.

Question number 1: Our estimate of friendly and enemy casualties.

Answer: From the beginning of the truce period—1800 hours, 29 January—the following casualties have been suffered by us or inflicted on the enemy in accordance with our best estimates. KIA, friendly, 421, which includes 189 U.S., 3 Free World, and remainder— 229—Vietnamese. Enemy 4320 KIA, 1181 detainees, a number of whom are prisoners of war.

Question number 2: How long do we estimate the present campaign will continue?

Answer: We see this as a three-phase campaign. The first involved preparation, build-up, sporadic attacks, and a well-orchestrated psy-war program. We are now in the second phase, which is an all-out military effort in South Vietnam, excepting the two northern provinces. The enemy has achieved some local successes, but there is evidence that the initiative is turning against him. However, we feel he has the capability of continuing this phase for perhaps several more days, at great risk to himself. The third phase involves a massive attack in Quang Tri and Thien Provinces. The enemy is now poised for this phase, which he considers his decisive campaign. Our air strikes may have blunted this attack, but we still give him the capability to strike at any time with large forces supported by an abundance of artillery and rockets.

Question number 3: Do we believe there is a relationship between activities in South Vietnam and those in Korea?

Answer: It would seem to us that there is a relationship.

Question number 4: The French press allege that there is an impasse in South Vietnam. What is our comment?

Answer: We do not consider the situation an impasse, since the initiative is turning in the favor of the government and her allies and the enemy is suffering unprecedented casualties.

Question 5: Is the enemy holding any towns in South Vietnam?

Answer: The enemy does not control any single town in South Vietnam. However, he has some degree of control in several towns. Specifically, he has forces in Quang Tri, Hue, Duyxuan, Kontum City, Chau Phu and Ben Tre, he has scattered elements in Saigon. Repeat, he does not control any single town. In those towns he has troops, they are confronted by Vietnamese troops and fighting is continuous.

Question number 6: What political problems do we anticipate as a result of this enemy activity? Will it have a psychological impact on the people and affect the stability of government?

Answer: It seems to us that initially there will be some psychological impact on the people and the government. However, if the government handles the matter carefully, they can seize an opportunity to strengthen their position with the people. President Thieu has the opportunity to exercise real leadership. The National Assembly has the opportunity to be more constructive. The President has declared martial law, but this will have to be approved by the Assembly after 12 days, in accordance with the Constitution. The situation should not slow down (for a prolonged period) major programs. It may well harden the government's position on negotiations with the Front. It may tend to set back civilianization of the government. Military successes should give the ARVN and its leadership self-confidence and encourage the acceleration of their improvement.

End of statement.

Source: *Foreign Relations of the United States, 1964–1968, Volume VI, Vietnam, January–August 1968* (Washington, D.C.: Government Printing Office, 2002), 96–98

Document 19

Memorandum from William J. Jorden of the National Security Council Staff to the President's Special Assistant (Rostow)

February 3, 1968

Subject: Situation in Viet-Nam

This memo contains some reflections on recent events in Viet-Nam and some thoughts on what should be done.

First, it is my opinion that the series of well-coordinated NVA/VC attacks in all parts of the country represents a distinct setback to the Government in Saigon and to us. But it may also offer some opportunities that should not be lost.

I regard these events as a setback because:

- among other things, they reflect probably the worst intelligence failure of the war. If the VC and the North Vietnamese can move probably 30,000 men into place for attacks in all parts of the country without detection, something is wrong with the GVN's intelligence network. It would have taken weeks to stockpile the weapons and ammunition used in these attacks. Thousands of Vietnamese must have been used in this process. Many thousands of others must have been aware of movements through or near their villages, and of unusual activity in their neighborhoods in the cities. Yet I have seen no clear evidence that any of these movements were reported or their significance correctly understood. We didn't have one single attack thoroughly anticipated, of the many that occurred. Something is rotten in the Vietnamese CIO, the Military Security Service and the National Police. And what about our intelligence work in the provinces?
- by these attacks, the NVA/VC have demonstrated an ability to hit any urban center they choose, and to carry out a level of coordination in their attacks heretofore unknown in Viet-Nam.
- I believe that the effectiveness of these assaults, despite their short duration in most cases, have severely shaken confidence in the Government's ability to provide security for its people. It is a virtual certainty that thousands of Vietnamese who have felt secure in the urban centers are

now telling themselves: if the VC can hit like this once, they can do it again; I better be more careful of what I say and do.

- these events cast serious doubt on any future statements that people in Viet-Nam's urban centers are "under Government control" or "free from VC threat." They clearly are not, if the VC are prepared to pay the price to hit them.

- finally it is clear from intelligence reporting of the last day or two that many Vietnamese are prepared to believe and to spread the wildest rumors about the Americans—that we helped the VC enter Saigon, that we are working with the VC to set up a coalition government, that we are looking for a chance to get out, etc., etc. This means to me that VC propaganda has been exceedingly effective and that ours and that of the GVN leaves a hell of a lot to be desired.

I recognize, of course, that the North Vietnamese and VC paid a heavy price for this adventure. Even if the reported losses are inflated—as they may be to some extent—they have sacrificed a lot of people, probably including some of their best sabotage and terror personnel. The effects of these losses should be felt for some time. But I doubt that either the VC or the general Vietnamese population are as impressed as we are by these losses. If the level of VC activity drops dramatically in the weeks ahead, it will indicate how badly they have been hurt.

In any case, it is my deep conviction that the Vietnamese people and the Government itself have been more seriously shaken by the events of this week than we now realize or than they are willing to admit.

This is not without potential benefit. It may cause people in the Government to take a more serious view of their situation and to pull up their socks—in strengthening their military forces and going after the VC with new vigor, in pushing forward programs of reform, in giving the people more protection and a higher stake in the future, in pushing personal rivalries and jealousies into the background.

But I am utterly convinced it will *not* have this effect unless we provide some strong pushing in the right directions.

I said at the outset that this week offers opportunities. But I would urge that we strike while the iron is hot. The moment can easily be lost.

I would recommend:

- that Bunker have a real heart-to-heart talk with Thieu. It should be private. He should tell Thieu that, in our judgment, the coordinated VC attacks and their extensive propaganda campaign have had a strongly negative effect on both Vietnamese and American opinion. It is of the highest urgency that the GVN act now and act decisively to meet the problem. The time for caution and for slow steps forward is past. We recognize that strong measures will entail mistakes. We can live with those and will not be throwing brickbats. But what we cannot live with is a "business as usual" approach to a grave crisis.

Thieu can count on our support. We will help him in every way possible. But we cannot support inaction and half-measures. We strongly believe that he, Vice President Ky and Prime Minister Loc should be a closely-knit team; that they should be working together and cooperating; that each should have his own clearly defined responsibilities and that each of them can move, knowing he has the support of the others and of the Americans.

We believe that it is urgent that he push ahead rapidly on:

- strengthening the ARVN and getting the most able officers in command positions, eliminating or shelving officers who are up to their necks in corruption;
- shaking up and getting more teamwork in his intelligence services. It is a disgrace that the VC can mount 30 or 40 simultaneous attacks all over the country and his Government doesn't know a damn thing about it in advance;
- improving the quality and honesty of his provincial and district leaders; the GVN's well-conceived reform program in this area should be pushed with maximum energy;
- a large-scale and effective drive on corruption. The Vietnamese people are sick and tired of sending their sons into the Army to receive $30 a month while they face death, when Vietnamese "operators" and black-marketeers are making millions a year on shady deals. It may be that the only approach to this knotty problem (given the involvements in deals of so many army officers, their wives, and other officials) is to declare an amnesty for all past dishonesty. But to make it clear that a new deal is now in effect, and the first officer or official who violates the new rules is going to get rapid and strong justice.

It may be the only way to get someone like General Vien (who is himself clean but whose wife has been busy in the marketplace) to take a strong supporting stand. Men like Vien are very worried about the effect of past activities of their friends and families. If they have a clean slate to start from, they can crack down.

Finally, they need to get cracking fast on national political organization to compete with the VC and the Front. My own personal belief here is that Senator Don and his Soldier–Farmer–Worker bloc has the best potential for something useful and we should be thinking about the most effective way of supporting it. They have no solid financial base. They need some kind of revenue-producing establishment whose profits can be fed into their organization. This is a better approach than a "black bag." I wouldn't talk to Thieu about the Don situation, but I would urge him to get together with Ky and begin real organizational work on a pro-government party, broadly based and national in scope. Every day that is lost is a day the VC use to their own advantage.

In sum, I think the time is ripe for a new approach in Viet-Nam. The Vietnamese deeply want a better shake. They do not want to be taken over by the Communists. They want a Government that they think is honest and effective. They want action. And they want it now. I think we should, too.

Otherwise, we are in for a year of trouble and heartbreak.

Bill

Source: *Foreign Relations of the United States, 1964–1968, Volume VI, Vietnam, January–August 1968* (Washington, D.C.: Government Printing Office, 2002), 111–14

Telegram from the Commander, Military Assistance Command, Vietnam (Westmoreland) to the Commander in Chief, Pacific Forces (Sharp)

February 3, 1968

1 The following is my assessment of the situation as it has developed.

2 The enemy's Tet offensive peaked on 30–31 January and has been ebbing over the past two days. Current actions result primarily from the mopping up of pockets of enemy forces in and around the urban areas of the country. The enemy has caused heavy damage to sections of Saigon, My Tho, and other cities and towns in his rampage of destruction, but he has failed to gain the objectives he sought. The costs to him in losses of manpower have been enormous. It is too early to accept any figure of enemy killed [garble—as legitimate], but I have no doubt that the enemy lost more men in the 72 hours beginning 1800 29 Jan than he has in any single month of the war.

3 The objectives, strategy and tactics of this enemy offensive are becoming clearer. Beginning on 31 January, the VC propaganda organs announced the existence of a new "revolutionary armed forces" responsive to a new political entity called "the Alliance of National and Peace Forces." This organization was touted as a collection of intellectuals, merchants, industrial, political and religious notables. The "revolutionary armed forces" are alleged to contain many elements including defected GVN troops. It is apparent that the enemy attempted to create the impression of spontaneous political and military uprising against the GVN and to suppress the role of the NLF and the VC/NVA military forces.

4 The use is transparent, but the goals and strategy of this Tet offensive are indicated in it. The enemy apparently hoped to seize a number of population centers or parts of them and set up an ostensibly non-VC political apparatus in the ensuing chaos. The initial assaults, where possible, were conducted by VC main and local forces and guerrillas infiltrated into populous areas under cover of the Tet celebrations. These were apparently to paralyze GVN control and generate a popular uprising within 48 hours. Then the remaining VC main forces and the NVA would reinforce to exploit the situation. This general pattern of the

enemy plan has been substantiated by numerous POW interrogations and by the actual movement and commitment of forces. There were, of course, modifications in various areas for local reasons.

[5 through 9 omitted]

10   Thus it appears that the enemy has generally followed his plan to commit VC forces and retain NVA forces for follow up attacks. He has achieved little success to exploit with follow up attacks, but his capability to recycle his offensive remains, and another round of attacks could occur in I, II and III CTZs at any time. In IV CTZ it appears that there are no large reserves for renewed attacks in the near future.

11   I expect enemy initiation of large-scale offensive action in the Khe Sanh DMZ area in the near future despite the failure of the Tet offensive to achieve its objectives. He has been hurt to some extent by friendly firepower and his losses around Cam Lo, but it is unlikely he would abandon his heavy investment in offensive preparation in that area. It is likely that the uncommitted NVA forces elsewhere in the country will conduct complementing offensive operations. If the enemy conducts these attacks he will no longer enjoy the cover of the Tet holidays, and he will lack the assistance of destroyed VC units. This presents us with an opportunity to inflict the same disastrous defeats on his NVA troops as we have on his VC forces.

Source: *Foreign Relations of the United States, 1964–1968, Volume VI, Vietnam, January– August 1968* (Washington, D.C.: Government Printing Office, 2002), 115–17

Telegram from the Embassy in Vietnam to the Department of State

February 4, 1968

For the President from Bunker. Herewith my thirty-seventh weekly message:

A   General

1   Because of the emergency caused by the widespread enemy attacks which began in the early hours of January 31, I have regretfully had to delay this week's message. It thus covers a period of ten days from January 25.

2   The early days of the period, although witnessing a continuation of the massive build-up of enemy strength along the DMZ and the northern part of I Corps, with anticipatory preparations for the Tet holidays underway, began in an atmosphere of relative calm. It began, however, with what to me was an occasion of great significance, an occasion largely overlooked as so many important developments here tend to be because of the concentration on the military situation. Appearing as the nation's freely elected President before the freely elected legislative branch, President Thieu delivered his first state of the union message. It was a sober, positive, and constructive speech, wide-ranging and comprehensive in scope, outlining plans to benefit the Vietnamese people. He began by a reference to the constitutional framework now in place and expressed the hope that the executive and legislative branches can work effectively together to serve the nation. He indicated his plans to move quickly in establishing the other institutions called for in the Constitution, notably the judiciary, the inspectorate, and the advisory councils. But he noted that the democratic system cannot exist only through an external form; that it demands fundamental changes in organizations and laws as well as in political structures and habits; and he noted the importance of the development of political parties.

3   While he mentioned some of the substantial achievements which had

already been accomplished, the main thrust of his speech looked to the future. Here he covered both plans for the longer term and short-range priority programs on which the government proposed to concentrate in the next six to seven months. These included judicial and administrative reform, expansion of educational opportunities; the development of industry and agriculture; the stimulation of land reform, in the social field, vigorous measures to improve the refugee situation; to expand public health measures; to improve the condition of labor and measures and incentives to bring the youth into the service of the nation. To carry out these programs, he presented a budget of 95 billion piasters which the Assembly is scheduled to take up as the first order of business when it resumes its session February 6. It is almost certain, however, that by mid-year the government will have to submit a supplementary budget since the amounts provided in its present submission for the military effort are inadequate.

4   In dealing with the government's position on the question of peace and negotiations, Thieu stressed the fact that the GVN is merely acting to defend itself against aggression and re-affirmed the government's adherence to the principles established by the Manila summit conference. Implicit in this program is the desire and intention of the GVN to strengthen its position before any negotiations open. The contrast between Hanoi's methods and that of President Thieu's government is very great and, I hope, instructive to the critics of this regime and our effort in support of it.

5   The massive, countrywide terrorist attacks on centers of population which began in the early morning hours of January 31 have been fully reported. I will not attempt to duplicate this reporting here. It is obvious that they were premeditated and planned well in advance. It is equally clear that they were coordinated and correlated with the massive and open invasion in northern I Corps by North Vietnamese forces.

6   It is evident too that the initial success of the attacks was due in part to the element of surprise and to the fact that they were made in flagrant violation of the Tet truce period which Hanoi as well as the GVN had proclaimed. I think it's fair to say also that there was some failure of intelligence on our side, for a sizable number of GVN troops and many GVN officials were on leave.

7   That these widespread, concerted attacks will result in a massive military defeat for the enemy is evident in the casualty figures reported Saturday morning. From 6:00 pm January 29, the beginning of Tet truce period, to midnight February 2, according to our figures, 12,704 of the enemy were killed, and 3,576, many of whom will become prisoners of war, were detained; 1,814 individual and 545 crew served

weapons were captured. Allied losses were 983 killed of which 318 were U.S., 661 ARVN, and 4 other Free World; the number of allied wounded was 3,483. Enemy casualties for these few days are considerably larger than for any previous month of the war. Based on the enemy casualties, I asked General Westmoreland for an estimate of the total number of enemy committed and he said he thought that this was probably in the neighborhood of 36,000.

8 Enemy military operations have been well orchestrated with their psychological warfare. As you know, for a considerable period, both Hanoi and the NLF have spread rumors that negotiations and a resulting coalition government were imminent after Tet. The inference, of course, was clear: if peace is so near, why go on fighting and getting killed? When the attacks came, the Liberation Radio called for everybody to rally to the revolution, alleged that many ARVN troops had defected, and of course claimed great victories, that the "U.S. bandits and their lackeys had never before been dealt such stinging blows." Liberation Radio also spread the rumor that U.S. forces were cooperating with Viet Cong attacks in order to put greater pressure on the GVN to agree to a coalition of government; and Hanoi Radio announced the formation of a "front of national, democratic and peace alliance" in Saigon and Hue.

9 Given the fact that the enemy has suffered massive military defeat, the question arises whether he has secured in spite of it a psychological victory; whether people's trust in the invincibility of the allied forces has been shattered; whether their confidence in the ability of the GVN to provide security has been shaken; or whether on the other hand Viet Cong perfidy in flagrant violation of the truce during the traditional Tet holiday, their use of pagodas, hospitals and residential areas as sanctuaries and their terrorist tactics have aroused people's indignation and resentment. While our information at this point on the reaction of the Vietnamese, especially in the provinces, is sketchy it seems apparent that both reactions have occurred. But it also seemed to all of us here that if the GVN would take prompt action, if Thieu would give evidence of strong leadership, would call in all elements in support of the government, that what might have turned out to be a Pyrrhic victory for the GVN and its allies could be turned into a psychological victory as well.

10 It is for this reason, as I have reported, that I saw Thieu Thursday morning and told him that I thought this was the psychological moment for him to demonstrate his leadership and to galvanize the nation by a statement which would constitute a declaration of national unity. I said it would not only reassure the civil population, especially in the provincial centers, but could also be a positive declaration to give

life and meaning to the main programs and priorities he had spelled out in his state of the union message. I suggested that he might want to meet with leaders of both houses of the Assembly and perhaps have them associate themselves with his declaration and intentions. I think Thieu was impressed with the arguments for taking advantage of the present situation to mobilize greater popular support. The next morning, he held a meeting of the National Security Council and included the presidents of both houses of the Assembly to lay out an action plan of relief and recovery for the civil population. In the afternoon, he recorded a speech to the nation which was delivered on TV and radio that same evening.

[Omitted here is discussion of the U.S.–GVN Joint Task Force on post-Tet reconstruction.]

13 One naturally considers what the motives and purposes of Hanoi and the Front have been in staging these massive attacks and apparently preparing momentarily to launch extremely heavy ones in northern I Corps. Were they prepared to suffer these tremendous casualties in order to gain a psychological and propaganda victory? There are some evidences that they might actually have had some expectations of popular uprisings, and in any case they are publicly claiming that these have occurred. The British Ambassador, who has had much Asian experience, remarked that the VC, having made these claims, will suffer, in Asian eyes, a very serious defeat if they prove to be not true. Had they planned these offenses hoping to put themselves in a strong position to enter negotiations, hoping to force a coalition government by demonstrating that the NLF commands the loyalty of the South Vietnamese people and must have a major voice in any peace settlement; conversely hoping to demonstrate that the GVN is a weak puppet government and can be ignored? Or is this part of a long winter–spring offensive which would endeavor to exert pressure to the extent to the enemy's capabilities at least until our elections, hoping if possible to score some major victory, but in any case to inflict heavy casualties on our troops in the expectation that they might create adverse psychological reactions in the United States and thus a change in policy?

14 I am inclined to the former theory. It seems to me that the primary purpose of this particular operation was probably psychological rather than military, that it was designed to put Hanoi and the Front in a strong position for negotiations by demonstrating the strength of the Viet Cong while shaking the faith of the people in South Viet-Nam in the ability of their own government and the U.S. to protect them. This would be consistent with the determination on their part to press towards peace talks.

[Omitted here is additional discussion of the Joint Task Force, politics, economics, Chieu Hoi, and casualties.]

Source: *Foreign Relations of the United States, 1964–1968, Volume VI, Vietnam, January–August 1968* (Washington, D.C.: Government Printing Office, 2002), 123–27

Document 22

Telegram from General Westmoreland, COMUSMACV, to General Wheeler, CJCS

February 4, 1968

After nearly five days of widespread fighting, the true dimensions of the situation are beginning to emerge.

From a realistic point of view we must accept the fact that the enemy has dealt the GVN a severe blow. He has brought the war to the towns and the cities and has inflicted damage and casualties on the population. Homes have been destroyed; distribution of the necessities of life has been interrupted. Damage has been inflicted to the LOCs and the economy has been disrupted. Martial law has been invoked, with stringent curfews in the cities. The people have felt directly the impact of the war.

A tremendous challenge has been posed to the GVN to restore stability and to aid the people who have suffered.

The enemy has paid a high price for his efforts. His losses from 291800H to 041200H stand at 15,595 KIA, 3,122 individual weapons and 682 crew-served weapons. He has committed a large percentage of his local forces, sapper units, and VC main force units into the battle. Our estimate indicates about 52,000. We do not know, at this time, how much of his guerilla force and infrastructure have been committed but, in the towns and cities, it must be a significant portion. Again, our estimate would be as high as 10,000. All of these forces have been badly hurt, some have been wiped out. The enemy has really failed to achieve his objectives. Politically, there have been no uprisings, none of the towns which he penetrated are now held by him, although he is holding out in parts of a few significant places such as Hue, Kontum City, Dalat, Saigon, and is continuing to launch new attacks against numerous towns in the IV CTZ. Specifically, in the Delta the battle surges in and out of the towns, some being hit repetitively, others temporarily occupied and then freed by friendly reaction forces. As of this writing, he has no significant hold on any town in the IV CTZ.

Militarily, the enemy has failed in his objectives and has not been able to sustain his attacks. Thus, he has demonstrated the lack of a basic capability to do so. All of our airfields are operational despite his attacks. We have lost a number of aircraft but these have not seriously influenced our ability to continue all facets of air support. He has failed to break communications. In fact, throughout this battle, communications have been completely dependable. He has failed to destroy any friendly units, although friendly casualties during the five day span are the heaviest of the war. As of 041200H, they stand at 415 U.S. KIA, 904 ARVN KIA, 13 FW KIA, and 2,385 U.S. WIA, 2,705 ARVN WIA and 102 FW WIA.

All FW and ARVN forces have the strength, disposition, and are in the proper frame of mind to keep at the enemy and inflict even greater losses if he persists in the attack. And, since many of his NVA/VC main forces have not been committed, we must accord him the capability of a second cycle of attacks either against the populated areas or, most likely, in the DMZ and other areas of NVA concentration. These may come in concert.

I have no doubt of the ability of the FW forces to meet this renewal. Also, I believe the ARVN has demonstrated that it can and will fight valiantly to stem this enemy surge. As for ARVN performance, there is no question but that they were caught in a "pre-Tet" posture. We do not have full details, but there is some evidence that units were reduced by Tet leave and were not fully alert despite President Thieu's assurance to me that 50 percent of each unit would be on the alert. From the opening of the fighting, however, they have moved their forces rapidly and towards the battles, and the troops have fought well. They are carrying the brunt of the city fighting, with the U.S. forces working on the outskirts, or in cooperative operations in the more critical towns. I am confident that the ARVN appreciates the enormity of the tasks ahead and, although the high command is understandably engrossed in clearing the capital, the rest of the machinery is functioning. The full impact of ARVN logistical losses has not been determined.

The immediate task facing us is to complete the clean up of enemy forces in the cities.

In Hue, the battle is still going on. Five ARVN battalions and one U.S. Marine battalion are operating in the city. Two battalions of the 1st CAV are employed just outside the city. I am hopeful that the next few days will see the situation cleaned up.

In Kontum, organized resistance has stopped and friendly forces are mopping up. We have a U.S. infantry battalion with APCs and tanks, and an ARVN infantry battalion in and around the city. The enemy has heavy casualties in the area.

Source: Tet Offensive Official History Research Files, U.S. Army Center of Military History, Ft. McNair, Washington, D.C.

Memorandum from the President's Special Assistant (Rostow) to President Johnson

February 6, 1968

We have gone through the accumulated materials resulting from interrogation of prisoners and documents captured last week, and sought the answers to three questions:

1 Did the VC/NVA troops expect the Vietnamese populace to rise up and support them in their attacks?
2 Did the VC/NVA have any known plans for retreat or withdrawal?
3 What is the VC/NVA evaluation as to success or failure of the campaign?

In general, the answers are as follows:

1 Yes, they did expect assistance and uprising as evidenced by the following responses to interrogation.

A prisoner captured on January 31 in Chau Doc City stated that the attack was to create conditions which would bring the U.S. Government to negotiate in order to proceed with peace. The time was ripe for an uprising. He said that the VC realized that they were committing everything and every person they had in this assault. It was obvious to all that the assault was a "go for broke" matter. He believes that few of the participants expected success, although most of them hoped that they would succeed.

Prisoners captured in Nha Trang (II Corps) state that they were told they could take Nha Trang because of the VC organization in the city. The NVA officers did not believe this but went on with the attack in order to support the nation-wide effort and make success possible elsewhere.

According to one of these who was captured on the morning of February 4, "The current general insurrection campaign will extend for the duration of the Winter–Spring Campaign. Many attacks will continue because the order has been given and cannot be countermanded."

He stated that "when the VC/NVA attached Nha Trang, they expected to be defeated; however, they believed in the general insurrection campaign of South Vietnam."

The Executive Officer of the VC Zone Committee II, Gai Lai (Pleiku), who was captured on January 30, stated that the aim of the present action is to achieve the goals set forth in Resolution 13 of the Lao Dong Party, that is, guide people to strike and demonstrate and to liberate all areas. He also advised that the present offensive was scheduled to last seven days and would end on February 5, 1968.

Three prisoners captured in the Bien Hoa area stated that they had believed that the population would assist in an uprising against the GVN and U.S. forces and in their opinion the anticipated support from the population has not been forthcoming.

2   All evidence points to the conclusion that orders were received to "hold at all costs." Prisoners captured on January 30 in the attack on Pleiku revealed that they had orders to "take Pleiku City or not return." Three prisoners captured in the Bien Hoa area apparently were not provided with withdrawal plans since there was no question about achievement of victory. The prisoners said their orders were to continue fighting until the victory. (Lack of a withdrawal plan and unfamiliarity with the local terrain may account in part for the large enemy losses.)

Four prisoners captured in the attack on Saigon provided the following: Casualties were to be left behind. After Saigon had been occupied, there would be a special detachment to take care of wounded. The Battalion was not to retreat. The objective was to be held indefinitely. Supplies would be brought in later. Troops were ordered to fight until Saigon was taken. A prisoner who died of wounds on February 1 revealed before his death that the major objectives in the attack on Saigon were the Presidential Palace, the radio station, and the Tan Son Nhut Airbase, with orders to hold at all costs, with no thought of retreat.

Another prisoner (believed to be a VC General and currently undergoing more intensive interrogation) revealed that the VC planned to take over Chau Doc Province at any cost. If this failed, then taking over the Province was to be completed before the end of the "Spring Phase," that is, before the end of March 1968. This all came about because of an order from COSVN to use the Tet period as a "unique opportunity to make sacrifices of their lives for the survival of the fatherland." There was no plan of retreat or withdrawal as the VC were convinced of success. This was part of a general uprising throughout South Vietnam, which would reduce the number of U.S. or GVN troops which could be sent in as reinforcements. Thus, if their first attack on Chau Doc City failed, they planned to keep attacking until they achieved success.

Approximately 100 VC prisoners captured in the attack on the city of Rach Gia, Kien Giang Province, with an average age being between 15 and 18 years, revealed during interrogation that the soldiers were given no contingency plan and were directed simply to take the town and hold it until a coalition government could be formed.

3   There is little hard evidence in the form of response to interrogation or captured documents which gives feel for their assessment of success or failure. However, the following does show that plans did not progress as anticipated.

A prisoner captured in Chau Doc City indicated that his troops had been told that the conditions were now right for an uprising of the population and that an aggressive and rapid assault would bring the people to the side of the VC and make untenable the positions of the GVN and American defenders. The uprising in fact did not take place during the attack and the prisoner said that it is likely that this lack of all-out popular commitment to the campaign is having a bad effect on the morale of the VC attackers.

A prisoner captured during the attack on Nha Trang stated that there would be a second attack of the city and that the Special Forces Headquarters, the 62nd Aerial Squadron, and the airfield would be shelled. Shelling had been intended during the first attack but the element in charge of transporting ammunition did not arrive on time.

W. W. Rostow

Source: *Foreign Relations of the United States, 1964–1968, Volume VI, Vietnam, January–August 1968* (Washington, D.C.: Government Printing Office, 2002), 132–34

Notes of meeting

February 7, 1968

Notes of the president's meeting with the National Security Council

General Wheeler: There is continued fighting in the Cholon section of Saigon. We have intelligence indicating there are two enemy divisions in the Saigon area. At Hue and Danang the situation is most serious. The enemy remains in Hue and the strength of the ARVN battalions is down. Early reports say the ARVN battalions are "running out of gas."

Bad weather on the coast has affected air activities, including some resupply. A new attack on Danang is expected.

General Westmoreland said he plans to reopen Highway One so he can take supplies in by road rather than by air.

In the Khesanh vicinity there was a heavy attack on a special forces camp 4 miles from Khesanh. For the first time, the attack was supported by 9 Soviet-supplied tanks. Some of the tanks were damaged or destroyed. The camp held out until daylight, but we have just learned that it was necessary to evacuate Lang Vei.

Khesanh was shelled against last night and there was a probing attack against Hill 861.

U.S. casualties so far are: 670 U.S. dead; 3,565 wounded. There have been 1,294 South Vietnamese KIA and 4,448 South Vietnamese wounded. Enemy dead now stands at 24,199 with 5,007 detainees. We have captured 6,216 enemy weapons.

General Westmoreland has established a field headquarters in Danang. It will be entitled "MACV Forward." General Abrams will command it for the moment. General Westmoreland and the Senior South Vietnamese Chief of Staff may move to this headquarters to coordinate the heavy activity in the neutral sections of I Corps.

There are some conclusions:

• The attacks have caused fear and confusion in South Vietnam.

- The attacks have aroused anger among the South Vietnamese people. The North Vietnamese and the Viet Cong had no regard for life and property in these raids. They also violated the Tet holiday.
- There is some loss of confidence, because of these attacks, in the government of South Vietnam and in the U.S.

General Loan said that his headquarters was getting many phone calls from private individuals in Saigon giving away locations of the Viet Cong. This is encouraging.

We are concerned about stepped up MiG activity. They have been conducting bombing practices. MiGs may be used for the first time in support of ground action or in an effort to shoot down our B-52s. They may also attempt to attack an air base, like the one at Danang. I sent a message to all field commanders alerting them to these possibilities.

Secretary Rusk: What about the possibility of the MiGs attacking a carrier?

General Wheeler: No, I do not think this likely. The carriers do have air caps and are distant from the MiG bases.

The President: Go in and get those MiGs at Phuc Yen.

General Wheeler: We will as soon as the weather permits.

Secretary McNamara: The MiGs would have negligible military effects but they would have spectacular psychological impact.

We do get the feeling that something big is ahead. We do not exactly know what it is, but our commanders are on alert.

The President: I want all of you to make whatever preparations are necessary. Let's know where we can get more people if we need to move additional ones in.

General Wheeler: I have a preliminary list on my desk. I am not satisfied with it.

Secretary McNamara: This would include Army, Navy, Air Force and Marine units.

The President: What about the allies?

General Wheeler: The Australians are incapable of providing more troops. The problems in Korea are such that it will be hard to get the South Koreans to even send the light division they had promised. The Thai troops are in training and to move them in now would be more detrimental than helpful.

The President: So it would be only American? Well, I want you to know exactly where you could get them, where they are located now and what we need to do. Get whatever emergency actions ready that will be necessary.

Secretary McNamara: All we would recommend at this time are the three items we had discussed earlier.

There may be some increase in draft calls but this would have no immediate effect.

The President: Do we have adequate hospitals and medical personnel?

General Wheeler: We have ample space, ample supplies, and enough doctors for the present.

Secretary McNamara: There are 6,400 military beds. Of that, 2,900 are occupied by U.S. troops and 1,100 by Vietnamese civilians. So we have an additional capacity of about 2,400.

The President: Look at this situation carefully. If we have another week like this one, you may need more.

Secretary Rusk: How do you interpret their use of tanks?

General Wheeler: They had to bring them all the way from Hanoi. This shows that this plan has been in staging since September. It represents a real logistic feat. They want to create maximum disruption.

Director Marks: Could they do anything at Cam Ranh Bay?

General Wheeler: They could. On this last attack, we caught frogmen in there. They could put rockets in the hills and fire on to the base.

The President: How many of the 25,000 killed were North Vietnamese Regulars?

General Wheeler: Approximately 18,000 were of a mixed variety of South Vietnamese enemy. Approximately 6,000 to 7,000 were North Vietnamese.

The President: How do things look at Khesanh? Would you expect to have to move out of Lang Vei?

General Wheeler: It was not planned that we would hold some of these outposts. We may have to move back that company on Hill 861.

The President: Bob, are you worried?

Secretary McNamara: I am not worried about a true military defeat.

General Wheeler: Mr. President, this is not a situation to take lightly. This is of great military concern to us. I do think that Khesanh is an important position which can and should be defended. It is important to us tactically and it is very important to us psychologically. But the fighting will be very heavy, and the losses may be high.

General Westmoreland will set up the forward field headquarters as quickly as possible. He told me this morning that he has his cables and his communications gear in. He is sending a list of his needs, including light aircraft. We are responding to this request.

The President: Let's get everybody involved on this as quickly as possible. Everything he wants, let's get it to him.

[Omitted here is discussion of the *Pueblo*.]

Then I went through the whole summary on Vietnam, similar to what General Wheeler gave here today. Most of them are concerned about the political significance of the offensive.

I pointed out that the Government of South Vietnam had not wavered or collapsed. There had been no reports of South Vietnamese defections. There have been no reports of a popular uprising. Not a single one of the provinces or district capitals is held by the Viet Cong.

I told them General Westmoreland made it clear that we can expect further attacks.

[Omitted here is discussion of military assistance programs.]

Source: *Foreign Relations of the United States, 1964–1968, Volume VI, Vietnam, January–August 1968* (Washington, D.C.: Government Printing Office, 2002), 141–44

Notes of meeting

February 9, 1968

Notes of the President's meeting with the Joint Chiefs of Staff

The President: I asked you to come here on the basis that we would hope for the best and expect the worst. I want to see what we should do in Vietnam.

We ought to look at everything that we should be doing. Get the requirements ready to do what needs to be done. Let's be fully prepared to move in the event we are required to do so.

We want to ask questions so that you can inform us of what the current situation is and so that we can determine what things we need to work on now in the event we get a call for additional help.

I want a military review of the problems confronting us if the enemy continues more of the same activities as during the past two weeks. I think we should anticipate all the surprises and determine what is going to confront us if the Viet Cong attack the cities, attack Khesanh, and pull off a few surprises elsewhere.

Two questions we will have to answer:

1   Will we have to put in more men?
2   Can we do it with the Vietnamese as they are now?

General Wheeler: During the past few days I have talked with General Westmoreland over the phone and received a number of cables from him.

Westmoreland reported the following:

* The enemy apparently will start new attacks on the 10th. That is tonight our time. This is based on communications intelligence and prisoners of war.
* The ARVN fought well. There have not been any defections that we know of.

- There is a question whether the ARVN can stand up after 12 days of heavy fighting if another series of heavy attacks occur.
- The enemy's objective may be fragmentation of the ARVN and the Government of South Vietnam. This fragmentation would be accomplished by attacks against our air bases with an effort to keep U.S. men concentrated in the north.
  Intelligence communications recognize this as one objective.
- The enemy may not be ready yet to attack Khesanh, General Chapman can elaborate on that.
- Westmoreland has moved the 1st Cavalry Division and elements of the 101st Airborne Division. These are his two strategic reserve elements which have been moved up North.
  Those units are there to take care of contingency operations in the area.
- Westmoreland has had to use other reserve elements to deal with the fighting around Quang Tri and north of Hue.
- He is now moving by LST an airborne battalion to the Hue area. The major problem is a logistical one.
  Westmoreland said he must have the use of Highway One in order to move supplies from Danang from the North and support Khesanh logistically.
- He has moved an army engineer combat battalion to clear the road area.
- He will move another battalion of the 101st to open "MACV Forward," his front headquarters. This will be done tonight our time.
- Yesterday was fairly quiet although Lang Vei was over-run and 27 U.S. men were killed. They killed 100 enemy.
- There was also an ambush on a truck convoy. It is obvious the enemy is trying to disrupt logistics.
- We are using water board craft to move supplies. The enemy is trying to disrupt this with frogmen.

The President: Are we doing all we can? Could we use civilians protected by military to help open that road? (The President also referred to civilian contractors who have been involved in construction projects.)

Secretary McNamara: I am sure that these units are being employed and I will check on this.

General Wheeler: Westmoreland needs reinforcements for several reasons. The reinforcements he has in mind are the 82nd Airborne Division and the Sixth-Ninth of a Marine division. This would total 15 battalions.

He needs these reinforcements for two reasons:

1 To prevent the ARVN from falling apart.
2 To give himself a reserve to use as quick response units to any initiatives by the enemy in Vietnam.

He said he would put the 82nd Airborne in Danang and north of Danang. That would permit him to move the 101st south and to keep Highway One open.

The Marines would give two capabilities:

1   Reinforcement in I Corps permitting amphibious forces to be available at all times.
2   Make available troops for an amphibious landing north of the DMZ if that action is decided upon.

The 82nd Airborne and the Sixth-Ninth of Marine division can only be deployed if we eliminate the restrictions on frequency of tours and length of tours in Vietnam.

Secretary McNamara: We should give some very serious thought to the proposal of scrapping the 12-month tour. It might have a very bad effect on morale.

Secretary McNamara: General Westmoreland said he needs the 82nd Division and two-thirds of a marine division. That would be 15 battalions.

In order to do that, it would be required to call up some Army divisions and the 4th Marine Division.

General Wheeler: We would propose to move the 4th Marine Division to Okinawa and Hawaii for ready deployment.

The 2 Army divisions should be in the U.S. to be ready to meet any contingencies.

The JCS will address themselves to this matter this afternoon.

There are 4 options:

Option 1 Slow movement. This would involve 265 aircraft and no draw down on airlift capacity in Southeast Asia.

This would put the 12,500 men in Vietnam in 15 days. The cargo would arrive in 29 days under this option. (There are 11,600 tons of cargo.) Under this option, the 5 Marine battalions would reach Vietnam in 8 days. Their cargo would get there in 17 days.

Option 2 This would involve 334 aircraft and a 70 percent draw down in cargo airlifts to Southeast Asia. This would put the 82nd Airborne Division in Vietnam in 6 days. The cargo would arrive in 17 days. The Marine battalions would reach Vietnam in 3 days, and its cargo in 10 days. Option 2 cuts by one-half the time as required under Option 1.

Option 3 This would involve 670 aircraft and the call up of the Air National Guard and other air squadrons. This would place the 82nd Airborne in Vietnam in 5 days (its cargo in 14 days). This option would put the Marines in Vietnam in 3 days and the cargo in 9 days.

Option 4 This would use civilian aircraft and would involve the cut down on airlift capacity to South Vietnam by 40 percent rather than 70 percent. General Holloway says the call up of Stage III craft would have no effect.

There would be considerable lost motion in refitting these civilian aircraft for military use.

General Holloway said that by leasing aircraft we could cut down on time required.

I would add a K factor to the times specified in order to alert the men and to assemble the airlift. This K factor would be plus 2 days to all times given.

If this program is followed, it will be necessary for the President to get authority to extend terms of service (to call up individual reservists) and to extend existing authority to call up reserve units past the 1968 deadline.

Based on my conversations with General Westmoreland, I believe General Westmoreland is now dictating a message to ask for early deployment of the units I have now mentioned.

The President: How many men does this represent?

General Wheeler: 25,000 men in these units plus support personnel.

Secretary McNamara: The total would run about 40,000.

Normally each battalion has 5,000 men. If one multiplies that times the 15 battalions, the total level would be 75,000 men. The difference between the 40,000 and the 75,000 is made up by the use of overhead manpower already in Vietnam which could be placed in these 15 battalions to raise them to full strength.

The President: How many men do we have there now?

General Wheeler: 500,000.

The President: Can we speed up the other infantry battalions we have already promised?

General Johnson: We have already curtailed training to the minimum. We must give these units proper training time. They are already squeezed. One battalion is scheduled to go the last week in March. Three battalions are scheduled to go the last week in April.

Secretary McNamara: If General Johnson says that is the case then I will accept it. I would like to look more at this. Perhaps these units could be sent on short training into rear areas.

General Johnson: Mr. Secretary, there are no rear areas in Vietnam anymore.

Secretary McNamara: What we are considering is a massive force structure. I think it would be unwise to leave these forces out there if the contingencies we have discussed do not develop.

Apart from the immediate contingency I do not think we will need them. We do need to extend the tours, but this should be only temporary.

To call up the forces we are talking about would involve a total of about 120 men.

General Wheeler: This emergency is not going to go away in a few days or a few weeks. In 3 months we may still be in an emergency situation.

The enemy is not in a position to really assault Khesanh. He is going to take his time and move when he has things under control as he would like them.

The reserve divisions we are sending must have a period of training and shake down before they can perform well. I would estimate this to take about 8 to 12 weeks.

I want to point out, Mr. President, that if you do make a decision to deploy the 82nd Airborne, you will have no readily deployable strategic reserves. I know this will be a serious problem for you politically.

In all prudence, I do not think we should deploy these troops without reconstituting our strategic reserves in the United States.

The President: All last week I asked two questions. The first was "Did Westmoreland have what he needed?" (You answered yes.) The second question was, "Can Westmoreland take care of the situation with what he has there now?" The answer was yes.

Tell me what has happened to change the situation between then and now.

General Wheeler: I have a chart which was completed today based on a very complete intelligence analysis. It relates to all of South Vietnam, Laos and the area around the DMZ. It shows the following:

- Since December the North Vietnamese infantry has increased from 78 battalions to 105 battalions. Estimating there are 600 men per battalion that is approximately 15,000 men.
- We have been able to get this information by 3 means:

  1   Contact with the actual units
  2   Communications intelligence
  3   Captured documents and POWs.

- This represents a substantial change in the combat ratios of U.S. troops to enemy troops.
- This ratio was 1.7 to 1 in December. It is 1.4 to 1 today.
- In the DMZ and I Corps area, there is a 1 to 1 ratio. There are 79 enemy battalions in the 1st Corps area (60 North Vietnamese and 19 Viet Cong). In the same area there are 82 Free World battalions (42 U.S.; 4 Free World; and 36 ARVN).
  This is about 1 to 1.

The President: What you are saying is this. Since last week we have information we did not know about earlier. This is the addition of 15,000 North Vietnamese in the northern part of the country. Because of that, do we need 15 U.S. battalions?

General Wheeler: General Westmoreland told me what he was going to put in tonight's telegram. This is the first time he has addressed the matter of additional troops.

Paul Nitze: I was not aware of this new intelligence.

General Wheeler: The last report was that there was approximately 15,000 enemy near and around Khesanh.

As of today, our estimates range between 16,000 and 25,000. Their infantry has been built up.

In addition, Westmoreland is now faced with the problem of the impact of these recent heavy attacks on the ARVN.

We do not know what is going to happen to the ARVN after this second round of attacks. All ARVN units are on maximum alert.

But in Hue, the ARVN airborne units are down to 160 men per battalion. Their strength is far below that required.

The President: We have to get the Government of South Vietnam to increase its efforts. Why can't we get them to do as we do, call up 18 year olds and give the American people the impression that they are doing as much as we?

Secretary McNamara: When I was in Vietnam I talked with Thieu and Ky. They told me then they intended to call up 18 and 19 year olds.

The President: I saw where Senator Kennedy pointed out that the South Vietnamese voted not to call up 18 year olds.

General Wheeler: I met last night with this unnamed group chaired by Nick Katzenbach and Paul Nitze. We are pressing for the South Vietnamese to lower the age limit at least to 19 and Bunker is pushing this hard.

Secretary Rusk: We must keep in mind that they consider a child 1 year old when he is born, so, their 19 year olds are our 18 year olds.

The President: Has either House voted not to draft these men?

Paul Nitze: I am unaware of any vote on it.

Secretary McNamara: I will look into this and follow through.

The President: Are there some things that we can get the South Koreans and the South Vietnamese to do to match all of these things we are planning to do?

Walt Rostow: The men at Hue have been drawn down by the very intensive action there. What is the state of strength of the ARVN units?

General Wheeler: I do not have the answers precisely. They have been mauled. As of 11:00 p.m. our time last night, 1,698 ARVN were killed; 6,633 were wounded seriously. This totals about 10,000 ARVN lost.

Mr. Rostow: Has the enemy switched from a slow attrition strategy to a "go for broke" strategy? Would an extension of tours in Vietnam be understood as far as morale is concerned?

General Wheeler: For a temporary period we can sustain an extension of tours without losing morale. For any longer period of time, however, you would face a loss of morale. We now have a rule that we will not send a man back without 25 months between tours in Vietnam.

General Johnson: We send men back now with special skills in less than 25 months.

As I see it there are two basic problems. The first is at Khesanh. The second is in the cities. What are they trying to do?

There are two postulates:

1   The enemy believed that the people would rise up. There were no withdrawal plans by the enemy.
2   The enemy suffered erosion over the last few months. They have seen a decoupling of its forces in hamlets and villages. U.S. troops have cleaned out the Viet Cong from many of the villages. So, he has concluded he must go for a psychological victory prior to negotiations.

We are in a critical state. We expect new attacks will begin on the 10th. There are two essential questions facing us:

1   What strength does the enemy have to renew the attacks with?
2   What strength does the ARVN possess to resist these attacks?

The President: What is the ARVN strength?

General Wheeler: Approximately 360,000 men now. Total forces about 600,000.

Secretary Rusk: I have been asking for several days if there was a new order of battle. This is the first time that I have heard of this.

The President: Because of their increase of 15,000 troops, is it true that we now need 15 battalions or 45,000 men? What mobile reserve forces does Westmoreland have between now and the time he gets more men?

General Wheeler: He has the bulk of the 1st Cavalry and one brigade of the 101st Airborne. Other than that, all of his forces are dispersed to meet the enemy. We are not getting much mileage out of the Australian or South Korean troops. They must go back to their home country for their orders.

The President: Do you mean that the Australian and Korean commanders have to go back to their capital before they can be deployed?

General Wheeler: Yes sir, they remain under the operational control of their government.

Secretary McNamara: I am under the very clear impression that they have been told by their home governments to do everything possible to hold down their own casualties.

Our losses are running six times the level of Korean losses on a percentage basis.

The President: We ought to try to bring all the allied forces under Westmoreland's command.

General Wheeler: In all fairness, the allies have operated well in areas where they have been located.

The President: Does Westmoreland have enough airpower to support his troops?

General Wheeler: Yes sir, we are moving in 2 more C-130 units.

The President: How is the supply problem at Khesanh? Will artillery and rockets knock this out? Can we rely on roads?

Secretary McNamara: There is no road available up there.

General Wheeler: We moved in 214 tons of supplies yesterday with helicopters and fixed wing aircraft. As long as we use B-52s and tactical air, we will be able to keep our resupply up. They are keeping about 10 to 12 days supplies in storage.

The President: Wouldn't we have one big problem if the airfield at Khe Sanh was out?

General Wheeler: Yes, we would have to link up by road some way. Of course we can use air drops and helicopters. The airstrip will be used from time to time.

The President: If you lost the air strip, would you evacuate Khesanh?

General Wheeler: That depends on the course of the fighting and their ability to resupply.

Secretary Rusk: When does the weather improve?

General Johnson: It is now beginning to improve. I have some concern about the loss of the air strip, because fixed wing aircraft carry so much more than helicopters.

Nobody can give a categorical answer. We think we have a 50–50 chance of sustaining our actions out there.

The men have 12 days of rations and 11 days of ammunition. Almost no COFRAM has been used.

Being cut off would hurt in the evacuation of wounded, but we can evacuate at night if necessary. This is one of the hazards you have to accept.

The President: How is the weather likely to affect actions along the border?

General Wheeler: The better the weather, the more it favors us.

The President: Have you anticipated air support from any of the communists?

General Wheeler: There is no evidence of any movement except the training flights and the Soviet bombers which were seen at Khesanh.

The President: What is his air capability if he uses it?

General Wheeler: His capability in using air is a nuisance and has propaganda value rather than any great military threat. He has 8 IL28s.

The President: What use does he have of these?

General Wheeler: I do not know.

The President: How many MiGs does he have?

General Wheeler: We know of 23 MiG 21s. There are other MiG 15s and 17s.

Most of these MiGs are in China.

The President: Keep the MiGs in sight at all times.

General Wheeler: We are doing the best we can. Admiral Sharp is moving a guided missile ship to the Gulf of Tonkin. It carries the Talos Missile. We are also sending in ships with the Terrier Missile.

The President: Get the JCS to work up all the options and let's review them together.

I want you to hope for the best and plan for the worst. Let's consider the extensions, call ups, and use of specialists.

Dean, should we have more than the Tonkin Gulf resolution in going into this? Should we ask for a declaration of war?

Secretary Rusk: Congressional action on individual items should avoid the problems inherent in a generalized declaration. I do not recommend a declaration of war. I will see what items we might ask the Congress to look at.

The President: Where are the problems in the cities?

General Wheeler: In Hue, we have one Marine battalion operating on the south side of the river. The ARVN units at Hue have been shot down to 160 men per battalion. In Cholon there are enemy forces being met by 3 Vietnamese. There is one U.S. battalion in the race track area.

The President: What would be the impact internationally to a declaration of war?

Secretary Rusk: It might be a direct challenge to Moscow and Peking, in a way we have never challenged them before. There would be very severe international effects.

Secretary Rusk: How can we get as many Vietnamese as possible returned to duty?

General Wheeler: The men are coming back. We do not know what numbers.

Secretary Rusk: I have skeptics [am skeptical?] of the enemy's ability to hit us again. Some of them have been very badly mauled.

Secretary McNamara: There is no question that they have been hurt, but I believe they have the ability to restrike.

Clark Clifford: There is a very strange contradiction in what we are saying and doing.

On one hand, we are saying that we have known of this build up. We now know the North Vietnamese and Viet Cong launches this type of effort in the cities. We have publicly told the American people that the communist offensive was: (a) not a victory, (b) produced no uprising among the Vietnamese in support of the enemy, and (c) cost the enemy between 20,000 and 25,000 of his combat troops.

Now our reaction to all of that is to say that the situation is more dangerous today than it was before all of this. We are saying that we need more troops, that we need more ammunition and that we need to call up the reserves.

I think we should give some very serious thought to how we explain saying on one hand the enemy did not take a victory and yet we are in need of many more troops and possibly an emergency call up.

The President: The only explanation I can see is that the enemy has changed its tactics. They are putting all of their stack in now. We have to be prepared for all that we might face.

Our front structure is based on estimates of their front structure. Our intelligence shows that they have changed and added about 15,000 men. In response to that, we must do likewise. That is the only explanation I see.

General Wheeler: The enemy has changed the pattern of the war. In the past, there have been instances of terrorism, but this is the first time they have mounted coordinated attacks throughout the country.

Secretary Rusk: I have a question. In the past, we have said the problem really was finding the enemy. Now the enemy has come to us. I am sure many will ask why aren't we doing better under these circumstances, now that we know where they are.

The President: Is there anything new on the *Pueblo*?

General Wheeler: No, except the North Korean Prime Minister says that North Korea is ready for another war.

Source: *Foreign Relations of the United States, 1964–1968, Volume VI, Vietnam, January–August 1968* (Washington, D.C.: Government Printing Office, 2002), 158–68

Document 26

Telegram from the Commander, Military Assistance Command, Vietnam (Westmoreland) to the Commander in Chief, Pacific Command (Sharp) and the Chairman of the Joint Chiefs of Staff (Wheeler)

February 12, 1968

Subject: Assessment of situation and requirements

1   Since last October, the enemy has launched a major campaign signaling a change of strategy from one of protracted war to one of quick military/political victory during the American election year. His first phase, designed to secure the border areas, has failed. The second phase, launched on the occasion of Tet and designed to initiate public uprising, to disrupt the machinery of government and command and control of the Vietnamese forces, and to isolate the cities, has also failed. Nevertheless, the enemy's third phase, which is designed to seize Quang Tri and Thur Thien Provinces has just begun. This will be a maximum effort by the enemy, capitalizing on his short lines of communication, the poor weather prevailing in the area for the next two months, and his ability to bring artillery and rocket fire to bear on installations from positions in the DMZ and north and from Laos to the west. Furthermore, he can bring armor to bear on the battlefield. It is clear that the enemy has decided he cannot "strike out" in this phase as a matter of fact. We can therefore expect him to exert on the battlefield the maximum military power available to him. In addition, we must expect him to try to regain the initiative in all other areas.

2   If the enemy has changed his strategy, we must change ours. On the assumption that it is our national policy to prohibit the enemy from seizing and permanently occupying the two northern provinces, I intend to hold them at all cost. However, to do so I must reinforce from other areas and accept a major risk, unless I can get reinforcements, which I desperately need.

3   To bring the maximum military power to bear on the enemy in Quang Tri and Thua Thien and to prevent the gradual erosion of these two

provinces, I must open up Highway 1 from Danang and Highway 9 to Khe Sanh. These two tasks are not unreasonable, provided that I can divert the troops to provide security and commit the engineers to the task. I therefore must make a down payment in troops in order to provide the logistics to support in fully adequate fashion troops now deployed and reinforcements that will be required. First, it will require a Marine regiment or an Army brigade to secure the Ai Van Pass from Quang Tri to Hue/Phu Bai. Another regiment or brigade will be required between Hue and Quang Tri. Finally, a third regiment or brigade will be required to secure Highway 9 to the Khe Sanh area. I cannot afford to divert troops now deployed in that area for the purpose and am therefore forced to deploy the 101st Abn Div from the III Corps; this is now in the process and will be done as fast as transportation can be made available. Even the commitment of the 101st will put be in no better than a marginal posture to cope with the situation at hand.

4   This has been a limited war with limited objectives, fought with limited means and programmed for the utilization of limited resources. This was a feasible proposition on the assumption that the enemy was to fight a protracted war. We are now in a new ball game where we face a determined, highly disciplined enemy, fully mobilized to achieve a quick victory. He is in the process of throwing in all his "military chips to go for broke." He realizes and I realize that his greatest opportunity to do this is in Quang Tri–Thua Thien. We cannot permit this. On the other hand, we must seize the opportunity to crush him. At the same time, we cannot permit him to make gains in the other Corps areas, and I am obligated to maintain the minimum essential troops in these areas to insure stability of the situation and to regain the initiative. Equal in priority to the enemy is the Saigon area and a high risk in this area is unacceptable. I now have approximately 500,000 U.S. troops and 60,981 Free World military assistance troops. Further contributions from the Thais and Koreans are months away. I have been promised 525,000 troops, which according to present programs will not materialize until 1969. I need these 525,000 troops now. It should be noted that this ceiling assumed the substantial replacement of military by civilians, which now appears impractical. I need reinforcements in terms of combat elements. I therefore urge that there be deployed immediately a Marine regiment package and a brigade package of the 82nd Abn Div and that the remaining elements of those two divisions be prepared to follow at a later time. Time is of the essence.

5   I must stress equally that we face a situation of great opportunity as well as heightened risk. However, time is of the essence here, too. I do not see how the enemy can long sustain the heavy losses which his new strategy is enabling us to inflict on him. Therefore, adequate

reinforcements should permit me not only to contain his I Corps offensive but also to capitalize on his losses by seizing the initiative in other areas. Exploiting this opportunity could materially shorten the war.

6   If CNCPAC concurs, request that the Secretary of Defense and Commander in Chief be informed of my position.

7   I have discussed this message in detail with Amb Bunker and he concurs.

Source: *Foreign Relations of the United States, 1964–1968, Volume VI, Vietnam, January–August 1968* (Washington, D.C.: Government Printing Office, 2002), 183–85

Notes of meeting

February 12, 1968

Notes of the President's meeting with senior foreign policy advisors

The President: Just now I said in a speech that we should keep in mind that President Lincoln lost 600,000 men and faced all of the division and adversity in this country that is imaginable. He said then "we have got to stick it out." I said today, "so will we." One man told me this morning that it doesn't look like the same person wrote the Westmoreland wire today and the one Friday. What reaction do you have to it?

Secretary Rusk: It looks to me like Westmoreland wants to take advantage of an opportunity to exploit the situation. I do not read it as a desperate need. He wants to shorten the war with it, and that has a certain attractiveness to all of us. It bothers me that we do not know what is happening to the South Vietnamese and their determination.

I don't appreciate Thieu saying he needed more American troops. I would think he would be looking for more ways to get more of his own men.

But if six battalions will help him exploit this opportunity, I am for sending them without a permanent commitment.

Secretary McNamara: I read the Westmoreland cable differently from Dean. I read that he needs these six battalions in order to avoid a defeat at Khe Sanh.

If he only wanted them to take advantage of the opportunity to do more, I would also send them.

I recommend today the following:

1 Send him the units he has requested.
2 Send the troops for the period of the emergency only, not a permanent augmentation.
3 Send General Wheeler out to meet with Ambassador Bunker, General Westmoreland and Cy Vance.

The President: Where will these units come from?

Secretary McNamara: It will include a brigade of the 82nd Airborne Division and Marine units.

The President: Do these units have Vietnam veterans in them?

Secretary McNamara: We will screen out the Vietnam veterans, those we can.

The President: How long will this take?

Secretary McNamara: 14 days.

General Wheeler: 14 days is correct.

The President: Are there any U.S. troops in the area we can use?

General Wheeler: No, sir.

Secretary McNamara: There is one battalion on the way.

General Wheeler: General Chapman wants to return that battalion to Hawaii because it includes some 17-year-olds and it was operating in the area on an exercise only.

The units will be sent from the following locations:

One battalion from Camp Pendleton.
Units from Camp Lejeune.
The 82nd Airborne from Fort Bragg, North Carolina.
Possibly some army from Fort Benning.

The President: How many men does that total?

General Wheeler: 3,800 from the 82nd and 6,500 from the Marines, for a total of 10,300.

The President: Does that give Westmoreland what he needs?

General Wheeler: Yes, sir.

Secretary McNamara: The loss of one brigade of the 82nd will not affect our ability to handle severe disturbances.

Clark Clifford: I would like to get some answers to several questions. In General Westmoreland's cable he says, "If the enemy has changed his strategy, we must change ours." What change in strategy has the enemy made?

General Wheeler: The enemy has been on a protracted fighting basis. Now he seeks to "grab" for immediate success. I think the enemy overestimates the degree of support in the Vietnamese populace and underestimates our strength.

General Wheeler: He is taking both actions concurrently. He is attacking the cities and also launching conventional attacks for the first time.

Clark Clifford: In his cable, General Westmoreland also points out that it is national policy to keep the enemy from seizing and holding the two northern provinces. Hasn't that been the situation all along?

General Wheeler: General Westmoreland believes that it would cost more to withdraw and go back later than to stand and fight now.

Clark Clifford: General Westmoreland says in his cable that he cannot hold without reinforcements. What change has taken place to keep him from holding?

General Wheeler: There have been wide-spread attacks in the South. General Westmoreland is unsure of the ARVN strength as a result of these attacks. He must also hold open Highway 1 and Highway 9. He has more troops committed around Saigon than he has in the past. He says that he cannot take more forces from the South without risk.

Secretary Rusk: Couldn't he take more out of the Delta?

General Wheeler: He does have contingency plans, both for taking units from the Delta and for, if necessary, withdrawal from Khesanh. But these are contingency plans only.

Clark Clifford: General Westmoreland also says that we are now in a new ballgame with the enemy mobilized to achieve quick victory. Is that something new?

General Wheeler: This thing has been building up for some time. There has been the greater build-up around the DMZ. There is a new determination for major attacks coupled with the Tet actions. Prior to now, the enemy has fought a piece-meal war.

Clark Clifford: General Westmoreland's telegram has a much greater sense of urgency in it. Why is that?

General Wheeler: General Westmoreland realized that his earlier low-key approach was not proper based on a full assessment of the situation.

Clark Clifford: General Westmoreland makes it clear that he cannot permit the enemy to make gains in other areas. He does not want to permit a reduction in strength elsewhere.

But he has now sent what is clearly an urgent message.

General Wheeler: General Westmoreland has been conservative in his troop requests in the past. Now he finds that his campaign plan has been pre-empted by enemy action.

Secretary Rusk: Can it only be done by additional U.S. forces? Can't we press them to brigade U.S. troops with Vietnamese?

General Wheeler: Before I answer that I need to know what you mean by brigading.

Secretary Rusk: By putting one battalion of U.S. troops with one battalion of ARVN.

Clark Clifford: General Westmoreland said it was time to open up key roads, Route 9 and Route 1. Can we use civilians under military protection to do some of this work?

Secretary McNamara: I authorized General Westmoreland to use whatever civilians he wished to use. I do not think he would want to use civilians in I Corps.

The President: I want a cable sent to Cy Vance to tell him to examine this. We should put civilian road and construction experts to work and replace military construction personnel so they may be sent up north.

General Wheeler: Westmoreland wants combat troops in construction brigades. Frankly I think he has underestimated what is needed to open and hold those two roads.

The President: Let's try to use what is out there if possible. I wanted Cy Vance to talk with him about it.

I am worried about the North Vietnamese Air Force and the possibility that many of our choppers will be destroyed.

Clark Clifford: I learned with great surprise that General Westmoreland does not have authority to control Korean and Australian forces. If he is short of men, can't Cy Vance get an understanding with President Park for greater utilization of the Korean troops in Vietnam?

Secretary Rusk: I think we should strongly consider a combined Allied Command with President Thieu as Commander in Chief and General Westmoreland as Chief of Staff.

Secretary McNamara: There are benefits to this with the Vietnamese. We have not moved in this direction because of the political problems.

General Wheeler: We have a similar thing to that in Thailand. On this, I think we need to get the advice of Ambassador Bunker.

The President: I would sure try to do this for maximum control of the South Koreans, the Australians and the South Vietnamese.

Clark Clifford: Are there any U.S. troops in the area of Japan, Hawaii or Okinawa we could use?

General Wheeler: Zero.

Clark Clifford: From a psychological standpoint, this would be a good time to get more Thais and South Koreans.

The President: Get Cy Vance to tell the South Vietnamese that we are accelerating our program and they need to accelerate theirs. In addition ask Cy to see what he can do about getting that extra division moving from Korea to Vietnam. What is the hold-up?

Secretary McNamara: They say equipment, but the equipment is on the way. The Thais cannot possibly be ready before July 1.

General Wheeler: All of our military people in Thailand say July 1 is the earliest time.

Secretary McNamara: The Koreans would send a division if they wanted to.

The President: What actions are the South Vietnamese taking on getting those extra 65,000 men?

Walt Rostow: The Cabinet on Sunday voted to do two things. The first is to call back veterans. The second is that they moved the date to begin the drafting of 18 and 19 year olds. They moved back from April 1 to March 1 the drafting of 19 year olds. They moved back the drafting of 18 year olds from July 1 to May 1.

The President: What is our average draft age?

Secretary McNamara: It's either 20.2 or 20.4 years.

The President: Get me the exact answers on that, Buzz.

What is our situation with equipment? I hear we lost quite a bit out there lately.

Secretary McNamara: That was a misleading report that you received today. We have had 57 choppers destroyed and 48 choppers which will require replacement. There will be between 97 and 137 to be replaced this month. We are shipping this month 246.

The President: How about observation planes?

Secretary McNamara: We are fine on those.

The President: I want to ask all the questions that I possibly can now so that we get answers to them before a situation develops and we didn't have them. I hope all of you see what has happened during the last two weeks. Westy said he *could* use troops one day last week. Today he comes in with an urgent request for them.

I want to look at all of these things now. I want to anticipate that more will happen to us than he had planned. I have very serious concerns about our equipment.

Frankly, I am scared about Khesanh.

I worry about that runway going out or those C-130s being knocked down. I think if the weather gets bad and if the runway gets knocked out we are going to have a hell of a problem on resupply. Then I guess we will have to use helicopters. I am afraid they will pick off the helicopters. So I want you to check the number of helicopters and fixed wing aircraft.

If we lost this big build-up we can't endure many losses. And we can look if we are out of ammunition, or out of fuel or didn't have medicine. I would feel better to get the answers here now. I have a mighty big stake in this. I am more unsure every day.

Secretary Rusk: Is General Westmoreland aware that he can choose his own place to fight?

The President: I want a crash program to get these men out there just as fast as they can. Dick, how do you feel about all of this?

Dick Helms: I have been meeting this morning with twelve of my top CIA people who have been in Vietnam. They believe the war is in a critical phase. They think Westmoreland should get the troops if he needs them. We cannot even find some of the forces. I am a believer in the old axiom "A stitch in time saves nine."

General Taylor: In my view, this is an urgent situation. The element of time bothers me. General Westmoreland seems to believe that he has time to open the roads. He seems to believe he has time to do all of the other things that are necessary. And I get the feeling that many of us here today feel the same way. I do not. This offensive could open up today. We should assume in our planning that it will open up tonight. I think Westmoreland's request is reasonable and we should act quickly to meet it.

The President: Do all of you feel that we should send troops?

Secretary McNamara: Yes.

Secretary Rusk: Yes.

Director Helms: Yes.

General Wheeler: Yes.

General Taylor: Yes.

Mr. Rostow: Yes.

The President: Is there any objection?

(There was no objection.)

General Wheeler: We will close these forces in Vietnam in 14 days.

The President: Is that the minimum time?

General Wheeler: Yes, it is.

The President: There is no schedule you can improve upon?

General Wheeler: We will move as quickly as possible.

We should maintain our current level of resupply to Southeast Asia. The Joint Chiefs will use these 62 aircraft which are normally withheld for emergencies. This is an emergency.

MAC and TAC will operate in war-time rates. We are utilizing voluntary civilian air lift.

We propose to call up the Air Force National Guard and Reserve C-124 squadrons. This will be augmented by 112 reserve aircraft and 48 Air National Guard aircraft. This would total about 10 squadrons.

The President: How many men?

Secretary McNamara: 2,000 to 3,000 men.

The President: Well, let's do it. Could you tell the Air Transport Association we will need to call up civilian aircraft?

General Wheeler: The Joint Chiefs feel that if you deploy these men there should be a call-up of the reserves.

If we send a brigade of the 82nd Airborne, we should call up two brigades from the Army National Guard. This would total about 30,000 men.

General Chapman feels that if we deploy this Marine unit, we should call up the Fourth Marine Division, one RLT now and the rest of the Fourth Division subject to call at any time.

The Marine reserves will be ready to go within two months.

The President: I want you and Bob McNamara to get together and come in with an agreed recommendation as to whom to call up. Let's not decide on that today. Go back and agree on what to call.

We must move as soon as we can. I was ready Friday. The clock is ticking.

We may waste valuable time and money, but it is better to have them there when they are needed than to need them there and not have them.

General Wheeler: I will call now and get my men drafting the order.

(General Wheeler left the room.)

The President: What is the status of Buttercup? I see where Ky agreed on the release of prisoners. Get Vance to follow through.

Walt Rostow: President Thieu also has agreed to this.

Secretary McNamara: My position on Vietnam is very clear. I do not think it wise to go to the Congress asking for additional legislation. I do not think the call-up is necessary.

The President: Well, if you cannot agree with the Joint Chiefs on what is needed, then submit to me a minority viewpoint and your separate recommendations.

Secretary McNamara: Do you want General Wheeler to go to Vietnam?

The President: No, I want him here. I don't want anybody substituting for him at a time like this. I feel better with him here.

My feeling is that if the Vietnamese aren't able to carry the load alone we will have to do it rather than let them all get defeated. I think Westmoreland is confronted with a defeat or a victory.

[Omitted here is discussion of Korea.]

The President, Dick Helms, George Christian, General Wheeler and Tom Johnson then went to the office where the President showed charts reflecting the ratio of enemy KIA to friendly KIA.

The President said that General Ridgway had told him that we are not prepared for another major problem elsewhere in the world. He said our preparedness is not that adequate.

The President said he would rather have more than is needed in Vietnam than to need something and not have it available.

Source: *Foreign Relations of the United States, 1964–1968, Volume VI, Vietnam, January–August 1968* (Washington, D.C.: Government Printing Office, 2002), 188–96

After action report, 716th Military Police Battalion

February 12, 1968

Subject: Synopsis of Events, 31 Jan to 12 Feb 68 (Tet Offensive)

At 0300 hours, 31 January 1968, the 716th Military Police Battalion received word that the United States Embassy in downtown Saigon was under attack. Within the next fifteen minutes reports were received that facilities we were guarding, and our motorized patrols were being attacked in the eastern, western, and northern side of the city. Within the first hour we had dispatched two MP reaction forces and they were engaged in major confrontations with the enemy; one at the U.S. Embassy and one at BOQ #3. Reports continued to come in that firefights were being carried out within the city between our static security posts and patrols and the enemy.

In the second hour military police reaction forces were sent to reinforce our unit at the U.S. Embassy and to extricate our force that had been ambushed at BOQ #3. The force that was sent to BOQ #3 had been warned not to enter by the main street. They attempted to attack the enemy from the rear using an alley that ran into the rear of the BOQ. While proceeding down this alley a claymore hit the 2½ ton truck exploded. Immediately the enemy racked the vehicle with small arms, and automatic weapons fire and grenades; most of the personnel were killed.

Two reaction forces were dispatched; one to cordon off and secure the 17th Field Hospital, and the other to secure the Columbia BEQ that was under heavy attack. Within the first two hours over 100 personnel in the form of reaction forces had been deployed. Of that 100, 20 had been killed in action and 24 had been wounded.

During the third hour one MP Patrol and one machine gun patrol were ambushed in the vicinity of the Meyerkord BOQ. A machine gun patrol was attacked in the vicinity of the Phu Tho racetrack and contact had been lost. Reports were received that the Butte BEQ had been overrun, and a military police reaction force was sent.

By the fourth hour all the above mentioned action was still in progress. A reaction force was dispatched to the racetrack to ascertain what had happened to the lost machine gun jeep. This force was subsequently pinned down with small arms and automatic weapons fire. The reaction force that was sent to the Butte, found that the BOQ was not overrun. It secured that area and was redispatched to the Royal Oaks BEQ which was reported under heavy fire. A platoon from C Co of the 52nd Inf was dispatched to the racetrack to reinforce our personnel that were already there—this platoon was ambushed three blocks south of the racetrack and took up a defensive position in a cemetery. Reports were received that Ambassador Bunker's Quarters was under attack. An MP reaction force was sent there and took the enemy under fire. MACV and MACV Annex were reinforced and were receiving fire. Subsequently, enemy mortar rounds were received at both MACV and MACV Annex.

A recapitulation of the first four hours showed the 716th MP Bn was operating in a city whose streets were VOID of any other allied or Vietnamese forces and were engaged in ten separate major confrontations with the enemy in an area that roughly formed a semicircle around the city. The battalion had committed 220 personnel in addition to 290 personnel who had been on duty at 0300 hours. An additional 125 personnel were standing by ready to dispatch in 5 minutes' notice as reaction forces. Beside the 10 major confrontations there were numerous small firefights going on throughout the city between our personnel on static posts, patrols, and the enemy. The battalion had located the enemy strong points and were engaged at these points. The MP casualties as of 0700 hours on the 31 Jan 68 were: 27 KIA and 41 WIA.

>Embassy—4 KIA, 5 WIA
>BOQ #3—16 KIA, 21 WIA
>Racetrack—5 KIA, 12 WIA
>Meyerkord—2 KIA, 3 WIA

In the fifth and sixth hours a platoon from BAC was dispatched to the BOQ #3 area—it made several attempts but could not get through to personnel from the first MP reaction force who had been trapped in an alley. The MP reaction force that had been dispatched to the Royal Oaks secured that area and was redispatched to the race track where it was pinned down and took up defensive positions in an ARVN Compound. C Co was notified to have a 20 man reaction force ready at the heliport between MACV and MACV Annex to be picked up and air lifted to the U.S. Embassy roof—this force was subsequently pinned down by enemy fire and eventually used to reinforce the MACV Annex.

The military police force had surrounded the Embassy but could not enter the compound because of the VC fire coming from the compound and from the roof of a building across the street. At daylight intense fire was directed at the enemy position on the roof across from the Embassy and that fire was silenced. At this time a MP jeep attempted to ram the front gate but was unsuccessful. The lock was then shot off. Once the gate was open MPs poured into the Embassy and over the walls and engaged in close combat with the remaining VC who were behind posts, building alcoves, and pillars. The remaining enemy were in the first floor of a house occupied by Col Jacobsen. An MP threw the Col a .45 cal pistol and he killed the last VC. At approximately the same time 20 members of the 101st Airborne Division landed on the roof and began to work their way down through the building. At approximately 0900 hrs the U.S. Embassy was secured. No VC were able to enter the main building.

A 33-man reaction force was dispatched from B Co to reinforce C Co at MACV. During this period small arms fire continued to be directed at most of the facilities we were guarding throughout the city. Except for the HAC Platoon the city streets were void of any allied or Vietnamese forces.

During the first 8 hours the battalion had no communication with any other command other than 89th MP Gp. The city was for all practical purposes ours—no other U.S. or allied forces were on the streets. We were using our basic load of ammunition and were quickly running out of ammunition: 89th MP Gp was asked for resupply and it was to be sent by chopper. We had retaken the U.S. Embassy and secured it; our reaction forces were holding the MACV Area and MACV Annex area; we were in contact with the enemy at his strong points—BOQ #3 and the race track; we were securing the two hospitals in the city and Ambassador Bunker's Quarters. Not a single U.S. billet or compound in the city had been taken by the enemy.

In the next four hours from 1100 to 1500 part of the personnel at the U.S. Embassy were returned to their companies. A request was made to 89th MP Group for 2 platoons from the 92 MP Bn to reinforce C Co—this request was approved and the 2 platoons were used to reinforce MACV and MACV Annex. The B Co force that had been sent to reinforce C Co was relieved by the 92nd MP Bn platoon and were dispatched to Saigon PX Depot on Plantation Road for security. Further attempts were made to get the wounded out of the alley by BOQ #3. There attempts were aided by an ARVN V-100, but each attempt was driven back by intense enemy fire. Several bodies were recovered due entirely to the bravery of the rescuers. The force that had been sent to the Air Force BOQ had secured the building and supported by 2 gun ships that were firing at an ARVN Compound where the enemy was firing on the BOQ. When ARVN APCs and tanks moved in and secured the GVN compound, the force returned to its company. One of the MPs was wounded in the engagement. A mechanized infantry unit from the 199th Light Infantry arrived at the Phu Tho race-track. These troops supported by our troops pinned down in the area were able to clear the enemy from the area. Once the enemy was cleared of the area the MP reaction force returned to their companies.

The first 12 hours showed the 716th was operating in a vacuum. There were some allied and Vietnamese troops in the Tan Son Nhut area, but the streets of Saigon were deserted of any other allied or Vietnamese military or police forces. Communication with higher operation control headquarters was non-existent. The men of the battalion had broken up two of the major enemy drives, one at BOQ #3 and one at the racetrack. None of the 130 billets, installations, and facilities which this battalion was guarding fell to the enemy, although many had been or still were under attack.

In the next four hours—1600 to 2000 hours on the 31st—the battalion was resupplied with ammunition by chopper by the 89th MP Gp. Word was received that four female USAID Billets, off Cach Mang, were under attack. A 12-man MP force was dispatched to secure them. Because of heavy fire in the area only two of these billets could be reached. The Helena BEQ, on Vo Tanh, was under heavy automatic weapons fire. Two MP patrols were sent to reinforce these billets.

All the facilities that we were guarding in the sixth Pet were reinforced. The Phu Tho Motor Pool came under attack from two sides. An MP force was sent and secured the area. Along with this numerous of our static posts were under small arms fire.

In the last four hours of the 31st most of the 130 facilities guarded by the battalion were still under either small arms or automatic weapons attack. Rockets and automatic weapons were directed at the Helena and Denoigh BEQs and 2 MPs were wounded. Several attempts were made to get ammunition and supplies to Air Force billets at 173 Huguyen Hue in the Tan Binh area, but all attempts were driven back by heavy fire. Small arms fire was directed at the International Hotel—Battalion Headquarters. Our patrols and alert [reaction] forces had been armed with M-79 and as many M-60s as were available. Patrols were paired up and located at selective positions to act as immediate reactions forces.

Resupply and reinforcement runs were made to our personnel located in the facilities throughout the city. The city was still empty of any appreciable allied or Vietnamese force other than the 716th MP Bn.

The first day the battalion committed more than 800 personnel to the defense of Saigon. Not a single U.S. billet or facility guarded by the 716th had fallen into the hands of the enemy, although most were under some type of attack. The battalion was securing the two U.S. hospitals in the Saigon area and had reinforced squads and platoons guarding the U.S. Embassy, the U.S. Ambassador's Qtrs, COMUSMACV, Headquarters MACV and BOQ #3. The casualties suffered by the battalion had been 27 killed and 44 wounded. Vietnamese or allied troops were still missing from the heart of the city. Decision had been made and action taken by the

Battalion Commander because there was no contact with higher headquarters that had operational control of the battalion. Because of the large number and dispersion of our static security posts and patrols throughout the city, the battalion had pinpointed most of the enemy strong points.

From 0500 hours to 1200 hours, 1 February 1968, the SA/AUT weapons fire continued throughout the city. The firing at MACV Annex, the Helena, and the Denoigh continued. Some of the billets that received fire were the Ambassador's Quarters, Metropole, 17th Field Hosp, PX Whse in the 4th Pct, Montana, Commissary Whse, Royal Oaks, Simmons, Cholon PX, Meyerchord and the Saigon PX Depot. During this period ARVN troops and Cahn Sats began to be seen in large groups in the city. Several sweep operations were begun. Reinforcements arrived at MACV Hq.

From 1200 to 1800 hrs, 1 Feb, the SA fire continued throughout the city. ARVN & Cahn Sats sweep operations continued. The cemetery by Ambassador Bunker's Quarters was swept—one of the ten times this cemetery was swept. V-100s from 89th MP Gp arrived and were being employed. Sniper fire was again reported in the BOQ #3 and in the Capital area.

The remaining USAID female billets were secured.

From 1800 to 2400, 1 Feb SA/AUT fire picked up throughout the city. USAID Female Billets, Koyler Compound, TV Station, BOQ #1, Saigon Depot, Bn motor pool and PX Warehouse in the 4th Pct. ARVN & Cahn Sat sweeps continued.

From 2400, 1 Feb to 0800 2 Feb, the situation continued in much the same—SA & AUT fire directed at various billets and facilities throughout the city.

From 0800, 2 Feb, sweeps were again made of the cemetery behind Ambassador Bunker's Quarters. Heavy fire was directed at the Cofat PX and the Capital area. The Cahn Sat Station by the racetrack was overrun. Cahn Sats and ARVN Troops continued to sweep the area. A joint patrol was pinned down in the vicinity of the Fish Market, and V-100s were sent to the scene. They drew fire and subsequently destroyed the MG Post with their twin 30-cal fire and M79 grenades.

From 1800 to 2400, 2 Feb, the small arms and automatic weapons fire at U.S. Installations decreased considerably from the previous night. ARVN and Cahn Sat sweeps of the city continued.

From 2400, 3 Feb to 1200 3 Feb, sporadic sniper fire continued—USAID billets, commissary whse, Cleveland, Annapolis, McCarthy, 5 Os, BOQ #1, 3rd Field Hospital and Walling. From this period, lasting for the next 12 to 13 days, there was continued ARVN and Cahn Sat sweeps throughout the city. Our mission reverted to the security of our facilities and personnel.

From 2400, 3 Feb to 1200 4 Feb, the situation continued much the same as it had been. 7 VC were scene [sic] in the cemetery across from the Ambassador's Quarters. ARVN and Cahn Sats continued to sweep.

From 1200 to 2400 4 Feb, scattered sniper fire continued. ARVN and Cahn Sats continued to sweep.

From 2400 4 Feb to 1200 5 Feb, heavy fire was received in the vicinity of the Royal Oaks, Splendid. The 90 mm team was dispatched to help clear the path for some ARVNs making a sweep of the 3rd Pct. area. The 90 mm team did its job, and the sweep continued as scheduled.

The remainder of the 5th and rest of the 6th day ARVN forces continued their sweep. SA fire was received at several of our posts, especially around the John Huston, Freeman and PMO.

On the 7th and 8th, the battalion received 2 APC's—on the 7th one was used to investigate the report of 2 dead MPs in the 6th Pct—which was under enemy fire. The V-100s were now used for convoying POL runs from Nha Bai to TSN Air Base.

Heavy to moderate SA/AUT fire continued on until the 12th; then it became very light to scattered. The ARVN and Cahn Sats continued to sweep the troubled areas. Race Track, area north of the PX and Go Vap.

Source: After Action Report, The Tet Offensive, 716th MP Battalion & 18th Military Police Brigade, VNIT 264, U.S. Army Center of Military History

PLAF Command salutes 20-day fight in Hue over Liberation Radio

(South Vietnam People's Liberation Armed Forces Command's message to the armed forces and people of Hue)

February 21, 1968

For nearly 20 days and nights of relentless fighting, the people's armed forces and compatriots in Hue have fought very heroically and resourcefully and have achieved splendid exploits, thus making all soldiers and people in the south and throughout the country both enthusiastic and proud.

During the early spring days of 1968, thoroughly implementing the NLFSV Central Committee Presidium's order, you comrades have launched very strong and resolute attacks. You have destroyed many leading military and administrative organs, military bases, and warehouses of the U.S. and puppet forces. You have joined with the people in smashing the enemy's entire oppressive control machinery, and have discarded the dishonored flags of the landgrabbers and countrysellers which have defiled the city's sky for years and hoisted the Front's glorious flag to the top of the city's flagpole.

Thus you have told the people throughout the country that the armed forces and people in the city of Hue have knocked down the U.S. aggressors and their lackeys and that the city is free and controlled by the people.

The enemy has mustered large numbers of U.S. and puppet troops, resorted to the most cruel and vile war tricks in an attempt to regain control of Hue. With extraordinary courage in victory and in iron-like determination, you comrades and compatriots have demonstrated your valor, skillfulness, and flexibility. You have developed revolutionary heroism and the comprehensive strength of the people's war to a high degree, and you have won, extremely brilliant new victories.

After nearly 20 days and nights of fighting, during which you have endured innumerable sacrifices and hardships, you are still maintaining your mastery over the city. You have pinned down the U.S. Marines and puppet troops and have made them incapable of making any headway. You have annihilated thousands, wiped out entire battalions of the U.S. and puppet troops, and taken the initiative in barring the enemy's advance, attacking him in the rear, and frontally attacking all troop columns he has sent to the city.

Even if the enemy launches five-pronged or ten-pronged counterattacks, regardless of whether he deploys his troops on land or on waterways, and even though he has used aircraft, artillery, bombs and shells, the most modern tanks, toxic gases, and warships of his 7th Fleet, he has not been able to shake your steel-like fighting determination or to save himself from defeat.

Along with these glorious feats of arms, you comrades have vigorously developed the fine characteristics and traditions of the People's Liberation Armed Forces which have come from the people, fought for the people, and scored many outstanding achievements in serving the people and in carrying out the revolutionary policies set forth by the Liberation Front.

You have unreservedly helped our people organize into fighting units in order to kill the enemy and get rid of traitors and to preserve order, security, and the revolutionary achievements, have guided the people to a return to normalcy, and have protected them against enemy shelling and bombing, and so forth. In achieving these glorious victories, you have greatly encouraged our armed forces and people throughout the country. You have proved worthy of being the citizens of the traditional, glorious indomitable city, of the heroic Tri-Thien provinces. You have set a shining example for all the PLAF to study. You have contributed substantially to the common victories scored by all our armed forces and people.

The PLAF command solemnly commends the Hue PLAF. It has been decided to award the military Liberation Medal Second Class to the victorious units which have been controlling Hue. It acclaims all cadres and fighters of the main forces, regional forces, and people's self-defense forces, fighting armed branches, and units and organizations which have served in the fighting.

The PLAF command acclaims and thanks the people and patriotic forces inside and outside the city for their unreserved support for the armed forces and the front, and their assistance to the PLAF in the fighting which has contributed substantially to the victories we have scored.

Dear comrades, although the Americans and the puppets have sustained serious defeats, they will squirm frantically and will perpetrate more crimes against our people.

All cadres and fighters of the Hue PLAF: Be extremely vigilant, persevering and most courageous; eagerly foster the revolutionary tempo; be active in the annihilation of the enemy; attack him continuously; closely cooperate with the people and patriotic forces; strictly carry out all Front policies and directives of Hue People's Revolutionary Committee; protect and develop the revolutionary achievements, and move forward to achieve complete success.

Our people and fighters all over the country await news of your victories every day and every hour. The command is waiting to commend your outstanding achievements. Take advantage of the victories to surge forward courageously. We will certainly win.

Source: PLAF Command salutes 20-day fight in Hue, 21 February 1968, Folder 12, Box 13, Douglas Pike Collection: Unit 05—National Liberation Front, The Vietnam Archive, Texas Tech University

Memorandum from the Ambassador's Special Assistant (Lansdale) to the Ambassador to Vietnam (Bunker)

February 27, 1968

Subject: Evaluation of Tet offensive

As desired by you, the Senior Liaison Office submits herein its spot evaluation of the enemy's Tet offensive. It contains both my personal opinion and also the opinions of the members of my staff (David Hudson, Calvin Mehlert and Charles Sweet). It's our first total attempt at sorting out and considering the lump sum of what we've seen in the Saigon–Cholon area, and what we've read in reports, and what we've heard from a wide variety of Vietnamese and other contacts. Here, then is our evaluation:

In brief

The enemy adopted the meanest attribute of the "Year of the Monkey," that of vicious trickery, to change the nature of the war in Viet Nam at the start of the lunar year. It will mark how the war is waged from now on. The high cost of the enemy was not vital to him. It could be made vital, if there were retribution from an aroused Vietnamese population who were led with more spark and spunk than the present Neville Chamberlain style of Vietnamese leadership. As it is, the enemy has the initiative in this war a month after Tet. Today, too many Vietnamese civilians and soldiers have a sinking feeling in their guts that the enemy is going to outwit us with this initiative. It will take some tough political and psychological judo on top of military muscle to throw down the enemy. There are initial thoughts about this at the end of the paper.

Pre-Tet

As a starting point, it would be useful to keep in mind the look of things in the enemy's "target area" before the attack. The enemy's immediate target was urban/suburban South Viet Nam, where the bulk of the people supporting the GVN live. On the eve of Tet, this target area presented a picture with many encouraging overtones. Although it also had less pleasing under-tones, such as the threat of a full-scale invasion from the North and the debilitating effect of official GVN corruption, these had been identified as problems and pertinent solutions were being tackled.

There was a fledgling Constitutional Government, elected by the people, learning to behave as an administrative–executive–legislative team; it had plans for progress and reform after Tet. There were more than a million and a quarter men under arms, including some 700,000 Vietnamese backed up by U.S. and Allied forces; RVNAF in many places had pushed out actively into the countryside after the smaller enemy, killing him at a high ratio, fighting him further and further away from cities and towns. There was an energetic, nation-wide "pacification" campaign to win back the countryside, with a heavy infusion of U.S. managerial techniques and with Americans to oversee the use of these techniques at every Vietnamese echelon. There was a stirring among the Vietnamese political elements towards the broadening of alliances, towards getting better roots among the people, as moves towards the founding of new political parties. The people of the population centers had a new feeling of more security; there was more safety from the terror of the enemy and there was more money to buy food and gifts for the family celebrations of Tet.

At Tet

The enemy moved into this target area at Tet, with effective new military weapons, with a hard core of dedicated fighting men who evidently had top generals and political cadre amongst them to share in the dangers, and with a beguiling exposition of political aims. The symbols of moral and political/administrative strength on our side were singled out for denigration or destruction. Thus, the U.S. Embassy, the Presidential Palace, the JGS compound, the Hue Citadel, most provincial headquarters, and police stations were attacked with great vigor; churches, temples, and pagodas were occupied; leaders among the people were sought out for quick murder or kidnapping. Enemy troops fought hard, notably so. Enemy troops behaved as good comrades towards the people, again notably so. Their new weapons were effective against our armor, once again notably so. With all of this, there was attractive political talk of the war soon ending, of the Americans making a deal and leaving Viet Nam to the Vietnamese, of the forming of a new government by the people.

The enemy who came into the cities and fought openly has been crushed militarily, with great loss of life to him, to our military, and to civilians, along with much destruction of public and private property. The physical wounds of the enemy's Tet offensive are being healed through a relief and recovery program which could ease the memory of them to a large extent within this year. The *psychological* wounds of the enemy's Tet offensive are different, deeper, more dangerous. If too little is done too late, the psychological wounds can fester and be fatal for us. The Tet offensive demonstrated that the enemy is still waging "people's war." He got in among the majority of the people on our side this time. Although he failed in his proclaimed objective of getting the people to rise up against the GVN and the Americans, the enemy has shaken the faith of the people in the ultimate success of our side. An enemy as skilled as this one in the manipulation of mass opinions can be expected to keep up the attack at a point he can recognize as being vulnerable.

One psychological fuse was lit during Tet that might bring a delayed explosion. It deserves attention. Both Vietnamese and American combat forces fought the enemy right out in plain view of hundreds of thousands of articulate city dwellers, the "home folks," instead of far off in the remote countryside or jungle. The Vietnamese home folks not only saw the brutal face of war up close, they also saw RVNAF in a harsh comparison with both Americans and the enemy. The comparison could become invidious, since RVNAF did not always show up well. From some of the emotional outbursts of civilian and military "young Turks" since then, it can be deduced that there is some feeling of shame among them. If reaction to this shame or "loss of face" is improperly channeled, it could turn into a virulent type of anti-Americanism as people acknowledge the obvious fact that the country would have been lost to the enemy if it weren't for American actions. The "young Turks" must be given a good way of "gaining face" again, fast.

Enemy objectives

When attempting to assess results of the enemy Tet offensive, we should ask what objectives the Communist leaders sought to attain. They told their combatants that people in urban areas would rise up against the government, that ARVN units would defect, and that "revolutionary" committees would be able to take over the administration in many cities. They also told their shock forces that reinforcements would arrive after the first period of battle.

The people and ARVN failed to respond to the Communist appeal, reinforcements failed to appear, and the cities remain under GVN control. Furthermore, the enemy took serious losses. On the surface, it would appear the Communists failed and that, on balance, their offensive resulted in a stronger position for the GVN.

However, it is likely that the Communists, while hoping to attain the larger goals, knew that the chance for success was uncertain, and had other, longer-range goals in mind, such as:

- striking fear into the hearts of the urban population by demonstrating the inability of the government to provide adequate security;
- terrorizing and demoralizing government civil and military personnel, and their families, the bulk of whom live in urban areas;
- exacerbating existing tensions among top GVN leaders by confronting them, with a major crisis, which caused them to view one another in frustration, anxiety, and fear;
- straining American/Vietnamese relations for the same reasons as above, and for others, i.e. seeking to portray the images that U.S. firepower destroyed the Vietnamese cities; that Americans in Viet Nam still live affluently while their Vietnamese allies are without homes, food, etc.;
- increasing pressure on the U.S. at home and abroad to withdraw, by seeking to demonstrate the hopelessness of victory and the immorality of our cause (for example, the image of U.S. firepower destroying friendly Vietnamese cities);
- forcing the government to abandon its efforts to expand its areas of authority in the countryside (i.e. the RD program) by compelling it to concentrate on urban defense and recovery; or alternatively, forcing the government to spread its resources so thinly that it is unable to do anything effective anywhere.

Enemy gains

The urban population, at least in Saigon–Cholon, is still somewhat fearful, unsure of the ability of the GVN to face repeated armed challenges in the cities. (For example, on the night of February 23, more than three weeks after the opening of the Tet offensive, VC were reported calling at the homes of people on Ly Nam De Street, District 5, asking for food. The people had no alternative but to provide food since there was no police protection on the streets after dark. Many people in Cholon believe stories that the VC have been cutting off the hands of persons who work for Americans.)

The excessive burden of the demands created by the offensive has further weakened the GVN executive branch which was already plagued by diffusion of power and internal political conflicts. The full powers required for handling the emergency were not invested in the Central Relief Committee nor were they effectively assumed by the President, causing considerable tension within the GVN as a result of its inability to act decisively in a critical period.

Destruction resulting from U.S./GVN bombing and artillery firepower has created some deep resentment against the U.S. and Vietnamese governments, particularly in the refugee camps where Viet Cong agitators are at work. Viet Cong atrocities have created mostly fear but not wide-spread antagonism, except in families which suffered personal losses. Viet Cong propaganda still seems to have more credibility with the people, on this point, than does the information campaign on our side. This can still be reversed, but time is running out.

The Viet Cong have sown the seeds of suspicion and distrust. The rumor of U.S./Viet Cong collusion in the attack is still alive, still talked about among the people. The allegations of Communist infiltration into private organizations, and collaboration by certain individuals with the Viet Cong, have also generated suspicions and have led the government to be overly cautious and at times suppressive in their dealings with private individuals and associations. (The arrest of CVT labor leaders at the moment they were generating an anti-Communist drive hurt our side, helped the enemy cause.)

Public criticism of U.S. policy in Viet Nam has intensified in the U.S. and elsewhere abroad.

GVN resources have necessarily been spread more thinly. In many areas of the countryside, RD teams and RVNAF units have been drawn back into more urban locations, inviting VC takeover of areas formerly under GVN control.

GVN response

The government's response, beyond defending and restoring security in the urban areas, centered on the formation of the People's Relief Committee headed by Vice President Ky. This Committee performed commendably in coordinating and expediting the emergency *welfare relief* measures of the involved GVN and U.S. agencies, including such action as:

(a) the re-supplying of Saigon and the shipping of emergency relief goods to the provinces;

(b) the distribution of rice and food to the refugees and public and the re-opening of rice retail shops with strict government price controls;

(c) the protection and repair of public utilities, allowing services to continue throughout the emergency;

(d) the resettling and registering of the 150,000 Saigon refugees;

(e) the intensification of the government's psychological operation by giving each refugee camp a radio and television, improving the news coverage on radio, and assisting 15 daily newspapers to begin publication;

(f) the soliciting of funds, supplies, blood and labor from Vietnamese private organizations and individuals and third countries;

(g) the gradual lifting of restrictions and extension of the blue (secure) areas in Saigon;

(h) the collection and burning of garbage; and

(i) the deployment of inspection teams to the provinces and establishment of a system for culling all pertinent data for Saigon and provinces.

Additionally, the imaginative action of assisting 2,500 RD cadre from Vung Tau to work in Saigon, the noteworthy performances of the Ministry of Health and the City Sanitation and Fire Departments throughout the entire emergency; and the visits of GVN officials to stricken areas brought definite political psychological gains to the government.

Both Houses in the National Assembly became actively engaged in the relief effort. Initially, each House sent representatives to attend the meetings of the Central Relief Committee. Senators and Lower House Deputies also inspected refugee camps and damaged areas in Saigon and the provinces; Lower House Deputies unable to return to Saigon assisted the provincial officials in the initial relief efforts. Both Houses have issued communiqués supporting the government's emergency relief efforts and have requested assistance for the victims from national legislatures of other countries.

Despite these positive actions, the GVN so far has been unable to capitalize on the opportunity the Tet offensive presented and emerge in a stronger position. Perhaps the principal reason for this is the excessive diffusion of executive and political power which is largely the result of the continuing rivalry between the Thieu and Ky camps. As a result, there has been no clear central point of executive and political leadership during the emergency. Because of this key executive decisions have been delayed or not made, particularly those involving joint civil/military considerations (for example, the curfew), and a trend has developed toward creation of two rival political Fronts.

Popular response

The enemy's biggest "calculated risk" in the Tet offensive was on how the people in the GVN centers would respond to him. True, the enemy asked for public uprising against the GVN and the Americans, which he failed to create. This was a tactical loss to him. The enemy's strategy still will aim for creating an eventual surge of popular support for his cause against ours in the urban/suburban population centers of Viet Nam. The enemy undoubtedly has this aspect of his Tet offensive under intense study right now.

The Communists must make sure that the people's reactions to their Tet violence do not crystallize into a purposeful hatred directed in an effective way against them. The enemy made this mistake against the Catholics and the Hoa Hao years ago. He risked doing it again with other large groups of Vietnamese, by his Tet attack. However, he seems to be getting away with it, although the final psychological effects are still not firm. The emotional flag-raising and the recaptured Citadel in Hue, witnessed by so many thousands of teary-eyed residents, may well spark the nation-wide tide against him that the enemy fears. However, there was no similar polarizing event in which the people could participate in Saigon or other centers. The Hue ceremony could remain an isolated incident instead of becoming the focal rallying point (such as "Remember the Alamo," "Remember the *Maine*," "Remember Pearl Harbor").

The initial response of the Saigon–Cholon–Gia Dinh population to the Tet offensive was disbelief—some even thought a coup was in process. As the critical nature of the situation became clear, concern for personal safety prevailed. The people soon started to wonder why their government could not protect them; stories of American and Viet Cong collusion in the offensive were widely spread and believed. As fear grew, there was a reluctance on the part of refugees and even volunteers from private associations to become too closely associated with the government although this feeling has now been reduced. On balance, although the people have appreciated the government's efforts to help them, there has also been a tendency out of fear for the urban population to assume a more moral neutral stance.

Political personalities, ARVN officers, civil servants, Northern Catholics, and other strongly anti-Communist groups also reacted initially with fear, for they would lose the most in a Viet Cong takeover; also, for the first time, the war was brought to their doorsteps. As the shock wore off, however, many of the elements came to believe that this may be the last opportunity for "all nationalists to unite and save the nation."

At the moment, many of the people in the capital—and possibly the same is true elsewhere—feel isolated into just their own family groups. Each family is an "island," separated apart from neighbors, the community, the government. In case of another enemy attack, individuals will feel highly vulnerable, their main recourse to comfort or safety being only within the immediate family. Much of this has been caused by the attitude and behavior of the police. Although the securing of Saigon–Cholon owes a big debt to the energy and resourcefulness of General Loan, he also portrayed the image of an emotionally unstable, suspicious, vindictive, and willful person. This image has rubbed off on the forces he commands, further tarnishing their reputation for corrupt venality and saving their own hides in time of trouble. Unless this image is changed, unless there is created some bond of trust and understanding between police and people, we will be leaving a grievous chink in our armor for the enemy to exploit.

Challenge—our thoughts

The enemy's Tet offensive demonstrated once again the ability of Communist leaders to make a hard strategic decision, marshal their resources in an extremely disciplined way, and deal us a hard blow. At present our strategy is less clear and our resources are not being used in as concerted and disciplined a fashion as the enemy's, at least in the political sphere.

If we are to achieve our goal of having a strong, popular-supported constitutional government and armed forces in South Viet Nam, we must make some hard political decisions now and carry them out with teamwork, skill and discipline of our own.

Specifically, I believe we must do the following:

1   Help Nguyen van Thieu rapidly become a strong President, under the Constitution. This action has two closely related facets: helping him develop his own capabilities as the elected leader of his country; and helping him acquire full powers delegated to the President under the Constitution. At present, he has far too little authority over the key elements of the executive branch, i.e. the cabinet, province chiefs, the police and the armed forces. Rapid emergence of Thieu as a strong President with full authority is the first, and absolutely essential step, toward creation of a GVN that works, that can really get things done, which is not the case today. Under a strong President, firm chains of command could be established in both the civil service and armed forces. Until this is achieved, however, the GVN can only muddle along in seeking to carry out critical programs, since the governmental mechanism for effective execution does not exist. We can no longer tolerate a two-headed, Siamese-twin central government with four separate "governments" between it and the people. Thieu and Ky, and their entourages, for many reasons, can never really work together to the extent required, and we should not delude ourselves that they can.

2   To assist Thieu, as discussed above, far more concerted U.S. political action is needed. As an immediate step, a small political working group should be established under your personal direction, composed of Arch Calhoun, Lew Lapham, a personal representative of General Westmoreland (such as Colonel John Hayes), General Forsythe and myself.

3   While helping Thieu consolidate presidential power under the Constitution, other critical actions should be taken to create a political base which would complement and reinforce establishment of a strong executive/administrative base. Immediate actions to create a political base include:

    (a) Real enforcement of the order recently issued by General Cao van Vien that looting by RVNAF personnel will result in summary court-martial, and execution, if warranted. This order should include, if it does not already, squarely placing responsibility for troop conduct on unit commanders. Another general order should be issued and backed up, stating that every officer and soldier has two duties of equal importance—to destroy the enemy, and to defend and help the people—and that any misconduct toward the people will result in severe punishment. (This is critical *political* action because the armed forces, along with the police and RD [Revolutionary Development] cadre, remain the principal link between the government and the people.)

(b) Acts of political leadership, starting with Thieu, but also by all nationalist leaders, within and without the government, which will create out of the emotions aroused by the Tet offensive, a new spirit of unity, sacrifice, pride and hope among Vietnamese nationalists. Full support by Thieu for the "People's Congress," as a single, united popular Front for emergency purposes, is one such leadership act critically needed now.

(c) Create psychological polarity to focus the people's emotions against the enemy as a beast who must be stopped. This can be done through a concerted campaign built around the battle-cry of "Remember Hue!" This requires a continuing revelation of information about what the enemy did to unarmed civilians and to cherished national heritages in Hue, through media that will spread these stories to the widest extent possible, over and over again. One such medium is the Vietnamese ballad; a song is needed, to be sung throughout the country, carried there by VIS [Visual Information Specialist], RD cadre, and student choral groups. "Remember Hue!" can be the theme of an address to the nation by President Thieu, of manifestos and speeches by patriots in the new "Fronts." "Remember Hue!" can be included in general orders of RVNAF, used by troops in counter-offensive operations. "Remember Hue!" can be imprinted with postal cancellation marks on all mail in Viet Nam. We must beat the Communists to the punch, before they use "Remember Hue!" first.

(d) Help put a stop to indiscriminate expressions of Sinophobia among the Vietnamese in urban centers, particularly Saigon–Cholon. You and the rest of us in the U.S. Mission can make a point of this when talking with Vietnamese leaders. President Thieu can be urged to meet with responsible and respected leaders of the Chinese-ancestry "congregations" in Cholon, to learn what has happened to them and what they have contributed to our common cause, to get a fix on enemy activities among those of Chinese blood, and to exchange pledges of mutual teamwork in the face of national peril. *Viet Nam Press* can do a feature news item on the favorable actions by the Sino-Vietnamese of Cholon; there have been heroic acts, heavy donations of money, goods, and services in this crisis. We in the U.S. Mission could see that this item is picked up by the world press, that it becomes known to police and other GVN officials where we have an advisory effort. This would give fresh heart to those in Viet Nam's most crucial commercial circles, to get the nation's economy moving again.

(e) Devise a feasible means of mobilizing the entire Vietnamese people into the war effort, in an organized way that will make good sense to them and gain their willing support. While this is especially needed by "young Turk" civilians and soldiers to channelize their energies and emotions into constructive channels, many others in the population are in need of having a practical, known way in which they can help against the enemy. The mobilization means and the duties assigned (which include self-defense) have a highly political import. GVN organizations, such as the Ministries of Interior, Youth, and RD, and the newly formed "Fronts" have concepts on mobilizing the people against the enemy. The U.S. Mission needs to crystallize its own policy on this matter, to gain maximum effect of U.S. support. It is urged that this subject be given early study by the small, political working group described above.

Source: *Foreign Relations of the United States, 1964–1968, Volume VI, Vietnam, January–August 1968* (Washington, D.C.: Government Printing Office, 2002), 251–60

Notes of meeting

February 27, 1968

[Participants]

Rusk, McNamara, Clifford, Katzenbach, Bundy, Rostow, Califano and McPherson

McN: Westmoreland wants

105,000 by 1 May
100,000 in two increments: part by 1 Sept., part by 31 Dec.
Total: 205,000 men, all but 25,000 (air) in Army and Marines.

This will require a sizeable reserve call-up (minimum 150,000) as well as increased draft. In total, an increase in uniformed strength of 400,000.

In expenditures, at least $10 billion extra in FY 1969. With automatic $5 billion in FY 1970, this will put FY 1970 DoD budget at 15 billion above current FY 1969 figure.

Alternatives for President's speech and program:

(1) Go with full 205,000. Ask for present surtax request plus additional taxes. Announce economic program (possibly controls on interest, production controls, etc.).
(2) Go with full 205,000, economic program, and announce new peace offensive.

Rusk: Basis for peace in Southeast Asia: ending of Communist assaults in Laos, Thailand; we will stop bombing North of the 20th parallel if NVN withdraws from Quang Tri province; or stop altogether in that event; or other specific proposal.

McPherson: This is unbelievable and futile.

(3) Status quo on forces, with a change in strategy. End U.S. commitment

to defend every province and district capital. Protect essential areas. Fight enemy wherever he fights; end search and destroy.

(4) (Clifford) Another possibility that should be considered—and I am not pushing it—is announcement that we intend to put in 500,000 to million men.

McN: That has virtue of clarity. Obviously we would have decided to put in enough men to accomplish the job. That and status quo both have the virtue of clarity. I do not understand what the strategy is in putting in 205,000 men. It is neither enough to do the job, or an indication that our role must change.

(5) (Bundy) We must also prepare for the worst. SVN is very weak. Our position may be truly untenable. Contingency planning should proceed toward possibility that we will withdraw with best possible face and defend rest of Asia. We can say truthfully that Asia is stronger because of what we have done in past few years.

Katzenbach took call from Habib in Hawaii. Reports Habib is "less optimistic" about political situation in Saigon than he was when he went out. Reports that there is serious disagreement in American circles in Saigon over 205,000 request. Bunker has doubts about this.

Rusk: If we have to call up reserves, we should take some of our troops out of Europe. Europeans will have to put some more in for their defense.

McN: Agree, if we call 400,000.

State of military situation:

Rusk: Rostow thinks enemy took beating in Tet offensive. Rostow says captured documents show enemy was disappointed, may be unable to mount heavy coordinated attack on cities. Rusk reminds that enemy took 40,000 casualties. No U.S. units out of operation. Rostow says if we can reinforce Westm. now, he should be able to handle situation until good weather comes to I Corps and NVN.

McN: What then? Let's not delude ourselves into thinking he cannot maintain pressure *after* good weather comes. (Rostow apparently had air attacks in mind.)

McN: We are dropping ordnance at a higher rate than in last year of WWII in Europe. It has not stopped him.

Bundy: SVN forces uncertain, but almost certainly not as strong as were before. Assessment due from MACV on Feb 29.

Clifford: Look at situation from point of view of American public and Vietnamese. Despite optimistic reports, our people (and world opinion) believe we have suffered a major setback. Problem is, how do we gain support for major program, defense and economic, if we have told people things are going well? How do we avoid creating feeling that we are pounding troops down rathole? What is our purpose? What is achievable? Before any decision is made, we must re-evaluate our entire posture in SVN. Unfortunately Pres. has been at ranch with hawks.

McN: Agreed. Decision must not be hasty. Will take a week at least to work out defense and economic measures, if we go big. Wheeler, Habib will meet with Secretaries Wednesday morning at breakfast with President. Decision should certainly not be announced that night.

General impression: prevailing uncertainty. Radically different proposals were offered and debated, none rejected out of hand. We are at a point of crisis. McNamara express grave doubts over military, economic, political, diplomatic and moral consequences of a larger force buildup in SVN.

Q[uestion] is whether these profound doubts will be presented to President.

Source: *Foreign Relations of the United States, 1964–1968, Volume VI, Vietnam, January–August 1968* (Washington, D.C.: Government Printing Office, 2002), 260–62

Walter Cronkite on *CBS News*

February 27, 1968

Tonight, back in more familiar surroundings in New York, we'd like to sum up our findings in Vietnam, an analysis that must be speculative, personal, subjective. Who won and who lost in the great Tet offensive against the cities? I'm not sure. The Vietcong did not win by a knockout, but neither did we. The referees of history may make it a draw. Another standoff may be coming in the big battles expected south of the Demilitarized Zone. Khesanh could well fall, with a terrible loss in American lives, prestige and morale, and this is a tragedy of our stubbornness there; but the bastion no longer is a key to the rest of the northern regions, and it is doubtful that the American forces can be defeated across the breadth of the DMZ with any substantial loss of ground. Another standoff. On the political front, past performance gives no confidence that the Vietnamese government can cope with its problems, now compounded by the attack on the cities. It may not fall, it may hold on, but it probably won't show the dynamic qualities demanded of this young nation. Another standoff.

We have been too often disappointed by the optimism of the American leaders, both in Vietnam and Washington, to have faith any longer in the silver linings they find in the darkest clouds. They may be right, that Hanoi's winter–spring offensive has been forced by the Communist realization that they could not win the longer war of attrition, and that the Communists hope that any success in the offensive will improve their position for eventual negotiations. It would improve their position, and it would also require our realization, that we should have had all along, that any negotiations must be that—negotiations, not the dictation of peace terms. For it seems now more certain than ever that the bloody experience of Vietnam is to end in a stalemate. This summer's almost certain standoff will either end in real give-and-take negotiations or terrible escalation; and for every means we have to escalate, the enemy can match us, and that applies to invasion of the North, the use of nuclear weapons, or the mere commitment of one hundred, or two hundred, or three hundred thousand more American troops to the battle. And with each escalation, the world comes closer to the brink of cosmic disaster.

To say that we are closer to victory today is to believe, in the face of the evidence, the optimists who have been wrong in the past. To suggest we are on the edge of defeat is to yield to unreasonable pessimism. To say that we are mired in stalemate seems the only realistic, yet unsatisfactory, conclusion. On the off chance that military and political analysts are right, in the next few months we must test the enemy's intentions, in case this is indeed his last big gasp before negotiations. But it is increasingly clear to this reporter that the only rational way out then will be to negotiate, not as victors, but as an honorable people who lived up to their pledge to defend democracy, and did the best they could.

This is Walter Cronkite. Good night.

Source: *Reporting Vietnam: Part One: American Journalism 1959–1969* (New York: Penguin, 1998), 581–82

Report by the Joint Chiefs of Staff

March 1, 1968

Analysis of COMUSMACV Force requirements and alternatives

Section I

Purpose

A   *The Problem.* To provide military advice on the military implications of several courses of action to defeat the enemy offensive and to regain the initiative in Vietnam.

B   *Study Objectives.* The study examines five alternative military courses of action. Each is examined as to its ability to attain the following military objectives:

     1   First, to counter the enemy offensive and to destroy or neutralize the North Vietnamese Army (NVA) invasion in the north.

     2   Second, to restore security in the cities and towns.

     3   Third, to restore security in the heavily populated area of the countryside.

     4   Fourth, to regain the initiative through offensive operations.

C   *Examination of the Options.* The following questions are posed which bring out the significance of each of the options examined:

     5   What military objectives are advanced by the option (in six months; 12 months)?

     6   What specific dangers is the option designed to avoid (in six months; 12 months)?

     7   What specific goals does the option achieve (in six months; 12 months)?

     8   Does it achieve the objectives? If not, where does it fall short?

     9   What personnel and procurement actions are required to support the option?

10   What specific units will be deployed and what time schedule?

11   How are these forces generated, and what combat forces remain in the CONUS?

12   What are the estimated dollar costs?

D   *Conclusion.* After this examination (of the pros and cons), the options are compared in order to provide a conclusion as to which of the options is the most advantageous from the military viewpoint.

Section II

Summary

1   The enemy, since November, has increased his forces in South Vietnam by at least 41 maneuver battalions, some armored elements, a large number of rockets, and additional artillery. There are indications he is preparing for the use of limited air support, including logistical air drops and bombing missions.

2   In the MACV proposal (options 1 and 1A), the number of maneuver battalions provided roughly offsets the increase in enemy forces. In the lesser options, the enemy buildup is not matched. Furthermore, there are indications now that additional enemy forces are on the move to RVN.

3   The basic strategy which must be followed by MACV in any circumstance is to defeat the current enemy offensive both in Northern I Corps Tactical Zone where it is the most formidable, in the Highlands where it is highly dangerous, and throughout South Vietnam in defense of the government and the cities and towns. In many places, allied forces have lost the initiative to the enemy. They are meeting the threat in the I Corps Tactical Zone, are in a marginal position in II CTZ, and elsewhere are committing the bulk of the South Vietnamese forces to the defense of cities and towns. Allied forces are not conducting offensive operations of any great magnitude or frequency and therefore they are not wresting control of the countryside from the enemy.

4   Under the smaller options, that is the current force plus 6 battalions already deployed (Option 2), or Option 3 which provides an additional 6 battalions within the 50,000 strength add on, the capability to meet the enemy offensive is definitely increased; however, this added capability may well be required in the II Corps Tactical Zone alone. It may permit MACV to break loose a small airborne or air cavalry reserve to conduct reaction or limited offensive operations. The intermediate Option 4 of 100,000 additional troops should permit the constitution of about a one-division reserve which could reinforce any threatened

area such as Khe Sanh or the Highlands or could undertake slightly expanded offensive operations. As long as the enemy employs the forces now available to him in synchronized attacks, it is not realistic to believe that this size force can guarantee security throughout South Vietnam's rural areas. However, the accomplishment of this mission of providing security in the populated countryside also depends very heavily on the speed with which they are able to operate.

5   If the enemy offensive can be broken with sustained heavy casualties, then, and only then, will the cities be secure and the countryside reentered. Even with the largest force contemplated (Option 1) it will not be possible to perform adequately all of the tasks unless the current enemy offensive is decisively defeated. This, therefore, is the first and most important task upon which all else depends. If the offensive can be broken, then all of the other tasks become possible with the forces in Option 1.

6   It is not possible to predict whether the forces now available in Vietnam will be able to break the offensive without additional help, considering the magnitude of the enemy buildup and his clear willingness to expend forces with small regard for casualties. Military prudence requires that we react and respond to his escalation and initiative. The larger and faster our response the better. It is not possible to draw clear and compelling distinctions between the effects to be expected from the incremental differences in the various options.

7   If the forces now in Vietnam or the forces under any of the options prove to be inadequate to break the enemy offensive, or if, conversely, the enemy sustained offensive breaks the Vietnamese armed forces (even short of destroying the GVN), then our objectives in South Vietnam, and the tasks associated with them will be unobtainable. Specifically, we would be unable to regain the initiative, that is, we would not be able to conduct offensive operations at the scope and pace required either to prevent further enemy buildup or to reenter the countryside. This would force U.S. and allied forces into a defensive posture around the major population centers.

8   The major risks involved in such circumstances are:

   (a) Enemy forces would retain the initiative and could move a number of divisions now tied down along the borders and around the Khe Sanh against the populated areas where their attacks by fire would be demoralizing.

   (b) By holding the countryside, enemy (particularly VC) strength would increase.

   (c) The enemy could consolidate both geographic areas and segments of the population and probably could establish a credible

Revolutionary Government which, as a minimum, would be a strong position for a negotiated settlement, but more importantly might bring about the collapse of the GVN and the removal of any reason for U.S. troops to remain in South Vietnam.

9 Therefore, immediate action to break the enemy's current offensive is not only the first but the decisive requirement.

10 In each of the options discussed in the following sections, sizeable support forces are included which will provide support not only for the additional combat troops but also for those of the recent (Feb 68) emergency deployments and the additional light ROK division soon to be deployed.

Source: *Foreign Relations of the United States, 1964–1968, Volume VI, Vietnam, January–August 1968* (Washington, D.C.: Government Printing Office, 2002), 292–95

Memorandum from the President's Special Assistant (Rostow) to President Johnson

March 6, 1968

Mr. President:

Herewith some personal thoughts on the war.

Objective The art of the next two or three months would be to produce a situation in which Hanoi decided to end the war. If that is impossible, the objective is to produce a situation in the second half of the year in which our side is clearly moving forward.

Present Situation We are clearly in the midst of an unresolved critical battle. The enemy is committed—having taken stock of his immediate post-Tet situation—to continue to throw forces into the battle at a rate almost four times his average for 1967; he is losing about 1,000 KIA per day as opposed to 241 per day in 1967. He did increase his order of battle in the days before Tet—with several additional North Vietnamese divisions, North Vietnamese fillers for VC main force units, plus hasty recruiting for VC units. But there is no evidence he can sustain present rates for more than a matter of a few months.

At the moment the enemy appears to be trying to pin Delta and Saigon allied forces close to the cities; draw Westy's reserves to the Western frontiers (Kontum-Pleiku); and strike a decisive blow in I Corps. The threat forming up around Hue is major (perhaps 5–6,000 enemy troops). Westy is trying to put his Delta and Saigon forces on to the offensive; deal with the Western highlands economically; fight a decisive battle in I Corps.

To maximize the chance that we achieve our objective, these things should happen:

- the ARVN and the GVN should put on a performance which convinces Hanoi, the U.S., and Moscow that they are viable and must be considered a major factor in settlement:
- above all, Westy must win as decisive a victory at Hue—and in I Corps—as he can;

- the U.S. must behave in the days ahead in a way to make clear we have the will and staying power to carry on;
- the supply prospects for North Viet Nam over the coming months and year must be worsened;
- the GVN—from a position of strength—must put forward a powerful new appeal and proposal for peace in the South.

The proper timing of this sequence is critical.

A proposal for consideration

The best trigger point would be:

- a major battle around Hue, initiated either by the enemy or by Westy going out to get these forces before they are set;
- plus some success in the battles Westy tells us are about to begin as Thang moves to the offensive in the Delta and our forces move out simultaneously against the enemy's Saigon divisions. This should happen in the next few days.

When the battle is joined we do two things:

- go for the Clifford package, beginning with a reserve call up;
- mine the North Vietnamese ports with delayed-action mines, telling international shipping to get out of North Vietnamese territorial waters.

At Tab A is a fresh analysis of the mining problem done by Bob Ginsburgh at my request. Mining by itself would *not* be decisive; but it will be costly to the enemy. The maximum predicated Soviet reaction would be to bring in mine-sweepers and shoot their way through. (This is what the Czech general, recently defected, has said; but since we're not blockading, there is nothing to shoot except mines.)

Against this background—and assuming some tactical success in the forthcoming battles—we persuade Thieu to take the offensive for peace:

- appealing to all Vietnamese to stop the bloodshed;
- offering to talk to any Southerners on the basis of converting the war into politics under a constitutional one-man–one-vote system.

We would accompany the offer with a temporary stoppage of bombing.

The whole sequence hinges, of course, on some tactical success on the ground in coming days and, especially, one clear-cut victory—hopefully at Hue. Thieu must feel he is operating from some strength.

Not since the Civil War has quite so much hinged for our country on immediate battlefield events.

As for Hanoi and the Russians: I do not believe a Communist takeover of South Viet Nam is regarded as a vital Soviet interest. The Chinese will oppose, but are not likely to occupy North Viet Nam. Hanoi may have entered the winter–spring offensive with the same judgment at high levels that they have conveyed to low levels; namely, 1968 must be the Year of Decision.

What happens if we fail in I Corps? I doubt that the North Vietnamese can drive Westy from I Corps; but a setback would not be a good occasion for a peace initiative. But we should proceed to lay the extra burden on the North Vietnamese supply system via mining.

This is a line of thought—not a firm recommendation. I believe it deserves some examination

Walt

Source: *Foreign Relations of the United States, 1964–1968, Volume VI, Vietnam, January–August 1968* (Washington, D.C.: Government Printing Office, 2002), 338–40

Document 35

Telegram from the Chairman of the Joint Chiefs of Staff (Wheeler) to the Commander, Military Assistance Command, Vietnam (Westmoreland) and the Commander in Chief, Pacific (Sharp)

March 8, 1968

1   I had a most interesting and informative conversation today with our new Secretary of Defense, Mr. Clifford. He is a very astute, intelligent and able man who is closely in touch with Congressional leaders, the business community, and the heads of the news media agencies. As you no doubt know, he has been the trusted advisor to four Presidents. In my judgment, apart from his important official position, he is a man of stature and achievement, one whose views must be accorded weight.

2   The main points he made with me this morning were the following:

A   The Tet offensive mounted by the enemy came as a great shock to the American public. He believes that this shock was the greater because of the euphoria engendered by optimistic statements in past days by various spokesmen supporting administration policy in South Vietnam.

B   He is concerned at the lessening support for the war effort; he cited satiric articles by Art Buchwald as reflecting the beliefs of many people that actualities in South Vietnam and what is said are poles apart.

C   He thinks that the American public cannot stand another shock such as that administered by the Tet offensive. He believes that we have laid ourselves open to the possibility of an additional setback with the American public by playing down the effects of the Tet offensive on the GVN, the RVNAF, and on the South Vietnamese public. One government spokesman (who shall be nameless) was ridiculed a couple of weeks ago for what the press considered to be wild overstatements in minimizing the strength and cunning of the enemy and the impact on the GVN.

D   He considers that additional substantial attacks over a fairly wide area of South Vietnam could create a credibility gap with the American public and the news media which would be virtually unbridgeable.

3   I must admit that Secretary Clifford's assessment is shared by me although, not having the contacts he enjoys, I cannot document the feelings in the business community and among the news media as can he. Nevertheless, I have been upset by views expounded in the news media, in the Congress, and in letters from the public to me that we are fighting a war which cannot be won; that unending hordes of North Vietnamese are surging against South Vietnam; that the GVN is corrupt and inept; that the South Vietnamese people are either solely interested in making money, largely by stealing from American sources, or are completely apathetic as to the outcome of the war, that the senior GVN military are war lords vying for power and are unconcerned about saving their country.

4   During our conversation, Mr. Clifford called my attention to a key article by Gene Roberts on the front page of the *New York Times* of 7 March. The article is datelined Saigon 6 March, and puts in quotes a number of expressions of opinion attributed to "a senior military spokesman." Among those which aroused the Secretary's concern are these:

A   A general statement that the military command is less worried now than at any other time during the last five weeks about a general second wave of attacks against Saigon and other population centers. This is followed by "I don't believe the enemy has any great capability to assume any general offensive in the near future. He has been hurt and hurt badly. He is tired. His logistic efforts have been adequate to support his campaign thus far, but there is evidence of developing logistic problems."

B   "But I do give him a capability in I Corps north where he has large forces near Hue. In my opinion, Hue is the next objective."

C   A general statement to the effect that supply and transportation problems and a steady pounding by American bombs have weakened the enemy's position around Khe Sanh and have decreased the possibilities of immediate attack. Apropos of the forgoing, Mr. Clifford remarked that of course he does not know whether the quotes attributed to the spokesman are correct. In this connection, he asked that I obtain the tapes of the press interview or stenographic notes if there are no tapes.

4   [sic] The Secretary continued that he believes our best course of action is to be conservative in assessments of the situation and enemy

capabilities. Otherwise, we could have the American public subjected to the second shock. In particular, he expressed the following views:

A   Do not denigrate the enemy.
B   Do not indulge in forecasting enemy plans or our plans.
C   Do not make predictions of victory.
D   Do express the view that there is tough fighting and that the enemy has residual capabilities not yet committed.
E   This conservative approach, he feels, would put us in a strong public information position. If we suffer some reverses, the public will not be shocked. If we achieve some successes, we can modestly and without overplaying the situation claim and receive some kudos.

5   The Secretary particularly stressed the impact of statements such as that appearing in the *Times* article on public opinion and in Congress in connection with your request for additional forces. He pointed out that your programs will require the call-up of on the order of 240,000 reservists, extension of terms of service, and authority to call to active duty individuals in the reserve pool. End strength of the armed forces will increase by 450,000 or more by end FY 69. In his view, these requests will be made much harder perhaps impossible to sell if we do not adopt a sober and conservative attitude as to the military, political, economic, and psychological situation in South Vietnam.

6   I pointed out to Secretary Clifford that you have a difficult problem facing you. No commander can afford to be pessimistic and apprehensive in dealing with his troops because such an attitude in the commander engenders poor morale and defeatism in his forces. The Secretary replied that he fully recognized the dilemma facing field commanders in this regard. Nevertheless, he feels that a conservative public stance will be in the over-all benefit to our public image and to the support we will receive for administration policies in pursuing the war to a successful conclusion. He considers that you can tell your senior commanders you are deliberately adopting this attitude for the purposes extensively discussed above and, at the same time, encourage them to approach the job with optimism and an [3 illegible words].

7   I believe this guidance from the Secretary of Defense is so critical to our military effort in Southeast Asia that you should devise some way of passing it on without attribution as command guidance to your commands and public information staffs. Needless to say, if you have comments, I will be please to have them. Warm regards.

Source: *Foreign Relations of the United States, 1964–1968, Volume VI, Vietnam, January–August 1968* (Washington, D.C.: Government Printing Office, 2002), 351–53

President Johnson's remarks to delegates to the National Farmers Union Convention in Minneapolis

March 18, 1968

Now, there is another area in which all Americans—mothers and fathers, farmers and city dwellers—must demonstrate that same courage, that same patience, that same determination.

For many years we have been engaged in a struggle in Southeast Asia to stop the onrushing tide of Communist aggression.

We faced it when the Greek Communists were a few miles out of Athens a few years ago. We faced it when we had to fly zero weather into Berlin to feed the people when that city was beleaguered and cut off. We faced it on the Pusan Peninsula when our men were fighting for the hills of Korea and everybody said, "They are not worth it."

We fight Communist aggression the same today in Southeast Asia. This tide threatens to engulf that part of the world, and to affect the safety of every American home. It threatens our own security and it threatens the security of every nation allied with us. The blood of our young men this hour is being shed on that soil.

They know why they are there. I read 100 letters from them every week. They do not have doubts that some at home preach. They have seen the enemy's determination. They have felt his thrust trying to conquer those who want to be left alone to determine their government for themselves, but whom the aggressor has marched over to try to envelop. Our fighting men know, from the evidence in their eyes, that we face a ruthless enemy. You make a serious mistake if you underestimate that enemy, his cause, and the effect of his conquest. They know from the carnage of the enemy's treacherous assaults that he has no feelings about deliberate murder of innocent women and children in the villages and the cities of South Vietnam.

They are not misled by propaganda or by the effort to gloss over the actions of an enemy who, I remind each of you, has broken every truce, and who makes no secret whatever of his intention and his determination to conquer by force and by aggression his neighbors to the south.

At the same time, during these past four years, we have made remarkable strides here at home.

We have opened the doors of freedom, full citizenship, and opportunity, to 30 million minority people, and we have sustained the highest level of prosperity for the longest period of time ever known.

But the time has come this morning when your President has come here to ask you people, and all the other people of this Nation, to join us in a total national effort to win the war, to win the peace, and to complete the job that must be done here at home.

I ask all of you to join in a program of national austerity to insure that our economy will prosper and that our fiscal position will be sound.

The Congress has been asked by the President—January, a year ago—to enact a tax bill which will impose upon the average citizen an additional one cent for each dollar in taxes. I ask you to bear this burden in the interest of a stronger Nation.

I am consulting with the Congress now on proposals for savings in our national budget—in non-defense, in non-Vietnam, in other items all across the board.

If I can get the help of Congress—and it is their will—we shall make reductions in that budget. They will postpone many needed actions that all of us would like to see taken in another time.

All travel outside the Western Hemisphere by Government officials and by all private citizens which is not absolutely essential to you should, in the interest of your country, be postponed.

I have already called for savings and cuts in expenditures and investments abroad by private corporations. We are going to intensify this program.

We have spent the weekend in an attempt to deal with the very troublesome gold problem. We have said that we are no longer going to be a party to encouraging the gold gambler or the gold speculator.

Most of all, I ask your help, and I come here to plead for your patriotic support, for our men, our sons, who are bearing the terrible burden of battle in Vietnam.

We seek not the victory of conquest, but we do seek the triumph of justice—the right of neighbors to be left alone; the right to determine for themselves what kind of a government to have. We seek that right and we will—make no mistake about it—win.

I am deeply aware of the yearning throughout the country, in every home of this land and throughout the Western world, for peace in the world. I believe all peoples want peace. I know that our peoples want peace, because we are a peace-loving nation. There is none among you who desires peace more than your own President and your own Vice President.

We hope to achieve an honorable peace and a just peace at the negotiation table.

But wanting peace, praying for peace, and desiring peace, as Chamberlain found out, doesn't always give you peace.

If the enemy continues to insist, as he does now—when he refuses to sit down and accept the fair proposition we made, that we would stop our bombing if he would sit down and talk promptly and productively—if he continues to insist, as he does now, that the outcome must be determined on the battlefield, then we will win peace on the battlefield by supporting our men who are doing that job there now.

We have a constitutional system. A majority of Americans have the right to select the leaders of their own choosing.

That is all we are asking for in South Vietnam.

You have provided your President with 100-odd ambassadors, the most trained men in every diplomatic outpost throughout the world.

Through West Point and Annapolis, you have provided your President with the best trained, best educated, most experienced and best led group of men that has ever formulated the strategy or tactics for any nation.

Your President welcomes suggestions from committees, from commissions, from Congress, from private individuals, from clubs, from anyone who has a plan or program that can stand inspection and can offer us any hope of successfully reaching our goal, which is peace in the world.

We consider them all, long and late. We work every day of every week trying to find the answer.

But when aggressors in the world are on the march, as they were in World War I and II, as they were in Korea, as they were in Berlin, and as they were in other places in our national history, then we must unite until we convince them that they know they cannot win the battle in South Vietnam from our boys, as they are trying to win the battle from our leaders here in Washington in this country.

That is very dangerous for them, to think for a moment that they can attack the moral fiber of our own country to the point where our people will not support the policy of their own Government, of their own men whom they have committed to battle.

You may not have a boy in the battle that is going on now—or you may. But whether you do or you don't, our policy ought to be the same. We ought not let them win something in Washington that they can't win in Hue, in the I Corps, or in Khe Sanh. And we are not going to.

Now, this one final word: We ask every Senator, every Congressman, every farmer, and every businessman to join with us in our program of trying to unite this Nation, and trying to support our commitment and our own security.

We thought in the early years of World War I, before the *Lusitania* was sunk, that we had no concern with what happened across the waters. But we soon found out that we couldn't stand on that position.

We thought in World War II that we had no concern with what Hitler was doing in other parts of the world, and he wasn't very dangerous anyway, and we could sit this one out.

But we soon found that we lived in a very small world.

Even though we hadn't gone beyond our shores, they sank our fleet at Pearl Harbor.

We soon learned that we must never permit an aggressor's appetite to go uncontrolled because the person he eats up today may make him more hungry for you tomorrow.

We want peace and we are ready to meet now, this minute.

But you may want peace with your neighbor, too, and you may be willing to go across the road and into his yard to try to talk him into it. But if he keeps his door barred and every time you call him the call goes unanswered, and he refuses to meet you halfway, your wanting peace with him won't get it for you.

So as long as he feels he can win something by propaganda in the country—that he can undermine the leadership—that he can bring down the government—that he can get something in the capital that he can't get from our men out there—he is going to keep on trying.

But I point out to you the time has come when we ought to unite, when we ought to stand up and be counted, when we ought to support our leaders, our Government, our men, and our allies until aggression is stopped, wherever it has occurred.

There are good, sincere, genuine people who believe that there are plans that could bring us peace soon.

Some think that we ought to get it over with, with a much wider war.

We have looked at those plans, and looked at them carefully.

We have looked at the possible danger of involving another million men.

We have tried to evaluate how you could get it over with, with less cost than we are now paying.

We do not seek a wider war. We do not think that is a wise course.

There is another extreme that thinks that you can just have peace by talking for it, by wishing for it, by saying you want it, and all you need to do is to pull back to the cities.

We had that plan tested in the Tet offensive. They killed thousands and thousands in the cities.

Those of you who think that you can save lives by moving the battlefield in from the mountains to the cities where the people live have another think coming.

If you think you can stop aggression by getting out of its way and letting them take over, roll over you, you have another think coming, too.

Most of these people don't say. "Cut and run." They don't say, "Pull out." They don't want a wider war. They don't want to do more than we are doing. They say that they want to do less than we are doing.

But we are not doing enough to win it the way we are doing it now, and we are constantly trying to find additional things that it is reasonable, and prudent, and safe to do.

So you have one extreme that says, "Let's go in with flags flying and get it over with quickly, regardless of the dangers involved."

You have another group that says, "We are doing too much. Let's pull out. Let's be quiet. We want peace."

Then you have third group that says, "We don't want to conquer you. We don't want to destroy your nation. We don't want to divide you. We just want to say to you that we have an obligation. We have signed 42 alliances with people of the world. We have said that when an aggressor comes across this line to try to dominate other people, and they call on us to help, we are going to come and help, until you decide to leave your neighbors alone."

We think that we are making progress on getting them to decide. They think they are making progress on getting us to decide to give up and pull out.

But I think they will find out in the days ahead that we are reasonable people, that we are fair people, that we are not folks who want to conquer the world.

We don't seek one acre of anybody else's soil.

We love nothing more than peace, but we hate nothing more than surrender and cowardice.

We don't ask anybody else to surrender. We just ask them to sit down and talk, meet at a family table and try to work out our differences. But we don't plan to surrender, either; we don't plan to pull out, either; we don't plan to let people influence us, pressure us, and force us to divide our Nation in a time of national peril.

The hour is here.

This Government has the best diplomats. This Government has the best generals. This Government has the best admirals. This Government has the best resources in every corner of the globe.

Although I have had more Secretaries of State than any President in modern times, or more would-be Secretaries of State, I still think this Government has one of the most able and patriotic men I have ever known sitting in that chair, and I think his policy is sound.

So as we go back to our homes, let's go back dedicated to achieving peace in the world, trying to get a fair balance here at home, trying to make things easier and better for our children than we had them, but, above all, trying to preserve this American system, which is first in the world today.

I want it to stay first, but it cannot be first if we pull out and tuck our tail and violate our commitments.

Thank you very much.

Source: *Public Papers of the Presidents, Lyndon B. Johnson, 1968–69, Book I: January 1–June 30, 1968* (Washington, D.C.: Government Printing Office, 1970), 409–13

Telephone conversation between President Johnson and Secretary of Defense Clifford

March 20, 1968

Clifford: One very quick item. I had a telephone call from Mac Bundy yesterday late in the afternoon. I thought he seemed exceedingly friendly and cooperative. Had no sympathy whatsoever for Bobby's entry into the race. We had a little talk about the problems of Vietnam. He said he knew we were going through quite a difficult and critical period and made the offer if he could be of any help at all, you only had to let him know and he would be glad to come down and help. Now I pass it on to you because I thought you might want to consider the advisability—if you thought well of it—of calling him and perhaps asking him to come down. This is a very important speech that has to be written. I spent a couple of hours with Harry McPherson yesterday afternoon and I had the feeling that maybe Mac could be quite useful during this particular period.

President: Yes, I think it would be very good. I think what we've got to do, too, is to get out of the posture of just being the war candidate that McCarthy has put us in and Bobby is putting us in, the kids are putting us in and the papers are putting us in. Lindsay is out advocating rebellions this morning and not responding to the draft and things of that kind. The Mayor urges youth to aid war resistance, and they've got four-column front-page pictures. Now when the head of the biggest city goes to doing things of that kind, you've got to really look at the picture. And I think that if we could get your people, your men like, I don't know who they are over there, I certainly don't want some of the civilians that are giving us trouble, but if we could get, if we had any young men at all, I think Goodpaster is one we ought to look at, DePuy maybe, sit down with some of Rusk's people, one or two there, maybe Habib and perhaps Bill Bundy, and see what it is that we could use with our left hand. Our right hand is going after their jaw with an offense on the war front, but we ought to have a peace front too simultaneously and use both fists—not just one, not fight with one hand behind us, so that we can say we are the peace candidate—but we are the true peace candidate. We're not the Chamberlain peace—we're the Churchill peace. We are not the guy that is going to throw in the towel and let them take Athens.

We are Truman who stands up and finally saves Greece and Turkey from the Communists. And that, of course, there is a temporary peace, and if we surrendered, you would have peace until they got their government installed and then by God you'd have a bigger war than ever. Now we have got to develop that. But in order to do it, we have got to come up with something. Now Goldberg's plan is not worth a damn, but if we could say that we are going to cut off Hanoi and Haiphong for a period, a specific period, now we are not going to touch them, and if they will cut off on the DMZ or some other area, where it's real reciprocation, then we'll respond and something of that type where it's really to our advantage, where the Russells just can't murder us. We ought to do that. We ought to have some kind of something on peace because they're concluding now that we are getting in shape and getting into pretty quick with McNamara's peace talks, his "Harvard stuff," and all the stuff they are putting out—you can see from Nitze's letter—where we are just the Goldwater of '68 and we can't take that.

Clifford: That is right. That is right.

President: We can't take it and hold because people like Daley and them are not going to hold.

Clifford: They won't hold. Really right in there, what it is, we are out to win, but we are not out to win the war—we are out to win the peace.

President: That is right.

Clifford: And that is what our slogan could very well be—win the peace with honor—and I think we have got to get that thought over. Now I have been giving consideration to offers of de-escalation. I don't know whether they have anything, but if we could begin to start a negotiation toward de-escalation, something to the effect that, now if we could have an agreement with the North Vietnamese, that we would let Hanoi alone if they would let Saigon alone. I don't know that it is very practical, but considering something of that kind, we can't stop, but if there is some program of a gradual de-escalation that the parties could get into, we could then get in a better posture.

President: This is right. I don't think they can do it because their announced thing is to do this job this year and that is why they are coming out of the woodworks and hitting us as they are—so they are not going to take anything off-limits. But if we could take something off-limits for a period that didn't really hurt us, and it seems to me that the weather is not too good anyway, and it seems to me that we could say that we're now going for several days without hitting Hanoi and Haiphong—it seems we have gone two months without it—we ought to say that to the public though. And we go in with a sporadic raid, we don't get any real benefit out of it but we say now we are going further, but if you want to respond you let us know and we will go to a Geneva Conference or something. I think you and Rusk ought to try to explore something that we could offer in that way. My own thought is that we ought to stress this peace thing and we ought to stress the permanence of it—and anybody can get an umbrella and have a temporary one, but that just means more people get murdered later—but that we are willing to have a Geneva Conference. We are willing to sit down and pull our troops out of there as soon as the violence subsides. We're willing to take our treasure and go back and help rebuild it as we did under the Marshall Plan and kind of add on to my Johns Hopkins speech a little, add on to Manila a little, but we've got to have something new and fresh that goes in there, along with the statement that we are going to win.

Clifford: Right. But we have to be very careful of what it is we say that we are going to win.

President: That is right.

Clifford: I think we would frighten the people if we just said we are going to win. They would think, "Well, hell, that just means we are going to keep pouring men in until we win militarily," and that isn't what we are after really.

President: Well, your President does and we don't want to appeal to them too much. We have got to appeal to them some but we sure as hell don't want to frighten the people. That's the thing that gives you the most support that you've got and I bet that if you pay a little attention to the 45 percent that want to do more instead of the 5 percent that want to pull out we will have a different attitude. But I just can't ever get Fulbright, but I can't afford to lose Russell. Now, if I lose him, we've got nothing. That's what we have got to remember. So we have got to get something that will not hurt our men materially, like Hanoi and Haiphong for a period, for a month, for two weeks, for something that Buzz Wheeler can tell them we wouldn't do anyway. Then we've got to make that public. We're not going to get these doves, but we can neutralize the country to where it won't follow them if we can come up with something.

Clifford: Yes, that's right. I think you put your finger right on it. We have a posture now in which Kennedy and McCarthy are the peace candidates and President Johnson is the war candidate. Now we must veer away from that and we can do it. What we need is a policy now that is a consistent far-ranging policy, but which we don't have. I think we need a policy of the kind that—say a five-step policy, Mr. President, that we will continue to exert the military pressure. That I know we have to do. We'll never get anything from them if we don't do that. So, as you say, with our right hand we continue to exert the military pressure, then I think we have to have a well thought-out program that we try with our left hand. Step number one. Then that might be some kind of mutual de-escalation that really doesn't hurt us. If it isn't successful, we might move to step number two. Now at some stage in this matter, if nothing else works, then I think we have to keep in mind that before the [Democratic Party National] Convention, then if not before the

Convention, before the election, I think we have to work out some kind of arrangement where we start some kind of negotiation.

President: Well, you can't do that but one way, you know, and these folks are not wanting to do that. They want to get rid of us.

Clifford: I know. Yes, that is right. But I still think there is a good chance to do that if it is prepared properly and if we work up to it in this plan. All I am saying is we don't have such a plan. The major task now is to come up with it and I intend to give a good part of my time and effort to see if we can't come up with such a plan. But what I think at the moment is, with this important speech coming, I think it would be a good idea if you felt well of it to call Mac back and say come on down and help us, Mac, and he offered to do it.

President: Thank you.

Source: *Foreign Relations of the United States, 1964–1968, Volume VI, Vietnam, January–August 1968* (Washington, D.C.: Government Printing Office, 2002), 428–31

Letter from 2nd Lieutenant Ray Smith, USMC, to Captain Batcheller, USMC

March 25, 1968

25 March 68
Phu Bai

Dear Captain Batcheller,

Well, sir, I'm sorry it's taken us so long to write, but we were pretty busy for quite a while. I really don't know how much you've found out about how we did in Hue, so I'll try and go through most of it for you.

As I'm sure you know, the Gunny took the company on in after you were hit. Naturally, he did an outstanding job and when I finally got there on the second of February, everyone had nothing but praise for him.

We got a new Lieutenant and a new—very good—Staff [Sergeant] and they made it up on 1 February. Lieutenant Garter took the company until I got in the next day. Sadly and shitly [sic] as it sounds, Lieutenant Perkins was killed more by accident than anything else. We went in on the 2nd by convoy and had to run a gauntlet of fire from the Phu Com River all the way to MACV. Lieutenant Perkins was on the back of a truckload of ammunition and in the rush the truck hit a huge hole left by a mine. The tailgate dropped and Lieutenant Perkins fell out the back and the truck and load came down on top of him, crushing his chest. We were, however, under heavy fire.

From the first to the 4th, we did no more than hold at MACV, but on the morning of the fourth, we started our attack to the west towards the building complex around the hospital and prison. This day casualty-wise was the worst for us of the entire fight, however we did a fine job. The Joan de Arc high school complex was our first objective—less than 100 yards from MACV. The building was square with an open compound in the middle and we found by about 0700 that it was heavily occupied. Before we secured the complex we lost 3 killed, including Sergeant Gonzales and 24 wounded. However, the large majority of these were minor. Sergeant Gonzales once again did a fine job and knocked out two B-40 rocket positions before he took a direct hit with a B-40. He has been recommended for and stands a good chance of getting the CMH [Medal of Honor].

On the fifth we once again had an extremely rough day, taking 19 casualties with 2 killed we advanced only about 75 yards in doing so. We ran into ARVN compound that the NVA had occupied and we couldn't get into it without crossing a road. We didn't cross the road that day, except for Alpha I, under Lieutenant Donnelly, who got there the evening of the fourth. They got across the street up a ways from the compound and occupied one fairly large building. They were forced to spend the night there and Lieutenant Donnelly plotted an H&I with our 60 mm right on top of his position. They could see the gooks all night moving back and forth from the compound, carrying dead and wounded out and supplies in. At daylight they had 9 NVA kills in the yard so close that the others couldn't get them to drag them away and no telling how many more further out. It was a night that I doubt Lieutenant Donnelly will ever forget. Incidentally, his platoon at that time numbered 19! The new Lieutenant—Garter—was wounded this day we lost him so were back to two officers.

From the sixth on, "A" began to roll and although we took many more casualties we never had another day to match those two.

2/5, 1/5, and "A" pushed west for 3 more days and cleared most of the "new" city west of MACV and east of the Phu Com–Perfume River junctions. On the tenth, along with a militia of cooks etc., that they called "B" company, we returned to MACV and began pushing east from MACV. We cleared about two whole blocks with little trouble and reached the stadium without a casualty. However, as we started east of the stadium we had another road to cross and we humped hard again. Our point was hit crossing the road and they opened up with automatic weapons all along the road. We had had 1 [?] attached since the 5th and he took two direct hits from a 57 recoiller and caught fire. Fortunately, the entire crew made it out with no more than scratches and bruises. They had given us really fine support— firing 700 rounds one day! And we missed them one hell of a lot in the next few days. Anyway, an ARVN major who was home for Tet leave made it out and it turned out we were knocking heads with an NAV battalion with two Soviet 57 recoillers and they even had a Chinese advisor. It turned out that their battalion HQ was in the house right beside the ARVN major's and he had hidden there for 8 or 9 days.

With his support, we got clearance for an [?] fire from the ARVNs—for the first time—so I just pulled back a little ways and started shooting. We fired 250—some 8", 483—155, and all the 81s that we had into that area that day and went in the next morning under gas from E-8 launches. We had some fairly heavy resistance but we cleared it out fairly easily, and found that we had done one hell of a lot of damage—though most of the bodies were carried out during the night. We found where they had had their battalion HQ set up—with NVA flags all around—and by a stroke of fortune we had hit it direct with an 8" round. We'll never know if we got the

Chinaman, but there was quite a lot of blood in the building so it is possible I guess.

From that day on, "A" got some rest and were used mostly for security until we left. We had contact nearly every day, but mostly just scattered snipers and die hards. We left the city on the 3rd of March and have been regrouping, resupplying, and remanning every [sic] since. The regiment is moving north in a few days—up by Khe Sanh—so we're probably not through.

All told, the company did a very fine job in Hue. We have 30-some odd U.S. awards going and 59 Vietnamese. Also, the battalion is supposedly in for the Navy Unit and the division in for the P[residential] U[nit] C[itation]—time will tell, I guess.

Oh, I forgot to mention that Al Courtney was stranded in Da Nang at that school and never joined us in Hue until the 11th of February. He was hit through the calf of his leg on the 13th but is back now.

Our company strength is back up to 157 and we have four lieutenants and—wonder of wonders—four staff [sergeants] and 1 E-5 who has already been picked up for staff [sergeant]. I still have the company—Lieutenant Donnelly has 1st Platoon, Lieutenant Bohlen has 2nd Platoon, and Lieutenant Courtney has 3rd. Al and Rick were just in and said to say "hello." Al says not to do much bug-a-lov-in.

A man couldn't have been with these Marines and Hue and not love them. I had several who had shrapnel in legs and arms who hobbled around and begged me not to medevac them. They did a tremendous job against real odds and I never heard a complaint. In my opinion, any man can be truly proud to say he had Alpha.

Well, I guess I've bragged long enough. You may have already heard all this, but wanted to tell it anyway so bear with it please.

[?] and Gunny both say hello and wish you luck as do I, and we all hope you're up and around soon. You may be pleased to hear that Gunny Conley, whom I consider the best there is, says you did a hell of a job and were definitely in the front and pushing. I'm really sorry that I got fouled up and was not there to help you out.

I guess that's all we have to report now. Again, best of luck to you and keep in touch.

Good luck from us all,
Ray Smith

Source: United States Marine Corps History Division, Gray Research Center, Quantico, Virginia, Box 24: Vietnam, Tet Offensive

Medal of Honor citation for Sergeant Alfredo Gonzales, United States Marine Corps

Rank and organization Sergeant, U.S. Marine Corps, Company A, 1st Battalion, 1st Marines, 1st Marine Division (Rein), FMF.
Place and date Near Thua Thien, Republic of Vietnam, 4 February 1968.
Entered service at San Antonio, Tex.
Born 23 May 1946, Edinburg Tex.
Citation For conspicuous gallantry and intrepidity at the risk of his life above and beyond the call of duty while serving as platoon commander, 3d Platoon, Company A. On 31 January 1968, during the initial phase of Operation Hue City, Sgt Gonzalez' unit was formed as a reaction force and deployed to Hue to relieve the pressure on the beleaguered city. While moving by truck convoy along Route No. 1, near the village of Lang Van Lrong, the marines received a heavy volume of enemy fire. Sgt Gonzalez aggressively maneuvered the marines in his platoon, and directed their fire until the area was cleared of snipers. Immediately after crossing a river south of Hue, the column was again hit by intense enemy fire. One of the marines on top of a tank was wounded and fell to the ground in an exposed position. With complete disregard for his safety, Sgt Gonzalez ran through the fire-swept area to the assistance of his injured comrade. He lifted him up and though receiving fragmentation wounds during the rescue, he carried the wounded marine to a covered position for treatment. Due to the increased volume and accuracy of enemy fire from a fortified machine gun bunker on the side of the road, the company was temporarily halted. Realizing the gravity of the situation, Sgt Gonzalez exposed himself to the enemy fire and moved his platoon along the east side of a bordering rice paddy to a dike directly across from the bunker. Though fully aware of the danger involved, he moved to the fire-swept road and destroyed the hostile position with hand grenades. Although seriously wounded again on 3 February, he steadfastly refused medical treatment and continued to supervise his men and lead the attack. On 4 February, the enemy had again pinned the company down, inflicting heavy casualties with automatic weapons and rocket fire. Sgt Gonzalez, utilizing a number of light antitank assault weapons, fearlessly

moved from position to position firing numerous rounds at the heavily fortified enemy emplacements. He successfully knocked out a rocket position and suppressed much of the enemy fire before falling mortally wounded. The heroism, courage, and dynamic leadership displayed by Sgt Gonzalez reflected great credit upon himself and the Marine Corps, and were in keeping with the highest traditions of the U.S. Naval Service. He gallantly gave his life for his country.

Source: Medals of Honor Recipients, Vietnam War, U.S. Army Center of Military History, http://www.army.mil/cmh-pg/mohviet.htm (accessed July 8, 2007)

President Johnson's address to the nation

March 31, 1968

Good evening, my fellow Americans:

Tonight I want to speak to you of peace in Vietnam and Southeast Asia.

No other question so preoccupies our people. No other dream so absorbs the 250 million human beings who live in that part of the world. No other goal motivates American policy in Southeast Asia.

For years, representatives of our Government and others have traveled the world—seeking to find a basis for peace talks.

Since last September, they have carried the offer that I made public at San Antonio. That offer was this:

That the United States would stop its bombardment of North Vietnam when that would lead promptly to productive discussions—and that we would assume that North Vietnam would not take military advantage of our restraint.

Hanoi denounced this offer, both privately and publicly. Even while the search for peace was going on, North Vietnam rushed their preparations for a savage assault on the people, the government, and the allies of South Vietnam.

Their attack—during the Tet holidays—failed to achieve its principal objectives.

It did not collapse the elected government of South Vietnam or shatter its army—as the Communists had hoped.

It did not produce a "general uprising" among the people of the cities as they had predicted.

The Communists were unable to maintain control of any of the more than 30 cities that they attacked. And they took very heavy casualties.

But they did compel the South Vietnamese and their allies to move certain forces from the countryside into the cities.

They caused widespread disruption and suffering. Their attacks, and the battles that followed, made refugees of half a million human beings.

The Communists may renew their attack any day.

They are, it appears, trying to make 1968 the year of decision in South

Vietnam—the year that brings, if not final victory or defeat, at least a turning point in the struggle.

This much is clear:

If they do mount another round of heavy attacks, they will not succeed in destroying the fighting power of South Vietnam and its allies.

But tragically, this is also clear: Many men—on both sides of the struggle—will be lost. A nation that has already suffered 20 years of warfare will suffer once again. Armies on both sides will take new casualties. And the war will go on.

There is no need for this to be so.

There is no need to delay the talks that could bring an end to this long and this bloody war.

Tonight, I renew the offer I made last August—to stop the bombardment of North Vietnam. We ask that talks begin promptly, that they be serious talks on the substance of peace. We assume that during those talks Hanoi will not take advantage of our restraint.

We are prepared to move immediately toward peace through negotiations.

So, tonight, in the hope that this action will lead to early talks, I am taking the first step to deescalate the conflict. We are reducing—substantially reducing—the present level of hostilities.

And we are doing so unilaterally, and at once.

Tonight, I have ordered our aircraft and our naval vessels to make no attacks on North Vietnam, except in the area north of the demilitarized zone where the continuing enemy buildup directly threatens allied forward positions and where the movements of their troops and supplies are clearly related to that threat.

The area in which we are stopping our attacks includes almost 90 percent of North Vietnam's population, and most of its territory. Thus there will be no attacks around the principal populated areas, or in the food-producing areas of North Vietnam.

Even this very limited bombing of the North could come to an early end—if our restraint is matched by restraint in Hanoi. But I cannot in good conscience stop all bombing so long as to do so would immediately and directly endanger the lives of our men and our allies. Whether a complete bombing halt becomes possible in the future will be determined by events.

Our purpose in this action is to bring about a reduction in the level of violence that now exists.

It is to save the lives of brave men—and to save the lives of innocent women and children. It is to permit the contending forces to move closer to a political settlement.

And tonight, I call upon the United Kingdom and I call upon the Soviet Union—as cochairmen of the Geneva Conferences, and as permanent members of the United Nations Security Council—to do all they can to move from the unilateral act of deescalation that I have just announced toward genuine peace in Southeast Asia.

Now, as in the past, the United States is ready to send its representatives to any forum, at any time, to discuss the means of bringing this ugly war to an end.

I am designating one of our most distinguished Americans, Ambassador Averell Harriman, as my personal representative for such talks. In addition, I have asked Ambassador Llewellyn Thompson, who returned from Moscow for consultation, to be available to join Ambassador Harriman at Geneva or any other suitable place—just as soon as Hanoi agrees to a conference.

I call upon President Ho Chi Minh to respond positively, and favorably, to this new step toward peace.

But if peace does not come now through negotiations, it will come when Hanoi understands that our common resolve is unshakable, and our common strength is invincible.

Tonight, we and the other allied nations are contributing 600,000 fighting men to assist 700,000 South Vietnamese troops in defending their little country.

Our presence there has always rested on this basic belief: the main burden of preserving their freedom must be carried out by them—by the South Vietnamese themselves.

We and our allies can only help to provide a shield behind which the people of South Vietnam can survive and can grow and develop. On their efforts—on their determination and resourcefulness—the outcome will ultimately depend.

That small, beleaguered nation has suffered terrible punishment for more than 20 years.

I pay tribute once again tonight to the great courage and endurance of its people. South Vietnam supports armed forces tonight of almost 700,000 men—and I call your attention to the fact that this is the equivalent of more than 10 million in our own population. Its people maintain their firm determination to be free of domination by the North.

There has been substantial progress, I think, in building a durable government during these last three years. The South Vietnam of 1965 could not have survived the enemy's Tet offensive of 1968. The elected government of South Vietnam survived that attack—and is rapidly repairing the devastation that it wrought.

The South Vietnamese know that further efforts are going to be required:

- to expand their own armed forces,
- to move back into the countryside as quickly as possible,
- to increase their taxes,

- to select the very best men that they have for civil and military responsibility,
- to achieve a new unity within their constitutional government, and
- to include in the national effort all those groups who wish to preserve South Vietnam's control over its own destiny.

Last week President Thieu ordered the mobilization of 135,000 additional South Vietnamese. He plans to reach—as soon as possible—a total military strength of more than 800,000 men.

To achieve this, the Government of South Vietnam started the drafting of 19-year-olds on March 1st. On May 1st, the Government will begin the drafting of 18-year-olds.

Last month, 10,000 men volunteered for military service—that was two and a half times the number of volunteers during the same month last year. Since the middle of January, more than 48,000 South Vietnamese have joined the armed forces—and nearly half of them volunteered to do so.

All men in the South Vietnamese armed forces have had their tours of duty extended for the duration of the war, and reserves are now being called up for immediate active duty.

President Thieu told his people last week:

"We must make greater efforts and accept more sacrifices because, as I have said many times, this is our country. The existence of our nation is at stake, and this is mainly a Vietnamese responsibility."

He warned his people that a major national effort is required to root out corruption and incompetence at all levels of government.

We applaud this evidence of determination on the part of South Vietnam. Our first priority will be to support their effort.

We shall accelerate the reequipment of South Vietnam's armed forces—in order to meet the enemy's increased firepower. This will enable them progressively to undertake a larger share of combat operations against the Communist invaders.

On many occasions I have told the American people that we would send to Vietnam those forces that are required to accomplish our mission there. So, with that as our guide, we have previously authorized a force level of approximately 525,000.

Some weeks ago—to help meet the enemy's new offensive—we sent to Vietnam about 11,000 additional Marine and airborne troops. They were deployed by air in 48 hours, on an emergency basis. But the artillery, tank, aircraft, medical, and other units that were needed to work with and to support these infantry troops in combat could not then accompany them by air on that short notice.

In order that these forces may reach maximum combat effectiveness, the

Joint Chiefs of Staff have recommended to me that we should prepare to send—during the next five months—support troops totaling approximately 13,500 men.

A portion of these men will be made available from our active forces. The balance will come from reserve component units which will be called up for service.

The actions that we have taken since the beginning of the year:

- to reequip the South Vietnamese forces,
- to meet our responsibilities in Korea, as well as our responsibilities in Vietnam,
- to meet price increases and the cost of activating and deploying reserve forces,
- to replace helicopters and provide the other military supplies we need,
- all of these actions are going to require additional expenditures.

The tentative estimate of those additional expenditures is $2.5 billion in this fiscal year, and $2.6 billion in the next fiscal year.

These projected increases in expenditures for our national security will bring into sharper focus the Nation's need for immediate action: action to protect the prosperity of the American people and to protect the strength and the stability of our American dollar.

On many occasions I have pointed out that, without a tax bill or decreased expenditures, next year's deficit would again be around $20 billion. I have emphasized the need to set strict priorities in our spending. I have stressed that failure to act and to act promptly and decisively would raise very strong doubts throughout the world about America's willingness to keep its financial house in order.

Yet Congress has not acted. And tonight we face the sharpest financial threat in the postwar era—a threat to the dollar's role as the keystone of international trade and finance in the world.

Last week, at the monetary conference in Stockholm, the major industrial countries decided to take a big step toward creating a new international monetary asset that will strengthen the international monetary system. I am very proud of the very able work done by Secretary Fowler and Chairman Martin of the Federal Reserve Board.

But to make this system work the United States just must bring its balance of payments to—or very close to—equilibrium. We must have a responsible fiscal policy in this country. The passage of a tax bill now, together with expenditure control that the Congress may desire and dictate, is absolutely necessary to protect this Nation's security, to continue our prosperity, and to meet the needs of our people.

What is at stake is seven years of unparalleled prosperity. In those seven years, the real income of the average American, after taxes, rose by almost 30 percent—a gain as large as that of the entire preceding nineteen years.

So the steps that we must take to convince the world are exactly the steps we must take to sustain our own economic strength here at home. In the past eight months, prices and interest rates have risen because of our inaction.

We must, therefore, now do everything we can to move from debate to action—from talking to voting. There is, I believe—I hope there is—in both Houses of the Congress—a growing sense of urgency that this situation just must be acted upon and must be corrected.

My budget in January was, we thought, a tight one. It fully reflected our evaluation of most of the demanding needs of this Nation.

But in these budgetary matters, the President does not decide alone. The Congress has the power and the duty to determine appropriations and taxes.

The Congress is now considering our proposals and they are considering reductions in the budget that we submitted.

As part of a program of fiscal restraint that includes the tax surcharge, I shall approve appropriate reductions in the January budget when and if Congress so decides that that should be done.

One thing is unmistakably clear, however: our deficit just must be reduced. Failure to act could bring on conditions that would strike hardest at those people that all of us are trying so hard to help.

These times call for prudence in this land of plenty. I believe that we have the character to provide it, and tonight I plead with the Congress and with the people to act promptly to serve the national interest, and thereby serve all of our people.

Now let me give you my estimate of the chances for peace:

- the peace that will one day stop the bloodshed in South Vietnam,
- that will permit all the Vietnamese people to rebuild and develop their land,
- that will permit us to turn more fully to our own tasks here at home.

I cannot promise that the initiative that I have announced tonight will be completely successful in achieving peace any more than the thirty others that we have undertaken and agreed to in recent years.

But it is our fervent hope that North Vietnam, after years of fighting that have left the issue unresolved, will now cease its efforts to achieve a military victory and will join with us in moving toward the peace table.

And there may come a time when South Vietnamese—on both sides—are able to work out a way to settle their own differences by free political choice rather than by war.

As Hanoi considers its course, it should be in no doubt of our intentions. It must not miscalculate the pressures within our democracy in this election year.

We have no intention of widening this war.

But the United States will never accept a fake solution to this long and arduous struggle and call it peace.

No one can foretell the precise terms of an eventual settlement.

Our objective in South Vietnam has never been the annihilation of the enemy. It has been to bring about a recognition in Hanoi that its objective—taking over the South by force—could not be achieved.

We think that peace can be based on the Geneva Accords of 1954—under political conditions that permit the South Vietnamese—all the South Vietnamese—to chart their course free of any outside domination or interference, from us or from anyone else.

So tonight I reaffirm the pledge that we made at Manila—that we are prepared to withdraw our forces from South Vietnam as the other side withdraws its forces to the north, stops the infiltration, and the level of violence thus subsides.

Our goal of peace and self-determination in Vietnam is directly related to the future of all of Southeast Asia—where much has happened to inspire confidence during the past ten years. We have done all that we knew how to do to contribute and to help build that confidence.

A number of its nations have shown what can be accomplished under conditions of security. Since 1966, Indonesia, the fifth largest nation in all the world, with a population of more than 100 million people, has had a government that is dedicated to peace with its neighbors and improved conditions for its own people. Political and economic cooperation between nations has grown rapidly.

I think every American can take a great deal of pride in the role that we have played in bringing this about in Southeast Asia. We can rightly judge—as responsible Southeast Asians themselves do—that the progress of the past three years would have been far less likely—if not completely impossible—if America's sons and others had not made their stand in Vietnam.

At Johns Hopkins University, about three years ago, I announced that the United States would take part in the great work of developing Southeast Asia, including the Mekong Valley, for all the people of that region. Our determination to help build a better land—a better land for men on both sides of the present conflict—has not diminished in the least. Indeed, the ravages of war, I think, have made it more urgent than ever.

So, I repeat on behalf of the United States again tonight what I said at Johns Hopkins—that North Vietnam could take its place in this common effort just as soon as peace comes.

Over time, a wider framework of peace and security in Southeast Asia may become possible. The new cooperation of the nations of the area could be a foundation-stone. Certainly friendship with the nations of such a Southeast Asia is what the United States seeks—and that is all that the United States seeks.

One day, my fellow citizens, there will be peace in Southeast Asia.

It will come because the people of Southeast Asia want it—those whose armies are at war tonight, and those who, though threatened, have thus far been spared.

Peace will come because Asians were willing to work for it—and to sacrifice for it—and to die by the thousands for it.

But let it never be forgotten: peace will come also because America sent her sons to help secure it.

It has not been easy—far from it. During the past 4½ years, it has been my fate and my responsibility to be Commander in Chief. I have lived—daily and nightly—with the cost of this war. I know the pain that it has inflicted. I know, perhaps better than anyone, the misgivings that it has aroused.

Throughout this entire, long period, I have been sustained by a single principle: that what we are doing now, in Vietnam, is vital not only to the security of Southeast Asia, but it is vital to the security of every American.

Surely we have treaties which we must respect. Surely we have commitments that we are going to keep. Resolutions of the Congress testify to the need to resist aggression in the world and in Southeast Asia.

But the heart of our involvement in South Vietnam—under three different presidents, three separate administrations—has always been America's own security.

And the larger purpose of our involvement has always been to help the nations of Southeast Asia become independent and stand alone, self-sustaining, as members of a great world community—at peace with themselves, and at peace with all others.

With such an Asia, our country—and the world—will be far more secure than it is tonight.

I believe that a peaceful Asia is far nearer to reality because of what America has done in Vietnam. I believe that the men who endure the dangers of battle—fighting there for us tonight—are helping the entire world avoid far greater conflicts, far wider wars, far more destruction, than this one.

The peace that will bring them home someday will come. Tonight I have offered the first in what I hope will be a series of mutual moves toward peace.

I pray that it will not be rejected by the leaders of North Vietnam. I pray that they will accept it as a means by which the sacrifices of their own people may be ended. And I ask your help and your support, my fellow citizens, for this effort to reach across the battlefield toward an early peace.

Finally, my fellow Americans, let me say this:

Of those to whom much is given, much is asked. I cannot say and no man could say that no more will be asked of us.

Yet, I believe that now, no less than when the decade began, this generation of Americans is willing to "pay any price, bear any burden, meet any hardship, support any friend, oppose any foe to assure the survival and the success of liberty."

Since those words were spoken by John F. Kennedy, the people of America have kept that compact with mankind's noblest cause.

And we shall continue to keep it.

Yet, I believe that we must always be mindful of this one thing, whatever the trials and the tests ahead. The ultimate strength of our country and our cause will lie not in powerful weapons or infinite resources or boundless wealth, but will lie in the unity of our people.

This I believe very deeply.

Throughout my entire public career I have followed the personal philosophy that I am a free man, an American, a public servant, and a member of my party, in that order always and only.

For 37 years in the service of our Nation, first as a Congressman, as a Senator, and as Vice President, and now as your President, I have put the unity of the people first. I have put it ahead of any divisive partisanship.

And in these times as in times before, it is true that a house divided against itself by the spirit of faction, of party, of region, of religion, of race, is a house that cannot stand.

There is division in the American house now. There is divisiveness among us all tonight. And holding the trust that is mine, as President of all the people, I cannot disregard the peril to the progress of the American people and the hope and the prospect of peace for all peoples.

So, I would ask all Americans, whatever their personal interests or concern, to guard against divisiveness and all its ugly consequences.

Fifty-two months and 10 days ago, in a moment of tragedy and trauma, the duties of this office fell upon me. I asked then for your help and God's, that we might continue America on its course, binding up our wounds, healing our history, moving forward in new unity, to clear the American agenda and to keep the American commitment for all of our people.

United we have kept that commitment. United we have enlarged that commitment.

Through all time to come, I think America will be a stronger nation, a more just society, and a land of greater opportunity and fulfillment because of what we have all done together in these years of unparalleled achievement.

Our reward will come in the life of freedom, peace, and hope that our children will enjoy through ages ahead.

What we won when all of our people united just must not now be lost in suspicion, distrust, selfishness, and politics among any of our people.

Believing this as I do, I have concluded that I should not permit the Presidency to become involved in the partisan divisions that are developing in this political year.

With America's sons in the fields far away, with America's future under challenge right here at home, with our hopes and the world's hopes for peace in the balance every day, I do not believe that I should devote an hour or a day of my time to any personal partisan causes or to any duties other than the awesome duties of this office—the Presidency of your country.

Accordingly, I shall not seek, and I will not accept, the nomination of my party for another term as your President.

But let men everywhere know, however, that a strong, a confident, and a vigilant America stands ready tonight to seek an honorable peace—and stands ready tonight to defend an honored cause—whatever the price, whatever the burden, whatever the sacrifice that duty may require.

Thank you for listening.

Good night and God bless all of you.

NOTE: The President spoke at 9 p.m. in his office at the White House. The address was broadcast nationally.

Source: *Public Papers of the Presidents of the United States: Lyndon B. Johnson, 1968–69, Book 1: January 1–June 30, 1968* (Washington, D.C.: Government Printing Office, 1970), 469–76

Report on Operation Bigbuild

c. July 1968

1   Purpose—To describe and analyze the building operation, deriving lessons of lasting value in Civic Action work there from.

2   Summary of operation—The original task was to put a roof over the head of every Vietnamese family who had lost their home during the Tet Offensive. Original estimates were around 2,000 houses destroyed during Tet and as many as 934 more during the May 5th Offensive and June 4th hostilities. It is submitted that these figures are subject to question in as much as there were different people using different criteria in determining the degree of damage or destruction to the houses. In other words, the totally destroyed figure was somewhat higher than the actual number of unrepairable houses.

The process was part of a three-step Revolutionary Development program involving the GVN primarily and augmented by the U.S.

(a) Step I—Payment of $3,000 VN for emergency refugee relief and $5,000 VN for total destruction of the house.

(b) Step II—10 sheets of tin and 10 bags of cement were distributed by the GVN and in some cases transported by 25th Infantry Division.

(c) Step III—Enough lumber was distributed by the 25th Infantry Division to build a 10 ft × 16 ft house. This was either delivered to the Village in packets as in Cu Chi District or placed on the building site as in Phu Hoa District. In addition, the 25th Infantry Division agree to provide 50 U.S. troops to help build in Phu Hoa District.

Another aspect of the program was for the U.S. to provide scrap lumber to help rebuild those houses which were not considered destroyed, and also the scrap lumber could be used for furniture, house sidings, and other uses.

3   Each local situation was unique, but generally the situations were as follows:

(a) During the Tet Offensive, the people had moved out of their ham-
     lets and sought refuge where they could.
(b) The people returned to find their homes damaged or destroyed and
     were provided shelter by neighbors or relatives.
(c) The people began to clear the land by hand and build lean-to's
     when possible.
(d) Later, the land was cleared by local contractors and U.S. engineer
     units when it was not possible to do it by hand.
(e) Even though some cement and tin was delivered, construction was
     not started to any great extent in either District until the lumber
     arrived.

Hau Nghia province, Cu Chi district

1   Tan Phu Trung Village (XT 7008, 6909, & 6808)

(a) Most of the 750 families whose house [sic] were estimated des-
     troyed returned to their hamlets and received their allotments from
     each of the three steps and also received scrap lumber. The U.S.
     troops did not actually help to build in this area.
(b) The people are still reconstructing their homes by themselves on
     the land cleared by the contractors and 169th Engr Bn. Their pro-
     gress has been slow but they have constructed over 600 homes to
     date.
(c) There was fair to excellent cooperation by local GVN officials and
     as each packet of lumber was handed out, a signature was received
     by the officials. In fact, 775 packets were handed out in this
     area since there were more houses destroyed during the May 5th
     Offensive.
(d) The People's attitudes towards the U.S. and GVN have improved
     slowly over the past few months. Their standard of living has been
     raised along with their improvement in health. The people are also
     proving to be a valuable source of information for the RF/PF
     elements in the area. This is natural since the role of the GVN
     was emphasized more that [sic] the role of the U.S.

2   Tan Thong Hamlet (XT 6610)

(a) This area received 220 packets of lumber for the houses destroyed
     during the Tet Offensive and the houses destroyed during the May
     5th Offensive. The area also received scrap lumber.
(b) The tin, cement, and money have not been delivered in sufficient
     quantities for the people to reconstruct as quickly as in other areas.
     This was due to the fact that the GVN has not yet declared the May

5th Offensive to be part of the Tet Offensive and therefore not under the program.

(c) It was decided by District Officials that these people should received [sic] the lumber packets on a priority basis since that may be all they will receive unless the GVN changes its decision not to put Tan Thong under the RD progress.

(d) The future of the project in this area depends upon the resources and energies of the people who have reconstructed around 40 houses to date.

(e) The people's attitudes vary quite a bit in this hamlet and there is still a strong VC faction in the hamlet which has not been disturbed by the program. However, some of the middle-of-the-road people are more loyal to the GVN and their friendliness is reflected in their cooperation in Medcaps and other RD programs such as rebuilding the school.

3   Bau Tre Hamlet (XT 6113)

(a) During the latter part of the Tet Offensive, the VC used the outside of the Hamlet as an ambush site. During the fight that followed, the Hamlet itself was hit. The 25th Infantry Division paid solatium immediately. In addition, the GVN and U.S. provided tin, cement, money and scrap lumber to the area.

(b) The people then rebuilt their homes with these assets and no further contribution was needed. However, the RF/PF outpost was strengthened to give the people more protection against the VC.

(c) This area is still contested and most of the psychological and intelligence advantage have gone to the GVN of late.

4   Cay Trom Hamlet (XT 5815)

(a) This Hamlet was hit recently during an ambush on a convoy. Over 60 houses were reported destroyed. The GVN and the U.S. reacted the next day with food, clothing, and scrap lumber. Solatium payments were made by the ¾ Cav.

(b) This area is already being repaired by the people.

(c) The people have reacted aggressively offering intelligence information concerning VC troop locations when those locations might endanger U.S. troops conducting Medcaps.

Binh Duong province, Phu Hoa district

1   Trung An Village (XT 7613)

(a) This hamlet is the model area where the project worked the best.

The lumber was taken out and distributed on the site as needed to build a 10 ft x 16 ft house.

(b) The 25th Infantry Division provided approximately 50 personnel and the GVN provided 59 RD Cadre and 50 ARVNs to help build the houses. The GVN also paid the $8,000 VN and provided the tin on location. The U.S. transported the GVN's cement to the site from Tu Duc.

(c) Construction went well until the May 5th Offensive which halted work by U.S. personnel. The people and the RD Cadre continued slowly until the U.S. troops returned and quickened the pace. The U.S. troops delivered 255 increments of lumber and cement and worked with the people until 200 houses were finished. The RD Cadre then asked that they and the people finish by themselves. This was done and 257 houses were finished.

(d) This village had been considered a VC/NVA stronghold up until the start of the program. After the program the [?] was considered contested on the Hamlet Evaluation rating. The people have been responsive, friendly, and an excellent source of intelligence information. A number of VC families have been turned in by the people. One individual was a VC paymaster who had been operating in the area for years without detection. VC tax collectors have also been shot at by the now aggressive RD Cadre. In addition, the people tell us that never again will the VC be allowed to cause the destruction of their homes.

2   Paris Tan Qui Village (XT 7214)

(a) The U.S. troops moved in without full cooperation of the village officials. The District Chief was hesitant about beginning construction around Paris Tan Qui even though he had been enthusiastic about it before the May 5th Offensive. He was also in the process of changing Village Chiefs and the new Village Chief was unfamiliar with what was going on. After several inquiries were made to District and Province level officials, cooperation was forthcoming from the GVN, District, and local officials. RD Cadre were moved in the area to help, but the people were still afraid of the VC and NVA and hesitant to relocate their homes.

(b) There were 71 houses constructed on a location around the hamlet of Paris Tan Qui which was to become the Village of Paris Tan Qui. About 710 sheets of tin and 300 bags of cement were used, but the project was stopped at that time because of the lack of cooperation from the people.

(c) Relocation was forced by the GVN and approximately 70 families have moved in from the hamlet of Bau Tram. The fear was caused by a combination of factors. The VC had fair control of the village and threatened harm to those who would move in. Another argument used by the VC was that the GVN would make prisoners of those who moved in. The people also wanted to be close to their fields, water holes, and Buddhist family altars. In addition the area was full of unexploded ordnance which was removed. These factors were overcome in part and are still being fought.

3   Tan Thanh Dong Village (XT 7511)

   (a) This project showed a great deal of promise from the start and worked quite well due to the strong leadership of the Village Chief and the aid of the ARVN 1/7th Bn and RD Cadre.

   (b) The project was underway when the U.S. troops arrived. The U.S. had delivered the GVN cement and U.S. scrap lumber. The tin had been delivered in part and 108 houses had been built by the RD Cadre and the people.

   (c) Around 250 houses were reported destroyed during the Tet Offensive and another 100 to 400 during the May 5th and June 4th Offensives. The building teams each consisting of 2 or 3 U.S. and 1 or 2 RD Cadre could construct about 2 frames a day with the help of the people. This meant that about 20 frames a day could be constructed under optimum conditions.

   (d) The people were helpful and learned to cooperate with the teams. The people also pointed out booby traps and unexploded ordnance which was taken care of by EOD Teams.

   (e) The people reacted well to the program and in some cases a citizen would come in and tell the ARVNs that the VC/NVA troops were in their homes or out in their fields. A large number of VC/NVA were killed and a few captured as a result of this information. It is interesting to note these people did this even though they knew their houses would be destroyed.

   (f) Other Civic Action work has been carried out in the area including festivals and Medcaps which have continued to improve the area for the GVN and erode away the control of the VC.

4   Phu Hoa Dong Village (XT 7118)

   (a) Original estimates of the destruction during Tet showed 230 homes destroyed.

   (b) By the time the U.S. team arrived with the materials, most of the houses had already been reconstructed by RD Cadre and the people or abandoned. The District and 3/7th ARVN Bn leaders desired relocation of some of the people from the hamlet of Phu Thuan (XT 7218 & 7219) which is reportedly a VC/NVA stronghold.

(c) A plan was decided upon and construction of the resettlement subdivision in the middle of Phu Hoa Dong (XT 715192) was begun.

(d) Construction was halted at 50 houses due to lack of cooperation of the people.

(e) The VC/NVA forces were also aware of the impact of the project and they fought hard to deep [sic] the people from moving into the new area. Even those people who hade [sic] made application were scared off by VC/NVA propaganda and terrorist attacks.

Conclusions

1   Almost 1,000 bd ft of scrap lumber have been delivered to the villages and District Subsectors. As many as 3,000 dwellings have been repaired with this material and hundreds of other uses have been made of this lumber. A careful study of its uses shows that most of the lumber benefited the people either directly or indirectly. Generally, this project carried a high impact effect on the two Districts and hopefully will save lives by reason of the loss of control of VC/NVA forces noted above.

2   The image of the GVN and U.S. has been enhanced since there was a promise of help and that promise was kept. A great deal of intelligence information has been gathered and will continue to be gathered as a result of the changes in attitude noted above.

3   There were different approaches taken by the 25th Infantry Division in each District.

(a) The first approach, used in Cu Chi, was to figure out how much lumber it would take to build the 10 ft x16 ft house bundle and deliver it to the Village. From there, it was up to the people to gather their tin, cement, and lumber and make their own house.

(b) The second approach used in Phu Hoa was to actually help build on the site chosen by District officials. This involved transportation of U.S. lumber and GVN cement to the site by the 25th Infantry Division soldiers, 59 RD Cadre, and 50 RF/PF soldiers helped build the houses or secure the building sites. The number of men varied in each area but the principal [sic] of total involvement was adhered to.

(c) Generally, both methods worked well but more houses were actually built where the 25th Division actually helped. That is even though 1,000 packets of lumber were delivered to the Cu Chi District, only 598 houses have been constructed to date. On the other hand, the people are still building in Cu Chi. In Phu Hoa District, 741 houses were built. However, a problem was encountered when it was decided by district officials to build on relocation sites rather than the site of the destroyed homes. This meant that the people were not as helpful nor were they as anxious to move in and finish their houses.

4   After weighing the advantages and disadvantages of both approaches, it is submitted that the second approach is better. The reasons for this are as follows:

(a) The U.S. soldiers had an opportunity to work in the field and meet the people.
(b) The people were enlightened by the contact with a different type of soldier than they had seen in the past.
(c) The impact on VC/NVA propaganda was greater in so far as it showed they had been lying about the U.S.
(d) The intelligence gathered was greater in Phu Hoa.
(e) The total involvement of U.S., ARVN, RF/PF, RD Cadre, District officials, and Province officials graphically demonstrated that all these people could get together and work for a common goal.
(f) The impact on the security of the area was greater as demonstrated by the change in the Hamlet Evaluation status of many of the Hamlets.
(g) The people were assured of getting enough lumber for their house and more importantly enough lumber of the right size.

5   All of the above benefits that have been received have not been as great as the benefits to the people themselves. Most of those who wanted a house and were willing to work for it now have it. Over 1,440 houses have been built, over 3,000 repaired, and another 295 were relocated in Trung Nhi with only scrap lumber assistance from the U.S. Also, the people are still building in both districts.

The main lesson learned is that the people must cooperate in order to get any Civic Action done. The VC/NVA element can be a detriment, but not a stoppage if the people really want the houses. All of the normal problems of supply and coordination can be solved, if and only if, the people are willing to work.

Source: "Operation Bigbuild," Civic Action Program, 25th Infantry, VNIT 233, U.S. Army Center of Military History, Fort McNair, Washington, D.C.

Notes

1 Military Institute of Vietnam, *Victory in Vietnam: The Official History of the People's Army of Vietnam, 1954–1975* (Lawrence: University Press of Kansas, 2002), 214–15.
2 Van Tran Tra, "Tet: The 1968 General Offensive and General Uprising," in Jayne S. Werner and Luu Doan Huynh, eds, *The Vietnam War: Vietnamese and American Perspectives* (Armonk, New York: M. E. Sharpe, 1992), 40.
3 Peter Macdonald, *Giap: The Victor in Vietnam* (New York: Norton, 1993), 260.
4 William C. Westmoreland, *A Soldier Reports* (New York: Da Capo Press, 1989), 310–11.
5 James H. Willbanks, *The Tet Offensive: A Concise History* (New York: Columbia University Press, 2007), 10–11.
6 William J. Duiker, *Sacred War: Nationalism and Revolution in a Divided Vietnam* (New York: McGraw-Hill, 1995), 208–10.
7 James Arnold, *Tet Offensive 1968: Turning Point in Vietnam* (Westport, Connecticut: Praeger Publishers, 2004), 13.
8 Don Oberdorfer, *Tet! The Turning Point in the Vietnam War* (New York: Da Capo, 1984), 54.
9 Gabriel Kolko, *Anatomy of a War: Vietnam, the United States, and the Modern Historical Experience* (New York: The New Press, 1994), 303.
10 Marilyn Young, *The Vietnam Wars: 1945–1990* (New York: HarperCollins, 1991), 216.
11 William S. Turley, *The Second Indochina War: A Short Political and Military History, 1954–1975* (Boulder: Westview Press, 1986), 100.
12 Gary R. Hess, *Vietnam and the United States: Origins and Legacy of War*, revised edn (New York: Twayne Publishers, 1998), 101.
13 George Donelson Moss, *Vietnam: An American Ordeal*, 4th edn (Upper Saddle River, New Jersey: Prentice Hall, 2002), 276–77.
14 Ronnie E. Ford, *Tet: Understanding the Surprise* (London: Frank Cass, 1995), 193.
15 George C. Herring, *America's Longest War: The United States and Vietnam, 1950–1975*, 4th edn (Boston: McGraw-Hill, 2002), 226–27.
16 John Prados, "Intelligence at Tet," in Jason Marc Gilbert and William Head, eds, *The Tet Offensive* (Westport, Connecticut: Praeger Publishers), 142–65.
17 James J. Wirtz, *The Tet Offensive: Intelligence Failure in War* (Ithaca: Cornell University Press, 1991), 252–75.
18 Ronnie Ford, *Tet 1968*, 167.
19 Larry Cable, "'Don't Bother Me with the Facts; I've Made up My Mind': The

Tet Offensive in the Context of Intelligence and U.S. Strategy," in Gilbert and Head, eds, *The Tet Offensive*, 167–80.

20 Willbanks, *The Tet Offensive*, 98.

21 Quoted in MacDonald, *Giap*, 290.

22 Westmoreland, *A Soldier Reports*, 336–37.

23 Neil Sheehan, *A Bright Shining Lie: John Paul Vann and American in Vietnam* (New York: Random House, 1988), 710.

24 John Prados and Ray Stubbe, *Valley of Decision: The Siege of Khe Sanh* (Boston: Houghton Mifflin, 1991), 451–56.

25 George R. Vickers, "U.S. Military Strategy and the Vietnam War," in Werner and Huynh, eds, *The Vietnam War*, 120.

26 Tran Van Tra, "Tet: The 1968 General Offensive and General Uprising," in Werner and Huynh, eds, *The Vietnam War*, 45.

27 Peter Brush, "The Battle of Khe Sanh, 1968," Gilbert and Head, eds, *The Tet Offensive*, 207–10.

28 Willbanks, *The Tet Offensive*, 104–5.

29 William S. Turley, *The Second Indochina War: A Short Political and Military History, 1954–1975* (Boulder: Westview Press, 1986), 105.

30 Wirtz, *The Tet Offensive*, 76–81.

31 Phillip B. Davidson, *Vietnam at War: The History, 1946–1975* (New York: Oxford University Press, 1988), 444–45.

32 Ang Cheng Guan, "Khe Sanh—From the Perspective of the North Vietnamese Communists," *War in History* Vol. 8, No. 1 (2001): 95–98.

33 Duiker, *Sacred War*, 213.

34 Oberdorfer, *Tet!*, 35–40.

35 Moss, *Vietnam: An American Ordeal*, 278.

36 William M. Hammond, *Reporting Vietnam: Media and Military at War* (Lawrence: University Press of Kansas, 1998), 109–13.

37 Ford, *Tet 1968*, 129.

38 Arnold, *Tet Offensive 1968*, 86–87.

39 Stanley Karnow, *Vietnam: A History* (New York: Penguin, 1984), 549.

40 Chester J. Pach, "The War on Television: TV News, the Johnson Administration, and Vietnam," in Marilyn B. Young and Robert Buzzanco, eds, *A Companion to the Vietnam War* (Oxford: Blackwell, 2002), 464.

41 Chester Pach, "TV's 1968: War, Politics, and Violence on the Network Evening News," *South Central Review* Vol. 16, No. 4 (Winter 1999–Spring 2000): 33.

42 Oberdorfer, *Tet*, 331–33.

43 Kathleen J. Turner, *Lyndon Johnson's Dual War: Vietnam and the Press* (Chicago: University of Chicago Press, 1985), 217–19.

44 Peter Braestrup, *Big Story: How the American Press and Television Reported and Interpreted the Crisis of Tet 1968 in Vietnam and Washington*, 2 vols (Boulder, Colorado: Westview Press, 1977), 1: 288.

45 Hammond, *Reporting Vietnam*, 122.

46 Daniel Hallin, *The "Uncensored War:" The Media and Vietnam* (New York: Oxford University Press, 1986), 170–78.

47 David F. Schmitz, *The Tet Offensive: Politics, War, and Public Opinion* (Lanham, Maryland: Rowman and Littlefield, 2005), 163–64.

48 Willbanks, *The Tet Offensive*, 117.

49 David Culbert, "Television's Visual Impact on Decision-Making in the USA, 1968: The Tet Offensive and Chicago's Democratic National Convention," *Journal of Contemporary History* Vol. 33, No. 3 (July 1998): 434.

50 Herring, *America's Longest War*, 241–45.
51 Michael Lind, *Vietnam: The Necessary War* (New York: The Free Press, 1999), 21.
52 Kolko, *Anatomy of a War*, 303, 337.
53 Ronald H. Spector, *After Tet: The Bloodiest Year in Vietnam* (New York: Vintage Books, 1993), 311–13.
54 Tran Van Tra, "Tet: The 1968 General Offensive and General Uprising," 60–61.
55 Cecil Curry, *Victory at Any Cost: The Genius of Viet Nam's General Vo Nguyen Giap* (Washington: Brassey's, 1997), 269–70.
56 Quoted in MacDonald, *Giap*, 269.
57 Westmoreland, *A Soldier Reports*, 333–34.
58 Duiker, *Sacred War*, 217–18.
59 Schmitz, *The Tet Offensive*, 166–67.
60 Willbanks, *The Tet Offensive*, 84–85.
61 Larry Berman, *Lyndon Johnson's War* (New York: Norton, 1989), 176–203.
62 David M. Barrett, *Uncertain Warriors: Lyndon Johnson and His Vietnam Advisors* (Lawrence: University Press of Kansas, 1993), 109–59.
63 George C. Herring, *LBJ and Vietnam: A Different Kind of War* (Austin: University of Texas Press, 1994), 170–79.
64 Lloyd C. Gardner, *Pay Any Price: Lyndon Johnson and the Wars for Vietnam* (Chicago: Ivan R. Dee, 1995), 535–37.
65 Victor Davis Hansen, "The Meaning of Tet," *American Heritage* Vol. 52, No. 3 (May 2001): 45–46.
66 Oberdorfer, *Tet*, ix.
67 Robert Buzzanco, "The Myth of Tet: American Failure and the Politics of War," Gilbert and Head, eds, *The Tet Offensive*, 231–33.

Bibliography

Anderson, David L. *The Vietnam War*. New York: Palgrave Macmillan, 2005.

Appy, Christian. *Patriots: The Vietnam War Remembered from All Sides*. New York: Penguin, 2003.

Arnold, James. *Tet Offensive 1968: Turning Point in Vietnam*. Westport, Connecticut: Praeger Publishers, 2004.

Bach, Vu, *et al. The 30-Year War, 1945–1975*. Hanoi: The Gioi Publishers, 2000.

Baritz, Loren. *Backfire: Vietnam—The Myths that Made Us Fight, the Illusions that Helped Us Lose, the Legacy that Haunts Us Today*. New York: Ballantine Books, 1985.

Barrett, David M. *Uncertain Warriors: Lyndon Johnson and His Vietnam Advisors*. Lawrence: University Press of Kansas, 1993.

Berman, Larry. *Lyndon Johnson's War*. New York: Norton, 1989.

Braestrup, Peter. *Big Story: How the American Press and Television Reported and Interpreted the Crisis of Tet 1968 in Vietnam and Washington*. 2 vols. Boulder, Colorado: Westview Press, 1977.

Brown, Jim. *Impact Zone: The Battle of the DMZ in Vietnam, 1967–1968*. Tuscaloosa: University of Alabama Press, 2004.

Brown, Richard L. *Palace Gate: Under Siege in Hue City, Tet, January 1968*. London: Schiffer, 1997.

Buzzanco, Robert. *Masters of War: Military Dissent and Politics in the Vietnam Era*. New York: Cambridge University Press, 1996.

Cable, Larry. *Unholy Grail: The U. S. and the Wars in Vietnam, 1965–1968*. New York: Routledge, 1991.

Campagna, Anthony S. *The Economic Consequences of the Vietnam War*. Westport, Connecticut: Praeger Publishers, 1991.

Coan, James P. *Con Thien: The Hill of Angels*. Tuscaloosa: University of Alabama Press, 2004.

Culbert, David. "Television's Visual Impact on Decision-Making in the USA, 1968: The Tet Offensive and Chicago's Democratic National Convention." *Journal of Contemporary History* 33, No. 3 (July 1998): 419–49

Curry, Cecil. *Victory at Any Cost: The Genius of Viet Nam's General Vo Nguyen Giap*. Washington: Brassey's, 1997.

Davidson, Phillip B. *Vietnam at War: The History, 1946–1975*. New York: Oxford University Press, 1988.

Duiker, William J. *Sacred War: Nationalism and Revolution in a Divided Vietnam*. New York: McGraw-Hill, 1995.

Elliott, David W. P. *The Vietnamese War: Revolution and Social Change in the Mekong Delta, 1930–1975*. 2 vols. Armonk, New York: M. E. Sharpe, 2003.

Errington, Elizabeth Jane, and B. J. C. McKercher, eds. *The Vietnam War as History*. Westport, Connecticut: Praeger Publishers, 1990.

Falk, Richard. *Appropriating Tet*. Princeton: Princeton University Center of International Studies, 1988.

FitzGerald, Frances. *Fire in the Lake: The Vietnamese and the Americans in Vietnam*. New York: Vintage Books, 1972.

Ford, Ronnie E. *Tet 1968: Understanding the Surprise*. London: Frank Cass, 1995.

Gaiduk, Ilya V. *The Soviet Union and the Vietnam War*. Chicago: Ivan R. Dee, 1996.

Gardner, Lloyd C. *Pay Any Price: Lyndon Johnson and the Wars for Vietnam*. Chicago: Ivan R. Dee, 1995.

Gilbert, Marc Jason, ed. *Why the North Won the Vietnam War*. New York: Palgrave, 2002.

Gilbert, Marc Jason, and William Head, eds. *The Tet Offensive*. Westport, Connecticut: Praeger Publishers, 1996.

Guan, Ang Chen. "Decision-Making Leading to the Tet Offensive (1968)—The Vietnamese Perspective." *Journal of Contemporary History* 33, No. 3 (July 1998): 341–53.

Guan, Ang Chen. "Khe Sanh—From the Perspective of the North Vietnamese Communists." *War in History* 8, No. 1 (2001): 87–98.

Hallin, Daniel. *The "Uncensored War": The Media and Vietnam*. New York: Oxford University Press, 1986.

Hammel, Eric. *Khe Sanh: Siege in the Clouds*. New York: Crown Publishers, 1989.

Hammel, Eric. *Fire in the Streets: The Battle for Hue, Tet, 1968*. Chicago: Contemporary Books, 1991.

Hammond, William M. *Reporting Vietnam: Media and Military at War*. Lawrence: University Press of Kansas, 1998.

Hansen, Victor Davis. "The Meaning of Tet." *American Heritage* 52, No. 3 (May 2001): 44–56.

Hearden, Patrick J. *The Tragedy of Vietnam*. 2nd ed. New York: Pearson Longman, 2005.

Herring, George C. *LBJ and Vietnam: A Different Kind of War*. Austin: University of Texas Press, 1994.

Herring, George C. *America's Longest War: The United States and Vietnam, 1950–1975*. 4th ed. Boston: McGraw Hill, 2002.

Hess, Gary R. *Vietnam and the United States: Origins and Legacy of War*. Revised ed. New York: Twayne Publishers, 1998.

Hoang, Ngoc Lung. *The General Offensives of 1968–69*. Washington, D.C.: U.S. Army Center of Military History, 1981.

Hunt, Michael H. *Lyndon Johnson's War: America's Cold War Crusade, 1945–1968*. New York: Hill and Wang, 1996.

Hunt, Richard A. *Pacification: The American Struggle for Vietnam's Hearts and Minds*. Boulder, Colorado: Westview Press, 1995.

Isserman, Maurice, and Michael Kazin. *America Divided: The Civil War of the 1960s*. 3rd ed. New York: Oxford University Press, 2008.

Karnow, Stanley. *Vietnam: A History*. New York: Penguin, 1984.

Kolko, Gabriel. *Anatomy of a War: Vietnam, the United States, and the Modern Historical Experience*. New York: The New Press, 1994.

Krepinevich, Andrew F. *The Army and Vietnam*. Baltimore: Johns Hopkins University Press, 1986.

LaFeber, Walter. *The Deadly Bet: LBJ, Vietnam, and the 1968 Election*. Lanham, Maryland: Rowman and Littlefield, 2005.

Langguth, A. J. *Our Vietnam: The War, 1954–1975*. New York: Simon and Schuster, 2000.

Lewis, Adrian R. *The American Culture of War: The History of U.S. Military Force from World War II to Operation Iraqi Freedom*. New York: Routledge, 2007.

Lewy, Guenter. *America in Vietnam*. New York: Oxford University Press, 1980.

Lind, Michael. *Vietnam: The Necessary War*. New York: The Free Press, 1999.

Long, Ngo Vinh. *The Tet Offensive and Its Aftermath*. Ithaca: Cornell University Press, 1991.

MacDonald, Peter. *Giap: The Victor in Vietnam*. New York: Norton, 1993.

McGarvey, Patrick J. *Visions of Victory: Selected Vietnamese Communist Military Writings, 1964–1968*. Stanford: Hoover Instituted Press, 1969.

McNamara, Robert S. *In Retrospect: The Tragedy and Lessons of Vietnam*. New York: Times Books, 1995.

McNamara, Robert S., James G. Blight, and Robert K. Brigham. *Argument without End: In Search of Answers to the Vietnam Tragedy*. New York: Public Affairs, 1999.

Military Institute of Vietnam. *Victory in Vietnam: The Official History of the People's Army of Vietnam, 1954–1975*. Translated by Merle L. Pribbenow. Foreword by William J. Duiker. Lawrence: University Press of Kansas, 2002.

Moss, George Donelson. *Vietnam: An American Ordeal*. 4th ed. Upper Saddle River, New Jersey: Prentice Hall, 2002.

Murphy, Edward F. *Semper Fi Vietnam: From Da Nang to the DMZ—Marine Corps Campaigns, 1965–1975*. Novato, California: Presidio, 1997.

Nolan, Keith W. *The Battle for Hue: Tet 1968*. Novato, California: Presidio Press, 1983.

Nolan, Keith W. *The Battle for Saigon: Tet 1968*. Novato, California: Presidio Press, 1996.

Oberdorfer, Don. *Tet! The Turning Point in the Vietnam War*. New York: Da Capo, 1984.

Olson, James S., and Randy Roberts. *Where the Domino Fell: America and Vietnam, 1945–2004*. 4th ed. Maplecrest, New York: Brandywine Press, 2004.

Pach, Chester. "TV's 1968: War, Politics, and Violence on the Network Evening News." *South Central Review* 16, No. 4 (Winter 1999–Spring 2000): 29–42.

Pearson, Willard. *Vietnam Studies—The War in the Northern Provinces, 1966–1968*. Washington, D.C.: Department of the Army, 1975.

The Pentagon Papers: The Defense Department History of United States Decision-making on Vietnam. Gravel Edition. 5 vols. Boston: Beacon Press, 1971–72.

Pike, Douglas. *PAVN: People's Army of North Vietnam.* Novato, California: Presidio Press, 1986.

Prados, John. *The Blood Road: The Ho Chi Minh Trail and the Vietnam War.* New York: John Wiley and Sons, 1999.

Prados, John, and Ray W. Stubbe. *Valley of Decision: The Siege of Khe Sanh.* Boston: Houghton Mifflin, 1991.

Rottman, Gordon S. *Khe Sanh 1967–68.* London: Osprey, 2005.

Schmitz, David F. *The Tet Offensive: Politics, War, and Public Opinion.* Lanham, Maryland: Rowman and Littlefield, 2005.

Sharp, U. S. Grant. *Strategy for Defeat: Vietnam in Retrospect.* Novato, California: Presidio Press, 1978.

Shore, Moyer S. *The Battle of Khe Sanh.* Washington, D.C.: Marine Corps History and Museums Division, 1969.

Shulimson, Jack, Leonard A. Blaisol, Charles R. Smith, and David A. Dawson. *U.S. Marines in Vietnam: The Defining Year 1968.* Washington, D.C.: Marine Corps History and Museums Division, 1997.

Shulzinger, Robert D. *A Time for War: The United States and Vietnam, 1945–1975.* New York: Oxford University Press, 1997.

Summers, Harry. *On Strategy: A Critical Analysis of the Vietnam War.* Novato, California: Presidio Press, 1982.

Thai, Hoang Van. *How South Vietnam was Liberated.* Hanoi: The Gioi Publishers, 1996.

Turley, William S. *The Second Indochina War: A Short Political and Military History, 1954–1975.* Boulder: Westview Press, 1986.

Turner, Kathleen J. *Lyndon Johnson's Dual War: Vietnam and the Press.* Chicago: University of Chicago Press, 1985.

Warr, Nicholas. *Phase Line Green: The Battle for Hue, 1968.* Annapolis: Naval Institute Press, 1997.

Werner, Jayne S., and Luu Doan Huynh, eds. *The Vietnam War: Vietnamese and American Perspectives.* Armonk, New York: M. E. Sharpe, 1992.

Westmoreland, William C. *A Soldier Reports.* New York: Da Capo Press, 1989.

Willbanks, James H. *The Tet Offensive: A Concise History.* New York: Columbia University Press, 2007.

Wirtz, James J. *The Tet Offensive: Intelligence Failure in War.* Ithaca: Cornell University Press, 1991.

Woods, Randall Bennett. "LBJ, Politics, and 1968." *South Central Review* 16, No. 4 (Winter 1999–Spring 2000): 16–28.

Worth, Richard. *Tet Offensive.* Philadelphia: Chelsea House Publications, 2002.

Young, Marilyn B. *The Vietnam Wars: 1945–1990.* New York: HarperCollins, 1991.

Young, Marilyn B., and Robert Buzzanco, eds. *A Companion to the Vietnam War.* Oxford: Blackwell Publishing, 2002.

Zhai, Qiang. *China and the Vietnam Wars, 1950–1975.* Chapel Hill: University of North Carolina Press, 2000.

Index

Note: figures in *italic type* indicate illustrations